Academic Entrepreneurship

How to Bring Your Scientific Discovery to a Successful Commercial Product

Michele Marcolongo, Ph.D.

Drexel University, Philadelphia, PA, USA

This edition first published 2017
© 2017 John Wiley & Sons, Inc.

Registered Office
John Wiley & Sons, Inc., 111 River Street, Hoboken, NJ 07030, USA

Editorial Office
111 River Street, Hoboken, NJ 07030, USA

For details of our global editorial offices, customer services, and more information about Wiley products visit us at www.wiley.com.

Wiley also publishes its books in a variety of electronic formats and by print-on-demand. Some content that appears in standard print versions of this book may not be available in other formats.

Library of Congress Cataloging-in-Publication data is applied for

ISBN: 9781118859087

Cover design by Wiley
Cover image: Courtesy of Michele Marcolongo

Set in 10/12pt Warnock by SPi Global, Pondicherry, India

10 9 8 7 6 5 4 3 2 1

Academic Entrepreneurship

Contents

Dedication   *ix*
Foreword   *xi*
Preface   *xiii*
Acknowledgments   *xv*
About the Author   *xvii*

1   So, You Have a Game-Changing Discovery… Congratulations!   *1*
Brief Review of Academic Entrepreneurship   *3*
State of University Technology Transfer   *5*
Study of Academic Entrepreneurship   *7*
Academic Start-Ups Are "Early Stage"   *8*
Overview of the Process   *13*
Summary   *18*
References   *18*

2   Now What? Protect Your Intellectual Property   *21*
Types of Intellectual Property   *22*
   Patent   *22*
   Trademark or Service Mark   *23*
   Copyright   *23*
   Trade Secret   *23*
Patenting and Public Disclosure Considerations   *25*
University Patenting Process   *27*
The Anatomy of a Patent   *34*
How to Read a Patent   *42*
Summary   *43*
References   *43*

3   Are They Buying What You're Selling? The Search Phase   *45*
Example   *48*
Example (Continued)   *51*

The Value Proposition   *54*
Summary   *56*
Reference   *56*

4   Friend or Foe: The Tech Transfer Office and Licensing   *57*
License Agreements with Existing Corporations   *58*
  Example   *58*
University IP Licenses to Start-Ups   *62*
Summary   *70*
References   *71*

5   Proof-of-Concept Centers: Bridging the Innovation Gap   *73*
Proof-of-Concept Centers (PoCCs)   *77*
SBIR/STTR Programs   *83*
Summary   *86*
References   *86*

6   Start-Up Management: You've Got to Kiss a Lot of Frogs...   *87*
Founder's Term Sheet for RegenLive   *99*
Management Structure   *102*
  Directors (Board of Directors)   *102*
    Board of Advisors   *105*
    Consultants   *105*
    Subcontractors   *106*
    Employees   *108*
Summary   *110*
References   *111*

7   Graduate Students and Postdocs, Start Up Your Career   *113*
Introduction   *113*
Why Do It?   *114*
Challenges and Opportunities Spinning Out from the University
for Students   *116*
Faculty Member Participation   *119*
Faculty Member Not Participating   *122*
None of the Above   *123*
Formal Education   *123*
Business Plan Competitions...Not Just for Undergrads   *125*
Conclusion   *126*
References   *127*

8   Incubators and Accelerators: It's Time to Move Out   *129*
Incubators   *130*
Accelerators   *136*

Summary   *140*
References   *140*

9   **Do You Believe in Angels? Financing Your Company**   *143*
Business Plan   *143*
Finding Investors   *149*
   Friends and Family   *150*
   Local Incubators/Accelerators   *150*
   Economic Development Organizations   *151*
   Individual Angels   *151*
   Angel Investor Groups or Networks   *153*
   Corporate Investors   *154*
   Crowdfunding   *155*
   Equity Crowdfunding   *157*
   Academic Crowdfunding   *160*
Venture Capital   *162*
   University Venture Capital   *165*
   Sample Problem   *168*
   Building and Expanding Value for the Academic Founder   *171*
Summary   *174*
References   *175*

10   **Your Roadmap: Avoid the Potholes**   **177**
How to Create a Successful Company   *183*
   Example 1: Uber   *183*
      The Concept   *183*
      Market Research   *183*
      Intellectual Property   *184*
      Proof of Concept   *184*
      The Team   *184*
      Financing   *184*
      Challenges for Uber   *185*
   Example 2: Genentech   *185*
      Discovery   *186*
      Intellectual Property   *186*
      The Team   *187*
      Market Research   *187*
      Financing   *188*
Summary and Going Forward to Your Successful Venture   *190*
References   *191*

Suggested Reading   *193*
Key Terms   *195*
Index   *199*

To all academic entrepreneurs and aspiring academic entrepreneurs, I hope this roadmap will save you time and increase your success.

To my husband, Paul, who is always supportive, loving, and amusing; our sons, Noah and Dan, who are innovative and inspire me every day; and my parents, who instilled in me a belief that I could make something from nothing.

Foreword

The research university as we know it today is, in many ways, a direct result of the needs of the nation during World War II. In response to the war effort, the federal government of the United States launched into an unprecedented expansion of investment in science and engineering-based research in, of all places, academic institutions. Powerhouse institutions, such as MIT and the University of California, Berkeley, led the way in developing significant technical advances that had a direct impact on the outcome of the war.

Because of the success of the partnership between academe and the federal government, Vannevar Bush, the head of the Office of Scientific Research and Development at the time, was asked to develop a plan to maintain and enhance federal programs for research. The result was the creation of his seminal work: "Science: The Endless Frontier." In it, Bush described the difference between so-called basic and applied research and made the case that the federal government should establish a systematic way of supporting basic research in academic institutions. Under this model, applied research was left to the private sector and industry.

The bargain that was struck in separating basic/academic research from applied research is the genesis of the so-called Valley of Death. This phenomenon is common to those who support the commercialization of technology out of academic labs and is a direct result of the structure Vannevar Bush used to distinguish between the type of research that takes place in academic institutions and the type of research that takes place in industrial settings.

For decades after World War II and in spite of the Valley of Death, the United States led the world in its ability to transform basic research into products and services to advance human progress. This ability is widely recognized as a source of comparative advantage around the world and has aided in the development of innovation hubs centered around leading institutions: most famously Silicon Valley in the San Francisco Bay Area.

Evidence suggests that technology can effectively be spun out of academic labs. The question before us now is can we do it better. My strong belief is that the answer to this question is yes, and *Academic Entrepreneurship* helps to point the way.

My work at the National Science Foundation (the brain child of Vannevar Bush), first as a program manager in the Small Business Innovation Research (SBIR) program and then as the founding lead program director for the Innovation Corps (I-Corps), has given me insight into business creation from academic institutions. During my time at NSF, I had an up-close and personal view of over 400 companies encompassing software and services, many of which had a direct connection to academic work. Through the I-Corps program, I was privileged to be involved with approximately 200 additional teams, all academic, and in multiple disciplines.

What I have found is a profound difference between the capacity for research and the success of innovation. Recognition of this difference is the key to improving the transformation of ideas into successful businesses.

Geoff Nicholson the former vice president of 3M had a saying, "Research is turning money into knowledge. Innovation is turning knowledge into money." It is true that great researchers are not necessarily great innovators and successful innovators are not necessarily competent researchers.

From my work with many academic spinouts, I have found the following things to be true. Academically trained scientists and engineers excel at discovery. Faculty, postdocs, and students have certain skills that enable them to identify potential commercial opportunity. They are able to ask, "Does this new technology provide value to potential customers?"

Despite the ability to ask and answer the important "exploration" questions, these highly creative teams struggle to pull resources together to turn their creative pursuits into valuable enterprises. It is *this* challenge that *Academic Entrepreneurship* addresses.

Academic institutions, with their vast intellectual resources, should be a breeding ground for great leaps forward in innovation. We need to break down the barriers of false dichotomy that exists between the separation of basic and applied research. We know that technology transfer from research institutions is a powerful source of human progress, but there is room for improvement. The future potential of academic venture creation is vast and not at odds with the endless frontier.

In the following pages, Michele explores the elements that lead to turning knowledge into money. *Academic Entrepreneurship* explores the importance of IP, customer discovery, team building, and early-stage financing. It is a significant contribution to our understanding of the commercialization process and represents an area of practices that deserves our attention.

Errol Arkilic, Ph.D.
Founding NSF Innovation Core (I-Core) Program Director
Founder of M34 Capital

Preface

What do Bose, Genentech, and Gatorade all have in common? They are all companies that were founded based on technology from academic research.

Academic research is fascinating. It allows you to explore and discover to the farthest reaches of your imagination and scientific skills. Academic researchers are trained through graduate school and often postdoctoral studies with a system of apprenticeship or mentorship under an advisor who guides the research. Under this system, we are taught the scientific method, how to pose relevant questions, critically review prior work, analyze data, report findings, financially support the work through grants, run a lab, and train the next generation of researchers.

Today, there is considerable interest of university faculty, national lab researchers, medical doctors, postdoctoral and graduate students in expanding academic research toward development of products or services that can directly serve society and drive economic development. More often than not, our graduate student and postdoctoral mentorship did not and does not include a systematic approach for translation of research to commercialization.

This book is intended as a guide to help you navigate the process of commercializing your academic discovery. While there are numerous outstanding books on entrepreneurship (see Suggested Reading), the academy offers some unique challenges to commercializing technologies for those on the inside. It's difficult to find a clear translational path to follow. The paths vary institutionally and geographically across the country. This book serves as a guide to academic entrepreneurship with all of its exciting opportunities as well as real challenges. Consider it a "how to" commercialize your academic findings.

The motivation for consolidating this "how to" was numerous requests for advice from colleagues in my university and across the country who were starting companies. From my position as a Professor of Materials Science and Engineering, I have been a cofounder of two start-up companies from my academic work and have cofounded a technology company outside of the university system. Work with my start-up companies has given me intimate insights into the start and in one case so far, to the finish line of the commercialization process. In addition, I've served in the university provost's office developing programs to better help researchers translate their scientific discoveries. My work was not done at Stanford or MIT, who have had great systems in place for translating research for decades, but at a top 100 university that was and is developing its methodologies around commercialization. So whether in Silicon Valley, Boston, or any other academic location, the strategies in this book will help to guide you through this exciting process.

But one person's perspective is limited, so I've interviewed numerous colleagues in university start-up ecosystems across the country to learn about their experiences and have included their insights as inserts in the chapters. You'll hear from technology transfer officers, regional economic development partners, venture capitalists, attorneys, faculty members, and students who have founded companies to translate academic research.

My hope is that this book will give you a framework for your technology commercialization. There is no "right way" or "only way" to proceed, but some considerations discussed here will make the commercialization path smoother for you and give you a foundation on which to base your many decisions. From my own experience in biomaterials and medical device research, it has been a great satisfaction to see a research concept evolve into a real patient treatment.

The book begins with a brief review of academic entrepreneurship for those interested in some historical context and data. In each of the subsequent chapters, you will find information on protecting your intellectual property, exploring market need, negotiating with the university technology transfer office, providing proof of concept for your product or service, assembling your management team, making postdoctoral and graduate students as founders of academic start-ups, hiring incubators/accelerators, and financing your company. In a final summary, the top reasons why start-ups fail (academic and nonacademic) as well as examples of how some succeeded are analyzed.

Additional topics addressed that are unique to academic start-ups include conflicts of interest (among you, the university, and the start-up company), tenure, and promotion considerations for faculty members in light of entrepreneurial activities, challenges, and opportunities, having academic colleagues as business partners, managing relationships between advisors and students in academic start-ups, keeping your day job while founding a company, or deciding to leave the academy entirely.

My hope is that by learning about the processes, stumbling points, successes, and general experiences of numerous people in the academic entrepreneurship ecosystem, you will have a roadmap to successfully commercializing your important research discovery. Welcome to the entrepreneurship community.

Michele Marcolongo
Philadelphia

Acknowledgments

I would like to thank numerous friends and colleagues who have provided advice and feedback during the writing of this book. From casual conversations to lengthy sit-down discussions, your input was essential. Each of the people in the university entrepreneurship ecosystem who agreed to provide an interview for this book helped to shape and bring the book personal insights from a variety of perspectives. Many thanks to each of you. As you all are extremely busy and talented people, your time and candor in our discussions were a great gift.

I appreciate the thorough reading of the manuscript by Tom Edwards and Errol Arkilic whose helpful feedback was both thoughtful and encouraging.

Thank you also to Leslie Campion who provided essential support in the preparation of the manuscript for publication and used her tremendous talents to create the cover art for the book. This necessary work takes a special skill to complete, and there is a good likelihood that without her talents the manuscript would not have been fully and finally published.

A special note of thanks goes to my family. My husband, Paul, and my sons, Noah and Dan, for their support of my sitting at the kitchen counter for many hours lost in the manuscript. Noah was especially kind to use his keen literary skills to edit the manuscript of the book before it could ever be given to the editor.

Thank you as well to Wiley for the editorial and production staff who were encouraging as well as skillful in finalizing the publication in every aspect.

About the Author

Dr. Michele Marcolongo, Ph.D., P.E., is the department head and professor of Materials Science and Engineering at Drexel University in Philadelphia. She has been a leader in the university entrepreneurship ecosystem where she has previously served as associate vice provost for research, associate dean of intellectual property development for the College of Engineering, and senior associate vice provost for translational research. She served on the Operations Boards of the Nanotechnology Institute and the Energy Commercialization Institute, which directed proof-of-concept commercialization funds for 14 universities in Pennsylvania. Dr. Marcolongo's field of research is biomaterials or materials that can be implanted into the body to replace diseased or damaged tissues. Dr. Marcolongo has cofounded two companies with from her research in biomaterials: the first, Gelifex, was sold to a major orthopaedics manufacturer, and the second, MimeCore, to commercialize a platform technology of biomimetic proteoglycans. In addition, she cofounded the health IT company, Invisalert Solutions. She is a fellow of AIMBE and Alpha Sigma Mu. Dr. Marcolongo received her doctorate in Biomedical Engineering from the University of Pennsylvania.

1

So, You Have a Game-Changing Discovery… Congratulations!

Vision without execution is hallucination.
—Thomas Edison

Some of the best days in the life of a researcher are those where you get the data back from a key experiment to find that you have proven your hypothesis, met your design objective, or just flat out made a new discovery. That excitement and sense of fulfillment is, in part, what drives academic faculty. The discovery and the dissemination of those important findings are the well-deserved products of tenacious research endeavors.

There may be a day when you realize that your discovery has real promise outside of the lab—it could be a game changer. But what's the best way to get this discovery from the lab to commercialization? Academics are trained in graduate school and during our postdocs in how to run a lab, design experiments and write grants, analyze data, write papers, present scientific findings, and teach. To date, the academic community has not used this same apprenticeship model for systematic training in aspects of entrepreneurship, especially academic entrepreneurship and all of the steps and decisions that need to be made to "translate" your discovery to commercialization (Figure 1.1), where it can become a product or service to meet a need in our society.

And yet, many academics roll up their sleeves and try anyway. Without training and often with little guidance, academics make their way through intellectual property (IP) law (United States and international), market assessment, value propositions, licensing agreements, negotiating business relationships, finding a good corporate partner, and starting and financing a new company. This book is intended to provide a process that will allow a step-by-step approach to evaluate and realize commercial potential of your research findings. To supplement the methods, there are summaries of

Academic Entrepreneurship: How to Bring Your Scientific Discovery to a Successful Commercial Product, First Edition. Michele Marcolongo.
© 2017 John Wiley & Sons, Inc. Published 2017 by John Wiley & Sons, Inc.

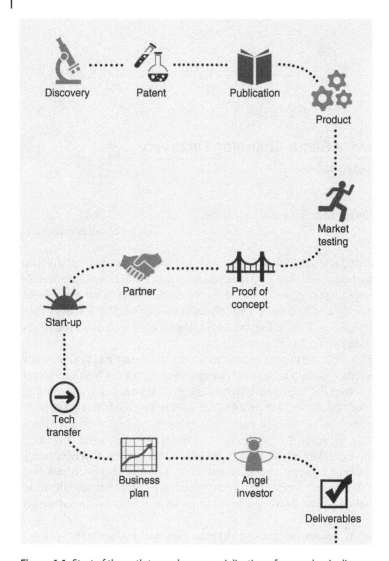

Figure 1.1 Start of the path toward commercialization of an academic discovery.

interviews with notable members of the academic entrepreneurship ecosystem including investors, heads of proof-of-concept centers, incubator directors, and numerous academic entrepreneurs themselves. To get started on your path to entrepreneurship, please go to Chapter 2. For a very brief history of how we got to this point in academic entrepreneurship, continue through the rest of this chapter.

Brief Review of Academic Entrepreneurship

How did we get to the point of academic research turning into commercial products and services? Some academics are not interested in commercializing a research finding (but probably not many of those reading this book). They're driven solely by the probing of new knowledge and not by bringing the fruits of that knowledge back to society in ways other than the traditional methods of publishing findings and training students. Indeed, if universities don't provide a place for fundamental research, where will it be done? With notable exceptions, corporations that used to have major internal research centers have cut those back dramatically with a preference for outsourcing or acquiring early-stage research. Early-stage research and discovery is a concept that is critical to the advancement of basic knowledge, but expensive to support with the constraints and impatience of real-world corporations today. The Bureau of Economic Analysis (BEA, 2014) cites a decrease in research and development (R&D) growth from 7% in 1965 to 2% in 2013, with a 50-year average of 4.6%. From 2007 to 2013, the average was 1.1%. This corresponds with, but may not be causal to, a reduction in the number of corporations that publish in scientific journals, which have gone from 17.7% in 1980 to 6.1% in 2007 (Fortune, 2015). A tremendous source of research is our national labs whose members contribute research, but with a focus that is primarily mission driven, potentially limiting the breadth of basic research questions. Along with teaching and service, research is a primary mission of an academic faculty member who then disseminates those findings openly to the scientific community. Can we maintain this "purity" while extending our definition of dissemination of findings to include translating discoveries toward commercialization where they can more directly address societal and technological challenges?

In the book *Open Innovation*, Henry Chesbrough summarizes the evolution of research within the government, universities, and corporations (Chesbrough, 2006). From the turn of the twentieth century until World War II, the US government was generally uninterested in supporting university research. The government's few scientific interests were in understanding gunpowder as well as in developing a system of weights and measures. For corporate protection, the US patent system was initiated. During this same period, basic science was in an amazing state of discovery in universities across the world. This was the time of Einstein, Bohr, Roentgen, Maxwell, Curie, Pasteur, and Plank. These were "pure" scientists. However, pre-World War II universities lacked funds to conduct significant experiments themselves. During this time period, Thomas Edison invented the phonograph and electric light bulb. Edison, however, was considered by the university scientific community to be a "tinkerer" of "lesser ability," who had compromised himself and corrupted the process of scientific discovery. Thomas Edison held 1093 patents.

Corporations during this time needed to work toward innovative products, so they began internal R&D within the companies. They were able to hire top scientists with jobs for life, creating academically stimulating corporate environments. Corporate scientists performed basic research that in some cases also led to product development. The centralized R&D organizations were critical to growth and business opportunities for the high-growth corporations. At that time there was little connection among government, university, and corporate research (each being mostly closed systems).

After World War II and through the 1970s, the US government's interest in supporting research was greatly enhanced. President Franklin D. Roosevelt realized that the United States needed to import much of its scientific knowledge and technology from Europe for weapons development during World War II. Roosevelt charged Vannevar Bush to study ways that the United States could increase the number of its own trained scientists. He wanted to simultaneously aid research activities in the public and private sector and increase federal funding of basic research in universities. Roosevelt envisioned a strong and independent scientific reservoir in the United States, in part as a defense strategy. To satisfy these needs, the National Science Foundation (NSF) was formed to coordinate efforts between government, universities, the military, and industry. The GI Bill of Rights was also enacted to fund tuition for veterans returning from war. As universities found themselves with a new influx of research funding from NSF, academic science was elevated to more equal partner with the government and industry. The government was now funding basic research in universities whose faculty, through open publication, were expanding the pool of knowledge available to society and industry.

After World War II, colleges and universities trained many new undergraduates and graduate students. This decentralization of knowledge enabled industry to increase internal R&D. There was expansion in Bell Labs, GE, and DuPont in addition to the formation of Watson Labs at IBM, Sarnoff Labs at RCA, and then others at HP and Xerox. Employees from Bell Labs and IBM received Nobel Prizes, and those at DuPont discovered new chemical fibers and materials. Chesbrough summarizes that this was the "golden age for internal R&D." The United States enjoyed growth of the postwar industry for over two decades. But the corporate closed innovation system was soon to come to an end.

Consider the US economy during the 1970s. The Japanese and German markets were taking off, and it looked as if the United States would lose the high-tech industry, while the economy was experiencing double-digit inflation and unemployment (AUTM, 2012). The federal government had a policy of taking all federally funded university inventions and licensing them to companies nonexclusively. With the lack of IP protection against competition (because of the nonexclusivity of the license agreements), companies were not actively pursuing the university inventions. The federal government held 28 000 patents with fewer than 5% licensed to industry (GAO, 1986). While numerous scientific advances were being made, it was felt that the great investment in university research from the American taxpayers, then billions of dollars, was not significantly making its way back to those taxpayers to advance the standard of living and economic viability of the United States.

In 1980, two US senators got together and formed legislation that again changed the innovation paradigm for the United States. The Bayh–Dole Act (1980) was motivated by widely held belief in the late 1970s that the United States would no longer be industrially competitive. Senators Birch Bayh (Indiana) and Bob Dole (Kansas) initiated a law that created a uniform patent policy for federal agencies that support research. The major focus of this law was to enable small businesses and nonprofit organizations (universities) to retain title to inventions made under federally funded research programs (http://www.autm.net/Bayh_Dole_Act1.htm).

Bayh–Dole Act led to new provisions to universities that are funded by federal agencies:

- Nonprofits, including universities, and small businesses may elect to retain title to innovations developed under federally funded research programs.
- Universities are encouraged to collaborate with commercial concerns to promote the utilization of inventions arising from federal funding.
- Universities are expected to file patents on inventions they elect to own.
- Universities are expected to give licensing preference to small businesses.
- The government retains a nonexclusive license to practice the patent throughout the world.
- The government retains march-in rights.

Now and for the past thirty-plus years, universities no longer provide free-of-charge, federally funded research findings to companies to advance industry. With the advent of Bayh–Dole, the universities themselves can protect the IP of their findings, and even though the research will still be published and knowledge shared openly, industry is no longer legally permitted to take the protected ideas of universities and use them to advance their products and profits. This primary change set a new dynamic for innovation that has undergone many iterations to bring us to present-day university policies. Corporations are able to license IP (exclusively or nonexclusively) directly from universities or national labs if they would like to commercialize discoveries from federally funded research. This option is extended to faculty members who are able to license university-owned IP through the vehicle of a start-up company.

State of University Technology Transfer

The Association of University Technology Managers (AUTM) was founded in 1974. In 2016, the organization had 3200 members from 300 universities. The mission of the organization is the support and advance technology transfer globally. AUTM has summarized the statistical productivity of university research toward innovation and economic development with citations from "The Gathering Storm," the 2006 report of the National Academy of Sciences. To summarize, since the initiation of the 1980 Bayh–Dole Act, university research helped create whole new industries, such as biotechnology. In addition,

- More than 5000 companies formed around university research resulted, many nearby the universities where the original research was performed.
- University patents in 2005 totaled 3278 up from only 495 in 1980.
- In 2005 alone, universities helped introduce 527 new products to the marketplace. Between 1998 and 2005, 3641 new products were created.
- University technology transfer creates billions of dollars of direct benefits to the US economy every year.

According to the former president of the NASDAQ Stock Market, an estimated 30% of its value is rooted in university-based, federally funded research results, which might never have been commercialized had it not been for the Bayh–Dole Act (AUTM, 2012). All the while, researchers in the United States led the world in the volume of articles published and in the frequency with which these papers are cited by others. US-based authors were listed in one-third of all scientific articles worldwide in 2001 (Committee on Science, Engineering, and Public Policy, 2007).

AUTM (2012) reports the following metrics:

- 22 150 total US patent applications filed
- 14 224 new patent applications filed
- 5145 issued US patents
- 5130 licenses executed
- 1242 options executed
- 483 executed licenses containing equity
- Total license income: $2.6 billion
- 705 start-up companies formed
- 4002 start-ups still operating as of the end of FY2012

There are some interesting inferences that can be drawn from this data. First, in consideration of the amount of federal research dollars spent in the United States in 2012 ($40 billion), there were 22 150 patent applications filed and 5 145 patents issued. Broadly, there is approximately 1 patent filed for every $7.7 million in federal research dollars spent. The long lag between patent filing and review makes the issued patents a lagging indication of productivity. The resulting licenses were 5130. There were 705 start-up companies formed, and these employed approximately 15 000 people. The data showing that 80% of licensed patents went to existing companies indicates that academia is still supporting corporate industrial growth in the

United States and that companies in some industries are interested in licensing directly from universities. The 20% of licenses that went to start-ups is interesting in that this segment is a significant portion of the licenses. This can be compared with 2002 data that showed 14% of university licenses went to start-ups (Shane, 2004). Pro and con Bayh–Dole advocates have fairly strong opinions of the consequences to this law, which was summarized in a quote by James Pooley who says, "At the end of the day, what we've learned from Bayh-Dole is that by harnessing the capitalistic system, we get a lot more technologies out to market and, arguably, a lot more spread into other areas as well" (Slind-Flor, 2006). Academic entrepreneurs now make up a growing and significant part of the industry that translates knowledge from universities toward commercialization. Because this is an important market phenomenon, academics in another part of the university, the B-school, have become interested in studying this population to learn about academic start-ups.

Study of Academic Entrepreneurship

Business school academics have developed an independent discipline that studies and analyzes academic entrepreneurship. The academic entrepreneurship literature is rich with insights of some key areas: characteristics of an academic entrepreneur, which universities are best adapted to successfully support academic entrepreneurship, organization, and policies of the technology transfer office and environmental context network of innovation, social networks, and relational capital. The motivation for understanding these drivers is clear: policymakers, universities, and business leaders desire a clearer knowledge of the characteristics of academic entrepreneurs and the policies and practices that promote them. Some characteristics of an academic entrepreneur and the likelihood of an academic becoming an entrepreneur have also been investigated.

The characteristics typical of an entrepreneur:

- Ability to take risks (but not excessive risks)
- Innovative
- Knowledge of how the market functions
- Manufacturing know-how
- Marketing skills
- Business management skills
- Ability to cooperate
- Good nose for business
- Ability to correct errors effectively
- Ability to grasp profitable opportunities

For 1780 academics examined for participating in technology transfer, "individual attributes, while important, are conditioned by the local work environment" (Bercovitz and Feldman, 2008).

Academics were more likely to become academic entrepreneurs if:

- They were trained in institutions that had accepted technology transfer.
- They were closer to their graduate training (those farther away from graduate training had less participation).
- Their department head was active in technology transfer.
- Respected members of their academic community were participating in technology transfer (sometimes known as the "Porsche effect").

If, instead, academics find the social norm of the department or the community is not supportive of technology transfer, even if they received training in entrepreneurship, they will conform to local norms rather than prior experience.

Tenure/tenure-track faculty taking on entrepreneurship were also affected by the standard by which their contributions are measured for tenure and promotion. Assessment for tenure and promotion for STEM faculty are scholarly output (typically analyzed by the amount of externally funded research support, scholarly papers and other scholarly work, training of doctoral students, and academic reputation) in addition to teaching and service accomplishments. Academic entrepreneurship is not included in the performance reviews of most academic faculty members, although several universities have recently adapted entrepreneurship activities into the tenure and promotion metrics. Therefore, especially during the critical pre-tenure years, as well as at the associate professor level, academics are indirectly discouraged from pursuing academic entrepreneurship by not being rewarded for these endeavors. As universities are becoming more interested in the advancement of their research innovations to commercialization, policy change will surely be necessary to facilitate this activity in a major way without penalty for the faculty member in tenure and promotion (Stevens *et al.*, 2011). For those who decide to pursue academic entrepreneurship anyway, there are some interesting findings of how start-ups from academics differ from other high-tech start-ups.

Academic Start-Ups Are "Early Stage"

Because university start-ups often initiate from a discovery and not necessarily from a clearly defined product and market need, university start-ups can take a great deal of additional R&D before they can become a viable businesses according to Lubynsky (2013). This is often a frustration to the academic inventor who has worked, perhaps many years already on the initial invention, only to hear repeatedly that the technology is really "early stage" by investors and the broader business community. Lubynsky studied 10 start-ups out of MIT, most of which were led by graduate students with concepts developed in collaboration with their faculty mentor during the course of their doctoral work. Even in MIT's entrepreneurial community with substantial resources and support for academic entrepreneurship, out of 10 start-ups, 2 failed after about 10 years, 2 were acquired after 8 and 10 years, and the remaining 6 were still in business with duration ranging from 0.5 to 10 years at the conclusion of his analysis. Regardless of the outcome, the research phase of the start-up lasted between 3 and 10 years. Lubynsky concludes that academic ventures are different. Many academic entrepreneurs believed that the only effective path to advance the technology was to form their own start-up. Another interesting finding of the study relates to the importance of students (graduate students and postdoctoral researchers) in academic entrepreneurship with students being major contributors to the academic start-ups. While the students were critical to the start-ups that were successful, they also found challenges in the companies that were studied. Two common conflicts for the student entrepreneurs were with their faculty advisors and with business student partners in business plan competitions. Part of the challenge for all of the academic entrepreneurs was the transition from well-developed academic networks to networks in the entrepreneurial community.

Robert Langer, Ph.D.
David H. Koch Institute Professor
Department of Chemical Engineering
MIT

Only a few more and MIT's Bob Langer will have more patents than Thomas Edison (1093), not to mention 1250 journal articles. Wow.

Bob's accomplishments for the scientific world are impressive by any standards, and he has been recognized with numerous prestigious awards. But what might be most notable is Bob's dream to "use his background in chemistry and chemical engineering to improve people's lives." Founder of 28 companies to date, Bob's academic entrepreneurial efforts have fulfilled this dream over and over again.

An entire book should be dedicated to understanding the brilliance and tenacity of Bob Langer. Here we'll focus on some of Bob's observations about academic start-ups.

An article on The Langer Lab by Harvard Business School (Bowen *et al.*, 2005) summarizes Bob's own process of the "four elements of an ideal research project" and notes the "symbiotic relationship between science and science-based business":

1) *A huge idea* conceived by recognizing a critical societal need that could be met by inventing a platform product
2) *A seminal paper* based on research to establish the science underlying the product concept and its efficacy
3) *A blocking patent* derived from patent disclosures written in parallel with the research process, the goal being to have patents filed before the research paper's publication
4) *Preliminary in vivo studies* in animals that demonstrated the efficacy of the research

Some academics are lucky enough to hit on these four elements a couple of times in a career, but Bob and his lab have the creativity, intellect, and drive to do this almost annually. The resulting companies have given Bob tremendous insights into the academic start-up process.

When discussing what he wished he had known before embarking as an academic entrepreneur, Bob had a ready reply: "1. How to find good investors; 2. How to find a good CEO; and 3. How important it is to have a really good plan before you do lots of research."

Bob has had a business partner for each of his companies. Now, he doesn't have any trouble finding a good CEO, but in the early days it was more difficult. "It's hard to know when you have a great CEO, but easy to know when you have a poor one."

With his broad experiences in start-up companies, Bob can offer many perspectives, but perhaps most unique is his vast experience with exits. Most academics with start-ups may have an exit opportunity one, two or maybe three times…Bob could do a statistical study on his!

Many founders have trouble letting go of control of their company with a sale. How does Bob approach exits? By the time there is a decision of an exit, he feels it's a joint decision. Aside from IPO's (to bring resources into the company), there are two reasons why exits occur: The first is financial interest. If a preemptive offer is extended (2–3X), then investors are interested in the deal. The second may be unique to the medical sector where the commercialization and sales process is complicated and a lot of capital is needed to do the work. Sometimes before the product is launched, another company will buy the start-up and put in the investment to take the product to the clinic. With mergers you lose control, but gain resources to advance the technology.

When you transition your start-up to a larger company, there still are challenges. Financially, "milestone-based payments are bad," especially when you don't have control over the budget or work any longer. Some companies do a good job of taking on technology, but others may have priorities that are not aligned to those of the start-up. What forces them to do a good job is the con-tractual arrangement. These terms can vary widely, but in general they are intended to cover what happens if there is a lack of progress after the sale, for example, additional payments are to be made or technology is to be given to the start-up.

There is "no particular answer for a company and many variables." Exits depend on whether the technology is a one-trick pony or platform. For a plat-form, Bob wouldn't want to sell quickly because you have more "shots on goal." "Developing the technology across lots of product spaces is a good thing."

Does Bob like all of the financials and board meetings that go with the com-pany management? Not really. He prefers more creative endeavors. However, Bob recommends that the founders have a representative on the board of the start-up. It's the best way to "really know what's going on, including understand-ing the financials."

How has Bob managed his tremendous success in translating his research findings to commercialized products to help people? I've had "lots of good stu-dents, lots of opportunities and made lots of mistakes."

All of our mistakes should be so fruitful.

Social capital describes the resources you use to execute your objectives through your network. There are differences in the networks that are neces-sary for academic research and academic start-ups. Social capital evolves from your network and helps you best complete your work (De Carolis and Saparito, 2006). For a faculty member, the social capital may be the dean, department head, the research office administrator, the registrar, program director, purchasing representative, students, and fellow professors, among others. For an entrepreneur, this network may include quite a different cir-cle, such as the patent and contract attorneys, business entrepreneurs in your sector, accountants, local economic development administrators, tech-nology transfer officers, corporate players in target sector, angel investors, and venture capitalists (Figure 1.2). The intersection of these networks of social capital is divergent for the most part with little overlap. A university system that provides a faculty member with the opportunity to develop social capital in the entrepreneurship ecosystem may more efficiently drive commercialization.

The current state of academic entrepreneurship is in different stages of matu-rity among the different research institutions across the country. Challenges include creating a supportive ecosystem, methods for navigating the university processes and policies, and moving a start-up forward while maintaining an active research lab. The National Academies Press has published a report (2013)

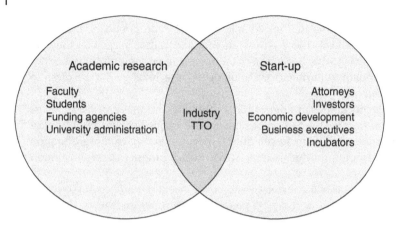

Figure 1.2 The social capital needed for academic research and translation of that research into a commercial product or service can be very diverse.

that discusses trends in the innovation ecosystem through a collaboration between the Academies of Sciences and Engineering and the Institute of Medicine. Their analysis summarizes the state of national universities toward supporting innovation (Olson and Dahlberg, 2013):

- The knowledge and experience of individuals are the primary drivers of innovation.
- Science and technology expertise alone is not enough to ensure innovation; the skills of finance, business development, production, and management are useful.
- Innovation is stimulated by the movement and interaction of individuals from different sectors.
- The culture of a region and its institutions shapes the nature of these interactions.
- Openness to new ideas and a tolerance for failure are important.
- Culture is not easily changed, and creating clones of Silicon Valley might be the wrong strategy.
- Innovation is a contact sport and might be facilitated by a concentration of talent that increases the rate of interaction.
- General principles do not explain everything. Significant differences exist among institutions, regions, industries, and sectors.

Among the most interesting observation by the members who collaborated on this report is that "general principles do not explain everything." It is interesting that while there is an overall process for translating research to commercialization, there is not a governing path to ensure success. The process is multifaceted, and each component of the business development has its associated risks that need to be managed uniquely for each case. This being said, there is a general process that can be put forth as a framework to take a scientific discovery on the journey to commercialization.

Overview of the Process

The challenge with creating value from a scientific discovery revolves around limiting the risk associated with the business proposition to secure investment and then executing on a well-considered plan using those resources. The types of risks may include technical risk of the product or service working, being scalable and cost effective; marketing risk so that there is a buyer when you are ready to sell; team risk, which may be the most important of all to investors, having a talented, coachable team that can deliver on promises; and for some industries regulatory or reimbursement risk. While the chapters of the book are laid out serially, the process is iterative. Constant analysis and associated minor adjustments or major pivots may be necessary throughout the process, iterative toward convergence. The first step begins in the university lab (Figure 1.3).

The first step toward value creation is the protection of your discovery and is discussed in Chapter 2. After deciding the mechanism of protection (patent,

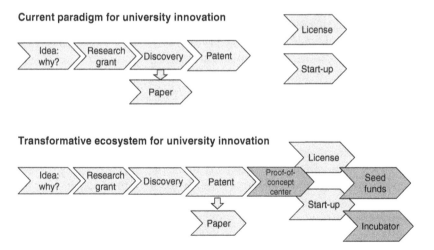

Figure 1.3 Research and dissemination of research findings typically follow the path (top) where there is a disconnect between the university flow to commercialization of the discovery as a product or service. To facilitate translation of research findings, a few key components to the process may be added to the university system, such as a proof-of-concept center, seed funds, and an incubator or accelerator in the region.

trademark, copyright, or trade secret), you will need to work with your tech transfer officer to disclose the IP, go through the university decision process for filing the IP, and work with a patent attorney to write the IP application in a smart way that will differentiate you from others. The protection of your IP needs to be addressed prior to disclosure of your invention external to your university in order for the patent to be valid. The concept will need to be described in the context of prior art, such as all pertinent previously published patents or patent applications, journal articles, abstracts, presentations, website descriptions, or the like. For a patent application, the description will have to be deemed novel and non-obvious by the patent examiner to be granted. You will need to make filing decisions on provisional or non-provisional follow-up with a Patent Cooperation Treaty and international filing. You may have more than one patent application for the work, so a portfolio of patents may be collated around the discovery. The protection of the discovery legally excludes others from making, using, selling, or importing the invention. This carves out the space for a business to operate by preventing competition from copying your invention (although it doesn't necessarily allow you freedom to operate, that separate analysis can be made of the patent landscape in your area). Once the patent application or patent has been filed, you can then publish your findings and discuss them publically (outside of the university or outside of a nondisclosure agreement) without risk of compromising the patent prosecution. At this time you are ready to move into a market analysis of your proposed product or service. Chapter 2 also discusses splits of inventorship among co-inventors, which may be unique to academic patent filing where potential rewards of a successful commercialization can be based on percentage contribution of the IP. With the IP protected, you are ready to explore the application of the discovery in the marketplace.

To take a deep dive into the market viability for your envisioned product or service, secondary and primary marketing analysis is needed. Secondary marketing data is compiled market analysis that tells of the overall size of a sector and then your niche within that sector. These analyses will give broad strokes to the market size and divisions to see if it is a fifty million or a billion plus dollar market. It may also tell the major competitors in the marketplace and their market share and growth. Secondary marketing data is typically sourced by companies that compile marketing research and sell it to customers like you. After framing the potential value of the market, primary marketing research is used to assess the need and value of your specific proposed product or service that may be derived from your discovery. This is a critical piece to the de-risking of your technology (market risk). Direct conversations with numerous (maybe 100) potential customers with targeted questions about the need for your product or service as well as the value will inform the market potential of your product or service. Feedback from potential customers, even at this early stage of development, is critical for examining the market need and willingness to pay for what you are offering. Feedback from the primary market research can be tabulated (scale of 1–10 type questions) and analyzed, and hypotheses can be tested. Results of the marketing research can tell you if you need to adjust the product (add features or simplify) and continue toward commercialization. The results can also tell you if your concept is interesting, but not commercially viable. This is a key step in the go-no-go decision process that you will make as you consider the development of your innovation toward commercialization. If you decide to go forward, the next step may be licensing the technology from the technology transfer office to an established company or to your own start-up.

The IP (application or granted) can be licensed from the university, who is the assignee. The university can choose to license the IP to an existing corporation or to a start-up company. While 80% of the IP is licensed to existing companies, more and more start-ups are spinning out of universities. An exclusive license of your IP to an existing company is the most straightforward way to transition your innovation toward commercialization. The license agreement is typically made in exchange for any combination of recovered patent fees, royalties, and up-front payment. There may be terms specifying the participation of the faculty member in the development of the technology through a sponsored research agreement and/or a consulting agreement. There is typically little conflict between the faculty member and the university around a direct licensing agreement. Sometimes, however, direct licensing is not desired either by the existing corporations or by the university. If the technology is "too early," sometimes major corporations prefer not to license. Some companies do not like to do business with universities because of a cumbersome negotiating and approval process within the universities. Other times the university does not have the resources to adequately market the technology. If a promising technology does not fit the model of licensing to an existing corporation, it may be suitable for a start-up company. If the faculty inventor is a founder (an equity holder) in a start-up and also eligible for a percentage of the share of the university in the license to the start-up, there is a conflict of interest to be managed. Centered in the middle of the conflict is the faculty inventor. This situation is another component of commercialization that is unique to university settings. In Chapter 4, negotiating with the technology transfer office and managing potential conflicts of interest are discussed. In addition, licensing agreements with existing corporations and how to manage that process as a faculty inventor are described, including how the match is made between the university and the existing corporations that might be interested in your IP and how to manage negotiations with "early-stage" technology.

One way to de-risk the technology behind your proposed product or service to transition out from the "early stage" is to do a proof-of-concept experiment. This experiment is not necessarily aimed at furthering basic scientific knowledge. Instead, it is a targeted analysis of the feasibility of your proposed product or service. This might be launch of a minimally viable product or a key animal model that conclusively shows that your proposed solution works. Chapter 5 describes proof-of-concept strategies. If you have strong proof of concept, investors are more likely to commit because you have begun to address the key technological risk in your business. Some universities have their own proof-of-concept centers like UCSD and MIT who were among the earliest academic proof-of-concept centers started in the early 2000s. It has been shown that proof-of-concept centers assist in technology commercialization and are a valuable part of the university entrepreneurial ecosystem. Even if your university does not have a proof-of-concept center, federal Small Business Innovation Research and Small Business Technology Transfer programs offered through numerous agencies can provide financial assistance by way of a grant (not investment) to further de-risk the technology. While these experiments may not be publishable, when designed correctly, they can answer key risk questions that will enable investment in a start-up or convince an existing corporation that the technology is robust enough for them to license.

If you decide to follow the start-up route toward commercialization of your university technology, you must assemble a group of people that will be able to drive the invention toward a product, define and test a viable market, and secure investment to provide the resources necessary to sustain the effort and communication among every member of the organization and its stakeholders. In Chapter 6, strategies are outlined for you as the founder to set up your company and to select key people who will help you execute your vision. You will have the opportunity to manage the company yourself and/or partner with a student (graduate student or postdoctoral researcher), technical colleague, or business partner. Considerations for how to select your partners are described. The team may consist of you as the founder, your business partner, students, or others who may join the start-up as employees, advisors, consultants, subcontractors, corporate partners, investors, and a board of directors. Discussion of structuring a bricks-and-mortar company versus a virtual company will allow you to think about strategy and associated financing needed to realize your business. Incentives for partners and employees will need to be considered. With a start-up on a tight budget, you may be limited in salary but can offer a share of a successful future with equity. Unique to academic start-ups is the business partnership with a graduate or postdoctoral student. Considerations of conflict and managing through this new type of relationship between advisor and student, now founder and employee, or founder and CEO are significant for the success of the start-up.

From the graduate student or postdoctoral student perspective, there are numerous considerations in joining a university start-up. In addition to the relationship with their academic advisor-turned business partner or employer, participating in a start-up after years of academic preparation will need to be weighed versus potential lost opportunity in pursuing a faculty position or industry or other position after graduation. Most (more than three quarters) of university start-ups have a student in a key role in the business. Chapter 7 explores university start-ups from the graduate and postdoctoral student perspective including potential conflicts with academic advisors, starting position in the company, negotiating compensation, evolving roles over progression and growth of the business, and furthering education in finance and management. For a student, choosing to launch a career with a start-up can be either an additional experience before returning to research or the beginning of an entirely new career path.

After securing your IP, negotiating a license to your start-up, doing a proof of concept, and assembling your team (not necessarily in that order and not without iteration), it will soon come time to move out of the university lab and into independent space for the start-up. Chapter 8 examines your options with incubators and accelerators. Incubators are generally nonprofit organizations that rent office and/or lab space to start-up companies. They are often associated with universities. The earliest incubators began around 1959. Typical time for a start-up in an incubator is 1–5 years. Accelerators are most often for-profit entities that select start-ups to join a cohort of companies that go through a three-month on-site program where the start-ups are developed to the point of succeeding or failing fast. In exchange for being in the program, the start-up receives some funding in exchange for equity in the company. The result of the accelerator is demo day, where the start-ups present their businesses to a group of investors. Ideally, this would serve as a jumping-off point for the company. Starting in an accelerator does not preclude a start-up from later using an incubator. Either way, accelerators and incubators are ways to transition from the lab to becoming an independent company.

From the very first day that a start-up is incorporated (and probably even before), the founders start to strategize about investment. Those who invest in start-ups are mavericks in the investor world, taking a major risk on a business that has no product and no sales. To convince an investor to put their money into your university start-up, you must put together an outstanding business plan. From our initial discussion, the objective of the plan is to lay a strategy for the business to build value. The value is built as the risks are addressed. Chapter 9 summarizes the components of a strong business plan and then describes strategies for securing investors in your start-up. Investment can be from friends, family, incubators/accelerators, economic development organizations, individual angels, angel investor groups, corporate partners, crowdfunding, and venture capital. Each investment comes with obligations and some money "costs more" than others. Dilution of the founder is a very real challenge in an academic start-up in particular. Because the technology is early stage at the time of incorporation and depending on the product or service, there can be an expensive and long timeline until a return is made to investors. Investment usually comes in rounds that build value with incremental infusions of investment. As each investor brings additional resources, the trade-off is equity, which can come from the founder's initial equity position. Numerous faculty members have started successful companies, but have not achieved financial reward themselves due to their negotiations through this process. Understanding the expectations with investment may help you to maximize your financial reward while still driving the business to a successful and viable company, getting your laboratory discovery into the hands of those who can directly benefit from it.

History affords us the ability to learn from others who have traveled the road before us. As it turns out, there are summaries of reasons why start-ups, both nonacademic and academic, have failed in their journey to sustain viable businesses. Interestingly, there is considerable overlap between the two categories of start-up pitfalls, although there are some particular challenges that are unique to academic start-ups. Equally important to analysis of the cause of failures is the study of what made a start-up succeed. A detailed study of great start-ups turned viable businesses allows us to see the exciting yet sometimes quite painful paths that companies who made it experienced.

The result of your reading of this book will be the understanding of the logical path to commercialization for your discovery. In a step-by-step introduction to the methods, lingo, considerations and points of potential conflict, you will be able to navigate the road, hopefully avoiding the biggest potholes.

Summary

Academic entrepreneurship is on the rise. The current US economy and society may greatly benefit from the potential products and industries across every sector initiated by an academic discovery. Universities that create instructive, supporting, and encouraging environments for academics to commercialize technologies are likely to have more successes in this domain. Academics who educate themselves in entrepreneurship and who expand their social capital to include the innovation ecosystem will have a necessary foundation for success.

References

AUTM (2012). AUTM Licensing Activity Survey FY2012 Highlights. https://register.autm.net/detail.aspx?id=2012_SUMMARY (accessed May 30, 2017).
Bayh-Dole Act (1980). P.L. 96-517, Patent and Trademark Act Amendments of 1980. https://www.gpo.gov/fdsys/pkg/CHRG-110hhrg36592/pdf/ CHRG-110hhrg36592.pdf (accessed May 30, 2017).

Bercovitz, J. and M. Feldman (2008). "Academic entrepreneurs: Organizational change at the individual level." *Organization Science* **19**(1): 69–89.

Bowen, H. K., A. Kazaks, A. Muir-Harmony, and B. LaPierre (2005). Langer Lab, The: Commercializing Science. Harvard Business School, Case 605-017, October 2004. (Revised March 2005.)

Bureau of Economic Analysis (BEA) (2014). Haver Analytics. https://www.bea.gov/ (accessed May 30, 2017).

Chesbrough, H. (2006). *Open innovation: The new imperative for creating and profiting from technology*. Boston, Harvard Business School Publishing Corporation.

Committee on Science, Engineering and Public Policy (2007). Rising above the Gathering Storm: Energizing and Employing America for a Brighter Economic Future. Washington, DC, National Academies Press.

De Carolis, D. M. and P. Saparito (2006). "Social capital, cognition, and entrepreneurial opportunities: A theoretical framework." *Entrepreneurship Theory and Practice* **30**(1): 41–56.

Fortune (2015). http://fortune.com/2015/12/21/death-american-research-and-development/ graphic from OECD; Duke University's FUQUA School of Business (accessed May 3, 2017).

General Accounting Office (GAO) report (1986). Patent Policy: Universities Research Efforts Under Public Law 96-517. http://www.gao.gov/products/RCED-86-93 (accessed May 30, 2017).

Lubynsky, R. M. (2013). From lab bench to innovation: Critical challenges to Nascent Academic Entrepreneurs. Kansas City, Ewing Marion Kauffman Foundation.

Olson, S. and M. Dahlberg (2013). Trends in the Innovation Ecosystem: Can Past Successes Help Inform Future Strategies? Summary of Two Workshops, Committee on Science, Engineering, and Public Policy, Policy and Global Affairs. Washington, DC, National Academy of Sciences, The National Academies Press.

Shane, S. (2004). *Academic Entrepreneurship: University Spinoffs and Wealth Creation (New Horizons in Entrepreneurship Series)*. Cheltenham/ Northampton, Edward Elgar Publishing.

Slind-Flor, V. (2006). "The Bayh-Dole Battle." *Intellectual Asset Management* (Dec/Jan): 26–31.

Stevens, A. J., G. A. Johnson, and P. R. Sanberg (2011). "The Role of Patents and Commercialization in the Tenure and Promotion Process." *Technology and Innovation* **13**: 241–248.

2

Now What? Protect Your Intellectual Property

Discovery consists of seeing what everybody has seen and thinking what nobody has thought.
—Albert von Szent-Gyorgyi, Nobel Prize Awardee in Physiology or Medicine

Value creation of your research discovery starts with protecting the discovery so that no one else can use it without your permission. When a company is first started from an academic lab, there is most often no "product" to speak of, which makes the company automatically "early stage." One way to start to bring value to a commercial activity is to secure intellectual property (IP) around the invention that may be used to protect the eventual product from others who wish to copy and sell it. IP can take the form of a patent, trademark, copyright, or trade secret. This discussion is an attempt to summarize a small fraction of the complicated patent law into some relatable terms to help you understand the concepts needed to protect your discovery. It is by no means legal advice, and as the laws change frequently, it is necessary to consult with your legal counsel for the current law and practices.

The road to product commercialization can be filled with pivots and repositioning of technologies that may be impossible to predict as you're reading this today. For a successful outcome, you may need a portfolio of IP that could include one or more patents, copyrights, and/or trademarks that will enable you to practice the technology used in your product or service. A patent will prevent others from selling what you have claimed, but will not necessarily allow you to sell what you've claimed without infringing on someone else's patent (Figure 2.1). For that consideration, you will also need to consider your freedom to operate (FTO), which will enable you not to infringe on any other company's IP with your product. The following describe some general IP terms.

Academic Entrepreneurship: How to Bring Your Scientific Discovery to a Successful Commercial Product, First Edition. Michele Marcolongo.
© 2017 John Wiley & Sons, Inc. Published 2017 by John Wiley & Sons, Inc.

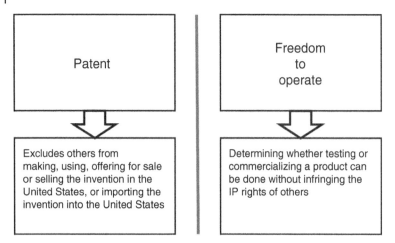

Figure 2.1 A patent can exclude others from selling your invention, but does not prevent you from infringing on someone else's patent.

Types of Intellectual Property

Patent

A patent for an invention is the grant of property rights to the inventor, issued by the USPTO. Generally, the term of a new patent is 20 years from the date on which the application for the patent was filed, subject to the payment of maintenance fees. The right conferred by the patent is "the right to exclude others from making, using, offering for sale, or selling" the invention in the United States or "importing" the invention into the United States. What is granted is not the right to make, use, offer for sale, sell, or import, but the right to exclude others from making, using, offering for sale, selling, or importing the invention. Once a patent is issued, the patentee must enforce the patent without aid of the USPTO.

There are three types of patents:

- *Utility patents* may be granted to anyone who invents or discovers any new and useful process, machine, article of manufacture, or composition of matter, or any new and useful improvement thereof;
- *Design patents* may be granted to anyone who invents a new, original, and ornamental design for an article of manufacture; and
- *Plant patents* may be granted to anyone who invents or discovers and asexually reproduces any distinct and new variety of plant. (direct quote USPTO website: uspto.gove/patents-getting-started)

Trademark or Service Mark

A trademark is a word, name, symbol, or device that is used in trade with goods to indicate the source of the goods and to distinguish them from the goods of others. A service mark is the same as a trademark except that it identifies and distinguishes the source of a service rather than a product. The terms "trademark" and "mark" are commonly used to refer to both trademarks and service marks.

Trademark rights may be used to prevent others from using a confusingly similar mark, but not to prevent others from making the same goods or from selling the same goods or services under a clearly different mark. Trademarks that are used in interstate or foreign commerce may be registered with the USPTO (direct quote USPTO website: uspto.gove/patents-getting-started: http://www.uspto.gov/patents-getting-started/general-information-concerning-patents#heading-2).

Copyright

Copyright is a form of protection provided to the authors of "original works of authorship" including literary, dramatic, musical, artistic, and certain other intellectual works, both published and unpublished. The 1976 Copyright Act generally gives the owner of copyright the exclusive right to reproduce the copyrighted work, to prepare derivative works, to distribute copies or phonorecords of the copyrighted work, to perform the copyrighted work publicly, or to display the copyrighted work publicly. Copyrights are registered by the Copyright Office of the Library of Congress (direct quote USPTO website: uspto.gov/patents-getting-started).

Trade Secret

Any practice or process of a company that is generally not known outside of the company. Information considered a trade secret gives the company an economic advantage over its competitors and is often associated with internal research and development. In order to be legally considered a trade secret in the United States, a company must take a reasonable effort in concealing the information from the public, the secret must intrinsically have economic value, and the trade secret must contain information. Trade secrets are the "classified documents" of the business world (Investopedia.com).

By law, in order for a patent to be granted by the USPTO, it must be found by the patent examiner to be novel and non-obvious. The description of novelty and non-obviousness, conditions for obtaining a patent, is as follows:

In order for an invention to be patentable it must be new as defined in the patent law, which provides that an invention cannot be patented if:

"(1) the claimed invention was patented, described in a printed publication, or in public use, on sale, or otherwise available to the public before the effective filing date of the claimed invention" or

"(2) the claimed invention was described in a patent issued [by the U.S.] or in an application for patent published or deemed published [by the U.S.], in which the patent or application, as the case may be, names another inventor and was effectively filed before the effective filing date of the claimed invention."

There are certain limited patent law exceptions to patent prohibitions (1) and (2) above. Notably, an exception may apply to a "disclosure made 1 year or less before the effective filing date of the claimed invention," but only if "the disclosure was made by the inventor or joint inventor or by another who obtained the subject matter disclosed… from the inventor or a joint inventor."

In patent prohibition (1), the term "otherwise available to the public" refers to other types of disclosures of the claimed invention such as, for example, an oral presentation at a scientific meeting, a demonstration at a trade show, a lecture or speech, a statement made on a radio talk show, a YouTube™ video, or a website or other on-line material.

Effective filing date of the claimed invention: This term appears in patent prohibitions (1) and (2). For a U.S. nonprovisional patent application that is the first application containing the claimed subject matter, the term "effective filing date of the claimed invention" means the actual filing date of the U.S. nonprovisional patent application (Figure 2.2). For a U.S. nonprovisional application that claims the benefit of a corresponding prior-filed U.S. provisional application, "effective filing date of the claimed invention" can be the filing date of the prior-filed provisional application provided the provisional application sufficiently describes the claimed invention. Similarly, for a U.S. nonprovisional application that is a continuation or division of a prior-filed U.S. nonprovisional application, "effective filing date of the claimed invention" can be the filing date of the prior filed nonprovisional application that sufficiently describes the claimed invention. Finally, "effective filing date of the claimed invention" may be the filing date of a prior-filed foreign patent application to which foreign priority is claimed provided the foreign patent application sufficiently describes the claimed invention.

Even if the subject matter sought to be patented is not exactly shown by the prior art, and involves one or more differences over the most nearly similar thing already known, a patent may still be refused if the differences would be obvious. The subject matter sought to be patented must be sufficiently different from what has been used or described before that

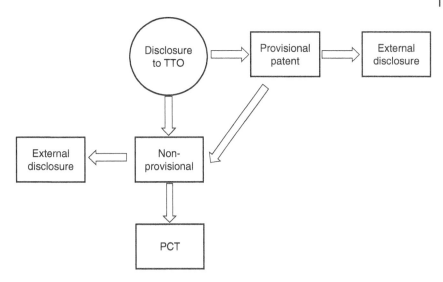

Figure 2.2 Preferred university disclosure and patent application process. Still possible to patent if you are 12 months past external disclosure.

it may be said to be non-obvious to a person having ordinary skill in the area of technology related to the invention. For example, the substitution of one color for another, or changes in size, are ordinarily not patentable (http://www.uspto.gov/patents-getting-started/general-information-concerning-patents#heading-2).

There can be quite a bit of strategy involved in writing a patent for your invention. You could follow the initial patent or other parent patents with a portfolio of expansive and/or defensive patents that preclude others from getting close practicing your technology.

This can get expensive very quickly due to both legal and filing fees. But these key pieces of IP are important because they are the initial foundation that you will use to build the value of a commercial product based on your technology. Spend the time to get it right.

Patenting and Public Disclosure Considerations

For a US patent a public disclosure is considered without limitation or obligation of secrecy. This is pretty broad but can be summarized by four categories (Northwestern INVO, no date):

1) Inventions described in printed publications
2) Inventions in public use

3) Inventions on sale
4) Inventions otherwise available to the public

For academics, perhaps the most widely applicable of these is the first. Printed publications can be those you would normally consider, such as book chapters, conference abstracts, journal articles, and theses. A public disclosure could be an email or other correspondence to someone outside of the university without stating that the information is confidential. Grant proposals to federal agencies are publications because they are accessible under the Freedom of Information laws. To protect confidential information in grants, the first page of the proposal should state that "Confidential Information-Pages X to Y of THIS PROPOSAL contain potentially patentable information." You must also write CONFIDENTIAL on the pages within the grant application that contain confidential information. Posters, Abstracts, and Proceedings all count as public disclosures as well. For oral presentations, there is a bit more subjectivity, but the rules state that if you distribute a copy of your presentation in which the invention is disclosed, it is a clear public disclosure. If no handouts are given, but an audience member takes notes that describe the invention, it would be a disclosure. Therefore, conference presentation, seminar, and thesis defense are potential public disclosures.

A public disclosure is information that is "enabling," giving sufficient details to allow "someone of ordinary skill in the art" to duplicate the invention. If you give limited information without describing details sufficient to enable duplication of the invention, then it will not be considered a public disclosure.

If you need to have a meeting with someone outside of the university around the invention before the patent is filed, it is critical to use a nondisclosure agreement (NDA), which both you and the designated representative from your university and the other party both sign. This should be discussed with the technology transfer office (TTO) and/or patent attorney to make sure that you are protecting your IP with the NDA. An NDA is a document that will describe terms of the agreement and secrecy of the discussion. An NDA will allow you much freedom for discussion around your market research and investment strategies and, in fact, is just good standard business practice even after you file your patent to protect confidential information. Your university will likely have a standard NDA available to you online or through the TTO. Otherwise, any attorney can provide you with a standard NDA template:

> **One Way Non-Disclosure Agreement:** A one-way non-disclosure agreement (NDA) is a legal contract between at least two parties that outlines confidential material, knowledge, or information that the disclosing party wishes to share with the receiving party for purposes of an actual or potential relationship, it wishes to restrict access to or by third parties. As such, and NDA protects nonpublic business information (www.upcounsel.com/one-way-non-disclosure agreement).

Two Way or Mutual Non-Disclosure Agreement: A mutual non-disclosure agreement (MDA) is a legal contract between at least two parties that outlines confidential material, knowledge, or information that the parties wish to share with one another for purposes of a potential or actual business relationship, but wish to restrict access to or by third parties. As such, and NDA protects nonpublic business information. (www.upcouncel.com/non-disclosure-agreement).

In 2013, US law for public disclosure on patentability was revised under the Leahy–Smith America Invents Act. Starting in 2013 (through the time of this writing in 2016), the United States converted to a first-to-file patent system, where a patent can be granted unless "the claimed invention was patented, described in a printed publication or in public use, on sale or otherwise available to the public before the effective filing date of the claimed invention." As summarized by Frommer Lawrence and Haug LLP (2016), a 1-year grace period prior to the filing of a patent application where public disclosure does not prevent patentability is in effect. The inventor's own publications and disclosures made within 1 year of filing an application do not constitute prior art (prior art is any public disclosure of the invention by anyone that occurred before your patent was filed). In addition, if someone else discloses subject matter relevant to your patent within 1 year after you have disclosed yours, it will not be considered prior art. This may lead you to think that you can disclose your discovery publically prior to filing your patent. While this strategy may work for you, there is risk in doing so. The US 2013 laws will need to be tested in court to see how they hold up when they are tested. Also, details that you think may not be important for the later patent application may become so as you progress through the process of writing and defending the patent by differentiating your discovery so that it is "non-obvious."

While the US laws have moved to the first-to-file patent system, international law is different. For Europe, Japan, and China, there is no recognition of a grace period for disclosures made prior to filing the patent application. This means that your own public disclosure can be used as prior art for your patent application, potentially making your patent "non-obvious." With our global economy, if there is no international coverage for your discovery, it may have greatly reduced value and, in some sectors, no value at all.

University Patenting Process

Protecting your invention may seem contrary to the open discussion of information that academics enjoy, but because this is the start of the transition from academia to commercialization for your invention, good business practices must be incorporated at this point forward.

Alyssa Panitch, Ph.D.
University of California Davis
Department Head and Professor Biomedical Engineering

Alyssa Panitch has co-founded three companies out of two universities and has learned a thing or two about start-ups. She is a highly innovative biomedical engineer with a knack for inventing new chemistries around peptides. Her first company, AzERx, was acquired after three years, while two others, Moerae Matrix and Symic Biomedical, are going strong.

Through the start-up process, Alyssa has developed business and management skills that have enabled her to be more efficient in entrepreneurship.

Alyssa served as CEO of her first company. She obtained financing, developed the value proposition, and managed the technology—everything to do with business. And she still had her day job as a professor. After the sale, she reconsidered her approach. For her next companies, her recommendation now is to bring in a management team. It's a big challenge to manage business and regulatory strategies, reimbursement, preclinical and clinical trials, payroll, hiring, and all of the twists and turns of a young business. Having a business team now allows her more time to be in the lab, creating new innovations, while the team is able to add value to the company. It took a little adjustment, though. "I had to accept someone else making decisions for the company, and losing control. We have to realize that we don't have the experience or time to do everything for the company, we have to rely on others."

While Alyssa has enjoyed much success with her companies, she does emphasize the time commitment involved in spinning out a technology from the university. Even with a management team, balancing the company activities with the additional obligations of a highly research-active faculty position as well as family, friends, and life was something that she underestimated at first. Before starting a company, she recommends that an academic consider the time commitment to the process that will be needed over many years.

A major skill that every academic entrepreneur needs is negotiating, which Alyssa found was one of the hardest things to manage early on. At first, academic entrepreneurs are negotiating what to in lab academically versus what to do for the interest of the company. Then, they're negotiating with the business team, the university, investors, and acquirers. The list goes on and on. Over time, she quickly developed strong negotiating skills, but those skills were well earned through numerous opportunities. "We need to understand that we can negotiate" as founders and participants in a company.

An observation that Alyssa notes is that university support has changed since she started her first company in 2002. At that time, she had to make the company happen on her own. There was little support within her university.

"The university didn't intentionally stand in the way, but didn't know how to help either." Starting her most recent company was a different experience. Her then university (Purdue) helped her meet the business team, helped with IP attorneys, gave early innovation funds, and catalyzed the company formation. The early innovation funds were helpful to fund proof-of-concept experiments and to build value proposition needed to get the company going. Purdue in particular has involved its alumni community to make connections for its start-ups. These alumni are spread throughout the country and mentor teams, get them ready for investment, and make introductions to VCs. These developing and helpful ecosystems will hopefully provide a rich environment to smoothly guide faculty along the path toward commercializing their technologies and bringing the innovations to society.

Or, they can just ask Alyssa.

In the university setting, this process begins with an internal disclosure (not considered public) to your TTO. The internal disclosure is a write-up on your concept and any supporting data that further substantiates the innovation. This could be a grant application with preliminary data, data that you are planning to submit in a thesis, a draft abstract for a conference, or an original text that gives some background to frame the innovation's significance. What you need to do is support the specific innovation with details of the design strategy, key features of the innovation, and some data that indicates that the concept can be put to practice. You or your TTO may take some time to do a prior art search, which is a search for anything close to your invention in the public literature or prior published patents. The more you know about the prior art in the field, the better you will be able to support the disclosure that will give you a better chance of success in the TTO moving forward with your disclosure to a patent application.

The TTO will evaluate the disclosure by whatever magic they choose (market potential, significance, likelihood of commercialization, their internal budget). Some TTOs have formal criteria and a committee that vets the disclosures, some use consultants, and others use their own analysis and gut reaction to the innovation submitted. Your TTO may be limited by budget, depending on your university's commitment to the area of technology commercialization. Real budget constraints force the TTO to prioritize IP decisions, limiting the amount of disclosures they can convert to patent applications. Typically, the TTO has a certain period of time by which they need to decide and inform you if your disclosure will be submitted as a patent application (typically a few months). This information is usually found in the university patent or IP policy. First thing to do is to check your university IP policy, which you may never have read before, to learn about the process. Also check the TTO website for any instructions and forms you might need.

If the TTO decides that the disclosure is *not* going to be patented, typically inventors are given the option to patent the technology themselves. This might be ok. After your own analysis and a conclusion that the technology is likely to lead to a viable business opportunity, you could still patent your invention hiring an attorney that is independent of the university using your own financial resources. In this case, you would bear the costs but would have ownership (you would be the assignee); therefore you would not have to license the technology from the university to pursue a business with this IP as a cornerstone for the commercial venture.

If, however, the TTO decides that they would like to protect your invention, then the university would own the potential patent that may be granted according to a form that you likely signed when you were hired to the university as part of your conditions of employment. Regardless of the approach, you have two options: you can file a provisional patent application or you can file a non-provisional (full) patent application. You may consider the provisional application option, because it allows you to submit to the US patent office, and hold your invention date (as long as a description of the invention is included) but still gives you *one year* from the provisional filing date until the full patent submission (including claims) must be made in the United States (USPTO, 2016). To hold your provisional filing date, you must include text and drawings in the provisional application in order to keep the provisional filing date in the non-provisional application. Further, the claims, which are not required in the provisional application but are necessary in the non-provisional application, must be supported by the text and drawings in the provisional application to keep the priority date. You may add additional text, drawings, and claims in the corresponding non-provisional, but the corresponding claims to the new matter will have the later priority date of the non-provisional, while claims supported by the provisional text and drawings will have the provisional filing date. The provisional application is not required to have a formal patent claim or an oath or declaration (USPTO, no date). The provisional patent application will *not* be reviewed by the patent office. It does, however, allow the term "patent pending" to be associated with the invention. Provisional patent applications are not published, with few exceptions. The provisional application is relatively inexpensive and can be done quickly, so often it is used as a placeholder before the consideration of the level of investment that a university will make in the protection of the technology.

Your other option is to directly submit a non-provisional patent application (without a provisional application), which is examined by a patent examiner and may be issued as a patent if all the requirements for patentability are met, such as all of the text, drawings, and claims. The non-provisional application will be published after 18 months, regardless of whether or not the patent has been issued. Each year the USPTO receives more than 500 000 patent applications. Most of the applications filed with the USPTO are non-provisional applications for utility patents.

It may also be worthwhile pursuing an international filing through the Patent Cooperation Treaty (PCT) that will allow your patent to be considered for protection in 148 countries simultaneously for one set of fees. The United States is part of the PCT. Generally, after the patent is filed in the United States, you have one year to file the international application under the PCT. During the national phase of the PCT review process, you decide in which countries that you'd like to proceed and then will be required to pay national fees (for each country) and in some cases filing translations with the application. The World Intellectual Property Organization (WIPO) administers the PCT (wipo.int).

The only eventual drawback to extensive filing is the considerable expense of filing independently in each country. This is a discussion that you will have to have with the TTO as you go along and you consider the likelihood of commercialization and the international market potential for a product or service that may result from your invention. If the university has decided to protect your invention with a patent application, the university will cover all expenses. However, each university has a different policy on whether they will file in the United States only or internationally and for how long they will continue to make payments on the patent through the long prosecution process. It is important to ask this from your TTO early in the process so that you get a sense of timing and what the plan is for the prosecution of your patent as well as any decision points in the process (such as the decision to abandon the patent or expand filings to additional countries).

After the provisional or non-provisional patent application has been made, you are free to present your findings and publish your work without the risk of interfering with the viability of your patent. This is an important point. *The protection of your IP should not preclude your ability to disseminate your research findings.* However, protection of your invention may delay the presentation or publication of your findings outside the university or at an open forum within the university, such as a thesis defense. If there is an imminent disclosure (talk you have to give next week), the TTO can often push a provisional application through in a day or two. Overall, the protection of your IP should not be a significant impediment to the dissemination of your knowledge as an academic researcher. The American Association of University Professors issued the following statement of IP:

> Inventions—despite distinctions often drawn in university policy statements—are a natural outgrowth of scholarly activities. The scholarly nature of university-based inventions does not simply disappear with the addition of a potential patent or other intellectual property rights.
>
> *AAUP, Statement of Intellectual Property, June 2014*

Once you decide that you will disclose your invention, you need to consider all the inventors who participated as co-inventors. By patent law, a granted patent can be invalidated if there is an inventor who was not included on the patent application. Think seriously about this part. We often have numerous colleagues for collaborative research: other faculty members, graduate students, postdoctoral students, undergraduate students, physicians, and others. There could be co-inventors outside your own university, which will require a few more steps of negotiation and agreements between your university TTO and theirs. This is done quite often but can result in a filing delay.

According to the terms of the typical university patent policy, each patent by a university employee (faculty member, postdoc, graduate student, medical doctor) is owned by the university. However, undergraduate students can fall into a category of their own. Because undergraduate students are not employees of the university, they can own their contribution to the patent themselves in some cases. Again, this varies from university to university. If an undergraduate is involved as a co-inventor of the patent, the university may offer them to sign their rights over the university, and in the future, the university will fully support the prosecution of patent. If undergraduates are the only inventors, the university may choose to finance the patenting of the technology or decline to patent the technology and enable the undergraduates to continue with the patent prosecution on their own.

For each invention, a percentage contribution to the invention from each of the inventors can be assigned. Some groups of co-inventors decide to split their contributions of the patent equally. *Whether you are going to divide inventorship evenly among your co-inventors or not, then the discussion of each member's relative contribution should occur at the time of the filing of the disclosure.* Failure to do so early in the process, before there even is a patent, before any value can be ascribed to the patent, and before any investment is made in a start-up based on the patent, can lead to ugly discussions/negotiations later in the life of the patent. After time has passed from the initial disclosure, the inventors have the opportunity to remember invention contributions with their own perspectives, which may not be the same among each inventor, leading to conflict among inventors. This cannot be emphasized enough. There are numerous examples of inventors who do not go along with the rest of the co-inventors and want to go on separately down path toward commercialization or inventors who feel they deserve a higher percentage of contribution in the patent either at the time of filing or as time goes on. **This is step one of how a company can fail before it even starts.** You have an opportunity for an honest discussion at the time of disclosure, when the promise is high but the stakes are still low because no fame or fortune is involved yet. The best advice at this time is to be honest about inventor contributions, with the acknowledgment that there would likely be no invention without each inventor's contribution. Work with each other in good faith and in a professional manner. Throughout the process, communication among inventors is critical to keeping everyone informed and involved in the patent prosecution to the extent that they want to be.

No matter how well you write the non-provisional patent application, years after you submit it, the patent examiner may come back to you with an office action describing numerous reasons why your patent is not unique and non-obvious (for at least some of the claims). Do not be alarmed. This is the patent examiner's job. The examiners need to ensure that each patent granted is differentiated from prior art in the field, so they will be conservative in the assessment.

The good news is, just like a grant review at NIH, you have a chance to rebut the critique. With the help of the patent attorney, you can use your data and analyses to build an argument to differentiate yourself from the patent examiner's cited prior art. You can adjust your claims so that they fall within the open space for granting the patent. Your rebuttal can be done in writing and when necessary by a call or visit to the patent examiner's office with your attorney and perhaps a member of the TTO. If you visit, you can bring demos or anything you like to help better explain your point to win claims for your patent.

Once the patent has been fully prosecuted, it will be granted with whatever claims you were able to secure. Are you now legally permitted to sell your product that uses the patented technology? Maybe...

Patent law will fill volumes more than this short chapter, and you should seek the advice of your attorney, no doubt. You should know at least enough to ask some important questions of your patent attorney. The first is: does the product, based on the IP we've secured, infringe on anyone else's patents, that is, do you have freedom to operate (FTO)? Investors can be concerned about the FTO and rightfully so. The FTO is an extensive search that can be quite costly and that will take all of the features of your final product and ensure that can you have "freedom" to use them as compared with all of the other patents that have been granted. This is critical to understanding the patent landscape of your product or service and usually not undertaken by the university, but by a start-up company or other company that is licensing your IP during due diligence.

> **Freedom to Operate:** Determining whether a particular action, such as testing or commercializing a product can be done without infringing the intellectual property rights of others (bios.net/daisy/patentlens).

What if there's something close to what you have? You then have some decisions to make in the product itself. One option is redesigning a feature so as not to infringe on another patent and to provide FTO. Another option is for your company to license the existing technology from the patent holder on whose patent you are infringing. Many business solutions may be able to work around this issue, but it is important to understand the starting framework and discuss this with your patent attorney as you go through development.

Another interesting aspect of patent law is that even if the patent is granted, you could still be challenged in court by another patent holder. A patent's validity can be reversed if it is challenged and decided by a court of law. This brings a potential level of uncertainty to the whole patent system. These challenges are not so common and typically occur only after you've had some level of success, but still something to be aware of in the patent business.

Are more patents better than one patent? The unequivocal answer is... maybe. A strong patent can be the basis for an entire business, but additional patents around it create a virtual fortress that not only protects the business with the original patent but also expands the reach of that patent with the additional IP to expand the territory and time frame in which you can operate and others can't. Patent strategies can depend on funding (GE's might be different from yours and MIT's might be different from another university's) and business strategy (some IP is never protected and maintained as a trade secret, like the recipe for Coke).

One thing is certain in the protection of IP. The quality of your patent attorney is priceless. A patent attorney who is sophisticated in your sector, with a knowledge of prior art and even a close technical background, will be better positioned to plan the patent strategy and help you to create a strong and defensible patent. If your TTO is not using the strongest attorney for your sector of technology, use your best persuasive skills to request a change to your suggested attorney. It is that critical that the patent be as strong as possible.

Investors and their attorneys will review your patents closely. If the patent has not issued yet, they are likely to solicit a patentability opinion from an independent attorney or an attorney of their choosing. A patentability opinion is a letter from a patent attorney (generally not yours) that assesses the likelihood that the patent will be granted. You may also have to get a patentability opinion yourself on unissued patents before investors will even talk with you seriously. Again, a large part of the value that an "early-stage" company has is dependent on the IP; make every effort to get it right from the start.

The Anatomy of a Patent

As you start to progress through protection of your IP and analysis of others, you will find yourself reading a lot of patents. It helps to understand the various coding and structure of those patents, so that you can best assess their relevance.

Jeffrey Lotz, Ph.D.
University of California at San Francisco
Professor, Orthopaedic Surgery
Director, Bioengineering Lab

Jeff Lotz got into academic entrepreneurship through an interesting pathway. While working in his orthopedic biomechanics lab with his close clinical collaborator and orthopedic surgeon, David Bradford, he started consulting to Bay Area venture capitalists and companies. Through this work, Jeff developed a deep network of VCs and strong industry collaborations.

At about this same time, another factor was at work. Every time Jeff took his kids to a soccer match or birthday party with their Bay Area friends, the adult conversation inevitably turned toward how the parents' start-ups were doing. "In the San Francisco Bay area, there are lots of people who take risks."

These factors along with a few innovative discoveries in the lab led to the development of Jeff's first start-up, Relievant, with his partner, David Bradford. Over the next several years, three additional start-ups followed.

One early observation that Jeff made about his research was that not every interesting scientific discovery translates to a clinically relevant product. When he and his clinical collaborators do find a sweet spot, early in the process they bring in a business partner (CEO). "An experienced CEO can do the detailed market analysis and bring investment to the start-up." He also partners with professionals who can guide the company in reimbursement and regulatory affairs. He takes an advisory role in the company and "passes the baton" to the professionals. He believes it's a mistake to assume an academic can do all that's needed for a company alone.

With all of these partners, Jeff recognizes that "science is worth something, but not everything." "Financially, by the time you take IP from a university and get a product through the FDA regulatory process, there is so much dilution, there is not much left for the founders." He goes into this process with eyes open. He doesn't believe that the start-up will lead to a "retirement event." He's realistic. Is this fun? Making life interesting? A start-up can be a serious commitment for the "long haul," with some companies needing ten years before they are profitable or can be sold. Jeff believes that you should enjoy the process, not be miserable and just trying to get to the end for the reward. If it's just about personal financial gain, it doesn't make much sense.

That being said, there are ways to retain your equity in the start-up. Early investing by angels is typically non-dilutive funding, the angels don't take control of the company and the company can still move forward. SBIR/STTRs are slow but non-dilutive methods to increase value in the company. Finally, bring in the VCs. "The VCs have incentives to make money for the people investing in their fund; they do not look out for the founder or the company." Still, at some point, you'll need some serious financing, and the VCs can provide this. Jeff manages this by negotiating his own matching shares to go along with VC investment. The VCs will re-up his shares if they find value in what he brings to the company. He has found that having good relations with the VCs has helped him protect his interest. But if different founders are awarded shares differently during this process, it can "get messy" within the operations of the company.

When asked about something he wished he had known before he started down the academic entrepreneurship path, Jeff is clear: interpersonal relationships. "Working around egos is tough." The process will be stressful and you need to know that your team has your back and that they will look out for the good of the team, not just themselves. When money is at stake, it's not always clear what people will do. You need to have a sense of yourself, who you can trust and who might be trying to use you to earn a quick buck. "Trust is important."

With all of the lessons Jeff has learned in the business world, perhaps the biggest educational challenge was within his own university.

It wasn't easy at first. Ten years ago, when Relievant was founded, the culture at UCSF took a "bipolar view of industry." Some faculty felt that any industrial relationships led to automatic bias and inherent conflict. Others took a different perspective and partnered with industry through the SBIR/STTR programs. The University rules made start-ups cumbersome. The start-up had significant frustration with the University. "There were lots of bumps and bruises."

More recently, UCSF is undergoing a transformation to a more industry-friendly environment. There is now a conflict-of-interest committee that promotes an active process to disclose any conflicts online to provide transparency and to manage conflict, rather than simply banning working with a company. UCSF is launching new programs in entrepreneurship and innovation, a turn of events that many universities are now exploring. This type of evolution in the policies of many universities across the country is positive for academic entrepreneurs and is the result of pioneers like Jeff who showed just how successful academic entrepreneurship can be.

Brown and Michaels legal firm has put together an easy-to-use process for reading patents (Brown and Michaels, PC, 2016a). The methods are summarized here. The front page of a patent has codes that give information about the patent (Figure 2.3). Referring to Figure 2.4, these are the following:

(12) Type of document: The US Patent is for issued patents. If the patent is not issued, there may be "patent application publication," "reissued patent," "defensive publication," or "statutory invention registration." Usually the last name of the lead inventor is under the document type.

(10) Identification of the publication
(11) Number of the publication
(12) Kind of the publication
(13) Kind of document code (according to ST.16)
(19) Country code (ST.3), or other identification, of the country of publication
(20) Local filing details
(21) Number given to the application
(22) Date of making application
(23) Other date(s) of filing, such as of complete application
(24) Date from which industrial property rights may have effect
(25) Language in which the published application was originally filed
(26) Language in which the application is published
(30) Priority details
(31) Number assigned to priority application
(32) Date of filing of priority application
(33) Country in which priority application was filed
(34) Priority filings under regional or international arrangements. At least one Paris Convention member state (or WTO member) must be named
(40) Date of publication
(41) Date of making available to the public by viewing, or copying on request, an unexamined specification which has not yet been granted
(42) Date of making available to the public by viewing, or copying on request, an examined specification which has not yet been granted
(43) Date of publication by printing of an unexamined specification which has not yet been granted
(44) Date of publication by printing of an examined specification which has not yet been granted
(45) Date of publication by printing of a granted patent
(46) Date of publication by printing of the claim(s) only
(47) Date of making a granted patent available to the public by viewing, or copying on request
(48) Date of issuing a correction
(50) Technical information
(51) International Patent Classification
(52) Domestic or national Classification or Cooperative Patent Classification
(53) Universal Decimal Classification
(54) Title of the invention
(55) Keywords
(56) List of prior art documents
(57) Abstract or claim
(58) Field of search
(60) Reference to other legally related domestic document(s)
(61) Related by addition
(62) Related by division
(63) Related by continuation
(64) Related by reissue
(65) Related by being the same application
(66) Related by filing after abandonment
(67) Related by filing as a utility model after filing as a patent
(68) Related by filing for a Supplementary Protection Certificate (SPC)
(70) Identification of parties
(71) Name of applicant

Figure 2.3 Standard field codes for patents (Brown and Michaels, PC, 2016).

---

(72) Name of inventor
(73) Name of grantee
(74) Name of attorney or agent
(75) Name of inventor who is also applicant—*Note: code (75) was used only for US patents applied for before September 16, 2012, since only the US had the requirement that the inventor and applicant had to be the same—after that date, US law changed to allow assignees to be applicants, so codes (71) and (72) should be used in the US as they had been in other countries.*
(76) Name of inventor who is also applicant and grantee—*same note applies as to code (75)—codes (71) and (72) will be used instead of (76).*
(80) and (90) Identification of data related to International Conventions and to legislation with respect to SPCs
(81) Designated State(s) according to the Patent Cooperation Treaty (PCT)
(83) Information relating to deposit of microorganisms under e.g. the Budapest Treaty
(84) Designated contracting states under regional patent conventions
(85) Date of supply of the international patent application to the national patent office
(86) Filing data of the international application
(87) Publication data of the international application
(88) Date of deferred publication of the search report
(91) Date on which an international document filed under the PCT fails to enter the national or regional phase
(92) For an SPC, number and date of the first national authorization to place the product on the market
(93) For an SPC, number, date and where applicable country of origin of first authorization to place the product on the market within a regional economic community
(94) Calculated date of expiry of the SPC, or the duration of the SPC
(95) Name of the product protected by the basic patent and the SPC
(96) Regional filing data
(97) Regional publication data

Figure 2.3 (Continued)

(10) Patent number: The United States typically precedes the number for a utility patent: AI is additional improvement, B is reexamination, D is design patent, H is statutory invention registration, NP is non-patent literature, PP is plant patent, RE is reissue patent, T is defensive publication, and X is for very old patents before numbers were issued.

(45) Date of patent: Date issued by the USPTO (always a Tuesday).

(54) Title: Full title of the patent.

(75) Inventors: All of the inventors with city of residence.

(73) Assignee: The owner of the patent, for example, your university.

(*) Term extension notice: Term of patent is extended due to the delays in processing, usually by a number of days.

(21) Application number: The identifying number of the application that the patent was based.

(22) Filing date: The filing date is the actual filing date, not necessarily the first filing date used for determining paten term.

US007214245B1

(12) **United States Patent**
Marcolongo et al.

(10) Patent No.: **US 7,214,245 B1**
(45) Date of Patent: **May 8, 2007**

(54) **ASSOCIATING HYDROGELS FOR NUCLEUS PULPOSUS REPLACEMENT IN INTERVERTEBRAL DISCS**

(75) Inventors: **Michele Marcolongo**, Landsdowne, PA (US); **Anthony Lowman**, Wallingford, PA (US)

(73) Assignee: **Drexel University**, Philadelphia, PA (US)

(*) Notice: Subject to any disclaimer, the term of this patent is extended or adjusted under 35 U.S.C. 154(b) by 106 days.

(21) Appl. No.: **10/111,782**

(22) PCT Filed: **Oct. 27, 2000**

(86) PCT No.: **PCT/US00/29874**

§ 371 (c)(1),
(2), (4) Date: **Dec. 23, 2002**

(87) PCT Pub. No.: **WO01/32100**

PCT Pub. Date: **May 10, 2001**

Related U.S. Application Data

(60) Provisional application No. 60/162,338, filed on Oct. 29, 1999.

(51) Int. Cl.
A61F 2/44 (2006.01)

(52) U.S. Cl. **623/17.16**; 623/17.11; 623/926

(58) Field of Classification Search 623/17.11, 623/17.16, 926
See application file for complete search history.

(56) **References Cited**

U.S. PATENT DOCUMENTS

5,106,876 A	*	4/1992	Kawamura 522/5
5,143,071 A	*	9/1992	Keusch et al. 600/397
5,192,326 A		3/1993	Bao et al. 623/17
5,262,475 A		11/1993	Creasy 525/58
5,314,478 A		5/1994	Oka et al. 623/18
5,458,643 A		10/1995	Oka et al. 623/18
5,534,028 A	*	7/1996	Bao et al. 623/17.16
5,824,093 A		10/1998	Ray et al. 623/17
5,846,214 A		12/1998	Makuuchi et al. 602/52
5,976,186 A	*	11/1999	Bao et al. 623/17.16
6,231,605 B1	*	5/2001	Ku 623/11.11
2002/0198599 A1	*	12/2002	Haldimann 623/17.16

FOREIGN PATENT DOCUMENTS

JP   09262279 A   * 10/1997

* cited by examiner

Primary Examiner—Paul B. Prebilic
(74) *Attorney, Agent, or Firm*—Stroock & Stroock & Lavan LLP

(57) **ABSTRACT**

A prosthetic nucleus prepared from blends of polyvinylal-cohol and polyvinyl pyrollidone or its copolymers for replacement of the nucleus pulposus in intervertebral discs is provided. Also provided are methods of replacing the nucleus pulposus and treating disc degeneration-associated pain in mammals using this prosthetic nucleus.

6 Claims, No Drawings

Figure 2.4 Sample front page of patent.

(65) Prior publication data: If the patent was published while it was a pending application, the publication number and date will be listed.

(60) Related US application data and (30) foreign priority data: If the patent is related to any other applications or patents, they will be listed.

(51) International patent classification: Classification by subject matter based on the International Patent Classification system that categorizes according to function or operation of the invention.

(52) US Patent Classification: Prior to 2014, the United States has its own classification system but now uses a Cooperative Patent Classification or CPC system.

(58) Field of search: The United States classes/subclasses the examiner search when examining the patent and can guide you toward places you should be looking for similar patents.

(56) References cited: Prior art that the examiner found in searching. Those with * are ones that the examiner found were particularly relevant to patentability of the patent.

Primary examiner: The examiner who did the examination of the application.

(74) Attorney, agent, or firm: Firm who filed and prosecuted the applications. (57) Abstract: Summary of the invention (less than 150 words).

Number of claims and drawing sheets: Summary of totals.

Representative drawing: The examiner selects one drawing, usually Figure 2.1, to put on the front page of the patent.

After the front page, the remainder of the patent document is called the "specification."

Title of the Invention
Cross-reference to related applications: If the patent is related to others, it will be stated after the title. A related patent might be a provisional, a divisional, or a continuation-in-part application.
Statement regarding federally sponsored research or development: If the invention was developed under a contract from a US government agency, the government retains some rights in the patent. The contract will define these rights, but at a minimum, the government will have a paid-up license to practice the invention.
Reference to a "Microfiche Appendix": If there is a long data list, it will appear as an appendix (e.g., code).
Background of the Invention:
1) Field of invention: Broad description of the area of technology for the patent. Usually stated in two sentences, it paraphrases the classification designation.
2) Description of the related art: Prior art or what was known before the invention. In the recent years, becoming more brief, but which may describe prior art and the limitations of that art in light of the invention.
Summary of the invention: General statement of the invention may point out advantages on the invention or how it solves problems discussed in the Background section. It most often encompasses the broadest claim that was in the initial application.
Brief description of the drawing: Reference to and brief drawing descriptions (one sentence).
1) Most patents have drawings that help to describe the invention. The drawings may be schematics of the design, flowcharts, images, graphs, or other ways to help explain the invention and embodiments.
Detailed description of invention: Description of the preferred embodiments is used to describe the embodiments in detail. Each of the figures explained

and every reference number in the drawings will be called out and explained. Examples can be used to demonstrate utility of the invention.

a) Embodiments: Versions or variations on the invention. They are examples that demonstrate the same invention.

The claims are last in the printed patent, but on the USPTO database, they come right after the abstract. The claims are the most important part of the patent in that they state what is covered by the patent. The only thing that the patent holder can prevent others from making, using, or selling is what is covered in the claims.

For design and plant patents, there is only one claim. For design the claims states, "A design as shown in the figures" and for plant "A new and distinct X plant named Y, as described and illustrated." Utility patents are those that have more of a structure and subtlety to them. Claims are numbered and typically start with claim 1 as the broadest claim. Grammatically, a claim is a long run-on sentence, sometimes with subdivisions a, b, c, and so on. There are two types of claims: independent and dependent. An independent claim is one that stands alone. The independent claim can have the following structure: preamble-connecting word list of elements.

From the patent of Figure 2.4, an independent claim reads:

Claim 1: *A prosthetic nucleus* for replacing at least a portion of a natural nucleus pulosus of an intervertebral disc, *comprising* an associating hydrogel, in said prosthetic nucleus, prepared from a blend polyvinyl alcohol and polyvinyl pyrollidone, wherein the associating hydrogel comprises from 0.5 to 2.5% polyvinyl pyrollidone.

In this case the preamble is "a prosthetic nucleus" and the connecting word is "comprising." In patent language, the connecting or transition words have specific meanings. Two commonly used connecting words are the following:

- *Comprising*: Comprising…(a list) means that the device has "at least" these things but might have other things also.
- *Consisting of*: Consisting of…(a list) means that the device has that list and nothing else.

A dependent claim is one that only has meaning when combined with a preceding claim. A dependent claim for the patent of Figure 2.4, which is dependent on the first claim, is claim 6:

Claim 6: The prosthetic nucleus of claim 1, wherein the associating hydrogel comprises about 1% polyvinyl pyrollidone.

In this case, claim 6 limits claim 1, but would not be able to be used without claim 1. Each dependent claim must be narrower than the claim on which it depends.

How to Read a Patent

Interpreting coverage of the claims of a patent is best done with the help of your patent attorney (Brown and Michaels, PC, 2016b). There are some strategies to reading patents, and for your discovery, you'll likely end up ready with many of them. The usual method that researchers use in reading journal articles, starting with the abstract, is not usually helpful for patents because their abstracts are intentionally vague.

To get an idea of the significance of the patent to you, go right to the claims. Separate the independent from the dependent claims. The independent claims usually start with the word "A." There are probably less than five independent claims, but there may be more. Google Patents displays dependent claims in gray text, saving you even more time. After reading the independent claims, you'll have a good idea of what the patent is about. If it is significant for you, look at the drawings. The drawings are useful in helping to describe the invention and may have a detailed illustration of a manufactured good, block diagram representing parts of a system and/or a flowchart for method or software. If you are still interested, or concerned, then spend the time to read the specification, starting with the summary, which will concisely tell what the patent is about.

You may find that you will be reading patents for different reasons. Jon Schuchardt (Dilworthip, 2013) describes four perspectives that you may consider when reading a patent:

1) *Reading for technical information.* To understand the technical accomplishments described in the patent, focus on the Background section and Summary, ignoring the detailed description. Experimental examples help to show what was accomplished and how it improves on prior art. Then focus on detailed description.

2) *Reading for patentability.* Is your invention patentable in light of this patent? The entire patent is relevant to patentability because of novelty. Asking yourself if your invention would be obvious to a skilled person with what is taught in this patent is a good way to view your reading. A common mistake is the assumption that if they didn't claim it, you can patent it, but that is incorrect because the entire body of the patent is taken into consideration with non-obviousness.

3) *Reading for infringement.* Infringement is being able to make your product without overlapping with what they have claimed. This is your assessment of what you are able to do, also called a FTO. The claims should be your concentration for a review of infringement.

4) *Reading for validity.* Here again, the focus is on claims, but with a focus on whether there are other references that would satisfy us that the claims lack validity. This is useful for especially broad claims.

Taking the time early in your path toward translation of your discovery toward commercialization to learn about the nuances of patenting and patent law will serve you well and help you to bring value to your discovery.

Summary

The first step toward developing a viable business is to protect the IP associated with your discovery. This starts with disclosure of the invention to the TTO, and a provisional patent and a year later a non-provisional patent application, if approved, will create value. The safest way for you to approach patenting is to limit public disclosure of your discovery unless you have confidentiality or your IP has been protected by a provisional or non-provisional patent application or appropriate copyrighting or trademarking.

References

American Association of University Professors (AAUP) (2014). Committee A on Academic Freedom and Tenure. Statement on Intellectual Property. American Association of University Professors Bulletin: 35–37, Washington, DC.

Brown and Michaels, PC (2016a). Intellectual Property Homepage. http://www.bpmlegal.com/ (accessed May 30, 2017).

Brown and Michaels, PC (2016b) How to Read a Patent, http://www.bpmlegal.com/howtopat1.html (accessed May 4, 2017).

Frommer Lawrence and Haug LLP (2016). "Not Your Parents One-Year Grace Period: Pre-Application Invention Disclosures Under the AIA," http://www.flhlaw.com/Not-YOur-parents-One-Year-Grace-period-Pre-Application-Invention-Disclosures-under-the-AIA/ (accessed May 4, 2017).

Northwestern University, INVO—Innovation and New Ventures Office (no date), https://invo.northwestern.edu/overview-public-disclosures (accessed May 29, 2017).

Schuchardt, J. (2013). "Basic Patent Law III: How to Read a Patent," www.dilworthip.com/basic-patnet-law-iii-how-to-read-a-patent/ (accessed May 4, 2017).

United States Patent and Trademark Office (USPTO) (no date), https://www.uspto.gov/learning-resources (accessed May 29, 2017).

Upcounsel.com, https://www.upcounsel.com/ (accessed May 4, 2017).

USPTO (2016). https://www.uspto.gov/ (accessed May 30, 2017).

Wipo.int.

3

Are They Buying What You're Selling?
The Search Phase

So often people are working hard at the wrong thing. Working on the right thing is probably more important than working hard.
—Caterina Fake, Cofounder, Flickr

Interestingly, not all amazing scientific discoveries translate into a product that the market is ready to adopt. When you ask any successful entrepreneur what the absolute first thing to get right, the answer is the market need. A major reason that start-ups fail is because they build a product that no one cares about. It's an easy trap for start-ups to forge ahead into the execution phase, designing and proving their product, without sufficient information about the market. You have an opportunity to get this critical information up front and all it really takes is time and energy.

When putting a business together, there are several points of risk. The idea of creating the business framework, especially when you're starting from a research discovery, is to de-risk the business opportunity. We typically think of de-risking the technology (through feasibility studies, manufacturing scale up, etc.; see Chapter 5), but the first part of taking risk out of the business is understanding and defining the real market needs. This data goes a long way toward convincing yourself as well as potential investors of the value of your business opportunity so that you can most efficiently get to the finish line (and can actually find it).

Steve Blank, a serial entrepreneur and lecturer at Stanford University, among others, has spent considerable time thinking about the best way to help entrepreneurs explore the real market need. Through his rich career as an attorney, serial entrepreneur, investor, author, and professor, he has learned a few things about starting companies (Blank and Dorf, 2012). His catchphrase, "get out of the building," summarizes his suggested approach to market research. Talking with potential customers about your product is a way to see what features

Academic Entrepreneurship: How to Bring Your Scientific Discovery to a Successful Commercial Product, First Edition. Michele Marcolongo.
© 2017 John Wiley & Sons, Inc. Published 2017 by John Wiley & Sons, Inc.

about your potential product excite them, which are functional and which they can easily live without. In recent years, Steve has modulated his tech start-up approach to academic start-ups. The NSF has adopted his model into their Innovation Corps (I-Corps) program. Shortly after that, Steve adopted his novel approach for the NIH I-Corps program. Fundamentally, his approach is consistent in that he uses his customer discovery and validation philosophy to help articulate a hypothesis about the market need for a product, then tests that hypothesis, and finally validates the customer base (Figure 3.1). This is an approach that resonates with scientists, who are used to setting and testing hypotheses. Who does all of this primary market research? There is no substitute for the key personnel involved with the innovation, so the I-Corps programs encourage the faculty member, grad student, or postdoc to engage in the primary market research. Steve's reasoning is that those who are deeply familiar with the technology can manage the customer conversations, allowing them to really probe for information to help them understand the real customer need. Steve believes that performing (not hiring out) your own primary marketing research (not hiring out your marketing research) is critical for digging down to the essence of the market need from the customers who you want to buy your future product.

Most academic researchers have not gone to business school. Some may not be comfortable having numerous conversations with potential customers. Steve recommends 100 interviews with potential customers for the NSF I-Corps model. This is the first part of business development for your invention that may push you out of your comfort zone. It's sometimes difficult for well-established experts in one domain, like you, to put themselves into a more unknown domain, like market research and conversations with potential customers. This requires leaving a bit of ego at the door, and from the NSF I-Corps experience, that has proven to be a major challenge to the success of those academics in the program.

Even finding the right people to talk to can be challenging. Technical markets are different from consumer markets. For example, a new way to process aluminum castings may only be interesting for a handful of metallurgical companies in the sector. These types of business-to-business

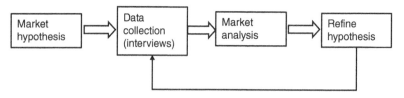

Figure 3.1 Test your market hypothesis by doing interviews and then refine your hypothesis. The endless loop is intentional to continue the process through product launch.

discussions will have a different customer composition than a new app that helps you get a beach body in 30 days. A highly efficient and inexpensive technology for a solar panel may be interesting to homeowners, government agencies, institutions, and corporations, among others. Your research may have to include these varied groups of stakeholders with purchasing power. Medical devices and pharmaceuticals as well as health IT will have different levels of customers, which may include patients, nursing staff, medical doctors, and/or health care administrators. Additional considerations may need to be made if the market is international or governed by regulations. How will different constraints in the marketplace affect the appetite for your product? The only way to know for sure is to talk to your potential customers.

Whatever your hypothesized customer base might be (and you may have to circle back a few times, learning as you go), "getting out of the building" or in your case, the lab, and talking with potential customers will be an education in itself. If 100% of your interviews come back positive for the product that you propose, congratulations, you are now ready to enter the next phase of business development. Are you really onto something? Can you expand the product in some way? Perhaps through your discussions you've learned about another critical market need and can make an additional product with your technology or new technology, then circle back with the customers to expand your business and product line.

What happens if the answer is, well, about half liked it? You have your first decision point in the preparation for your business. Can you move the percentage of likes higher? How can your discovery better meet the market need? Can the product be tweaked to add features, can the price be reduced, or will combining your discovery with another technology solve the problem and make $2 + 2 = 10$? You can try a few scenarios, refining your hypothesis, and continue the market research.

Sometimes the potential customers will emphatically and decisively say no to your concept. Be sure you have the right group of customers, and if you do, the best thing you can do for yourself is listen to them. If you can rework your product and get a positive response, then great. But, sometimes the answer is really no, about half of the time according to Steve's studies. Think of this as a gift. You now know this marketing study has just saved you lots of time and resources. Publish some papers on your technology. Maybe the next time you're proposing some work to the NSF or NIH, you'll have this marketing experience in mind. It may help you pose a different research question. You may take a new direction in your lab that might better address the science behind the customer needs that you learned about. In the start-up world, every experience is good. There is no single recipe for success, and the experience that you have had and contacts that you have made may come back to help you later.

Example

You and your team have discovered a new way to sense and monitor patient data in real time using an e-diagnostic protocol and sensor. The patent application is filed. You are now poised to collect some data on the market potential for this system. Your first hypothesis is that the e-diagnostic can be used in smart hospital rooms to better ensure care of the patients in a minimally invasive manner. You quickly determine that this e-diagnostic can be used in the general/surgical area of the hospital.

Who are your customers? You may start by discussing the e-diagnostic with surgeons and clinicians who are responsible for hospitalized patients. You interview 5 general surgeons and ask them to rate their response from 1 to 10 (low–high) on two questions: Would this system help your patients? Would you buy this system?

Your 5 data points are really informative. Of the 5 surgeons, all seemed to like the e-diagnostic concept. The answer to the first question, "Would this system help your patients?," resulted in an average of 6/10. When probing this question more deeply, you find that the patients are already being monitored for the data that you will collect with the e-diagnostic. However, this system would provide the added benefit of not having nurses continually interrupt the patients' rest to collect the data manually. It may help the patients get more rest but would not necessarily change the outcome of the patients' care because they really don't need to collect the data continually. What they really need is to know when an adverse reading is detected that does require a change in patient care.

In answer to the second question "Would you buy this system?," the average from the 5 surgeons was only a 2. It turns out that surgeons do not select patient monitoring systems. That falls entirely on the nursing staff. The surgeons will not be the proper customers.

This is a great first exercise. You're starting to learn more about the real market need or desire and are homing in on the target customers. Time for round two!

Next, you set up five meetings with nursing directors of general surgical units in hospitals. You ask question number 1 and the nursing directors give an average response of 8. They like the system and the idea that you could have a constant monitor on the patients, but they reiterate that it would be great if they didn't have to monitor all this data on all their patients 24 h a day. They also recommend an alarm to tell them that the patient is out of normal range using your sensor. If they had that, when asked question number 2, they scored it a 9/10. Do they have authorization to purchase this type of device? The reply was no; there is a hospital CFO who is in charge of major purchases and the CTO of the hospital would have to approve it because it would need to integrate with the existing electronic medical record system that they are using.

Example | 49

In those 10 interviews, you have learned so much about the actual market need, the key stakeholders (the nurses, not the doctors), the purchasers (the hospital administrators, not the nursing directors), and integration and product feature desires in order for the system to be useful to all of the stakeholders, including the patients.

If you stayed in the lab and continued with development, you might have missed the alarm feature or not have understood the importance of integration with the electronic medical record or even have known who your real customer within the hospital system would be. You are proving and/or disproving your marketing hypothesis as you go through the market research phase, like investigating a hypothesis for your research questions. As you get more data, the hypothesis is refined until you feel that you significantly understand the market demands and, in tailoring your potential product offering, can provide a commercially viable product that will truly meet the market needs.

Roy Rosin, MBA
University of Pennsylvania
Chief Innovation Officer
University of Pennsylvania Health System

Roy Rosin likes to go fast.

As the first chief innovation officer for the University of Pennsylvania Health System, Roy is working to accelerate innovations for Penn's Health System, not an easy task.

Roy developed his methods of product testing over 18 years as the vice president of Innovation at Intuit. There, he managed Intuit Brainstorm, which is akin to an internal incubator to make "ideas into actions and outcomes." His system for quickly developing ideas into products at Intuit was based on the strong use of outcome measures, even for the earliest prototypes.

His approach used the scientific method for product market testing. First, he determined a clear hypothesis that could be validated or invalidated. By "measuring what you care about," he found that he could better understand the market response to the product offering. For new product concepts (new IT platforms or products), he measured outcomes to experiments that were not yet validated by the marketplace. For validated products, he used the measures to help scale the product. This early and quick feedback was used to redesign products or to allow products to fail fast.

How does this experience translate to the Health System? He wanted a better response for the patients who interacted with the website and thought that offering same-day appointments, virtually immediate access to some of the world's top medical doctors, would be a huge improvement in patient satisfaction, rather than the typical system where a patient would wait weeks to months to see a specialist. To test his hypothesis, his team constructed a front-end portal with a false back end. He was able to test if this system would work and quickly found that it did without all of the time and expense of programming the back end of the system. Now, he's working to scale the operation.

Roy is also using his insights with quick product development to streamline numerous processes in the Health System including IRB and contract negotiations. Where university approval processes often go in series, he is trying to use concurrent review panels to improve the speed of review. He's working to change the pace of research and getting treatments to patients.

And Roy is moving in the fast lane.

Sometimes research discoveries lead to a platform technology, which is quite interesting because one innovation can be used in a variety of applications (Figure 3.2). If your lab developed a new nanoparticle that can target specific types of cells and deliver genes or drugs to them—amazing. It's exciting because it will open numerous possibilities for different products. For example, you could target cancer cells or maybe chondrocytes (cartilage cells) to treat arthritis. How about osteoblasts (bone cells) to help fracture healing or treat osteoporosis? Or maybe you could use them to influence the differentiation of stem cells to treat Alzheimer's disease!

The blessing of a platform technology is having the broad platform, but the challenge is where you start. Should the first application be cancer? Huge market potential, but tough problem, long development time, and serious clinical trials may be competition that is doing something close.... How about arthritis? In thinking through the product possibilities, the paths

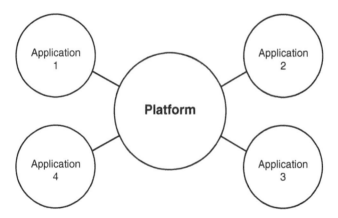

Figure 3.2 Platform technologies can result in multiple products and applications, making them attractive for investment, and market analysis will inform which application(s) to focus on first.

to commercialization and market potentials are just some of the factors that will go into your decisions. Testing the market is the best way to explore different scenarios by trying to focus on one or two applications to start the search phase. Investors typically like platform technologies, because if the technology is sound, but the market does not develop, then there is an opportunity to pivot and apply the technology to another application. However, investors also typically advise to prove the technology in one application first when you start the business. An abundance of riches, to be sure, but a platform technology may take a little more time in the market analysis and the discipline to stay focused.

Example (Continued)

As you refined your product offering for your e-diagnostic, a few of the interviewees from the general surgical world suggested that you talk with their colleagues in the emergency department. As it turns out, in the emergency department they have the same needs but have fewer staff to monitor patients as closely as they would like, and they can get distracted when a life-or-death case comes into the unit. They would like a few variations on the system, but generally, they could really use it. Now you've discovered that your system is really a platform technology. You have the technical capability to adapt the system not only to the general surgery hospital rooms but also to the emergency department. In fact, you can adapt it to critical care units as well. This platform now opens up far-ranging opportunities that you hadn't really considered initially but that you learned about through your market analysis. This has helped to broaden the technology platform and increase the total market potential of the e-diagnostic system.

The TTO may be another source of information to help your market analysis. Perhaps they subscribe to marketing reports (secondary market research) in your area of interest, which may tell the size and growth rates along with details and competitors in your market segment. For many universities, this has been a difficult part of the process to handle. Marketing information is expensive and since universities have so many sectors to consider, their budgets may not meet the need for this information. It's worth asking what resources they have. Being able to quote a reputable market report lends credibility to your analysis of market size and potential, essential components for understanding the market need, and competition.

Steve calls this overall process the "search phase." He and others have found that start-ups that are not successful and have often confused the search with the execution phases of business development. This can happen if you go forward with a product development, prototype development, and alpha and beta products without testing the market by talking with a significant number of potential customers. And, he notes, it's important to continue to test the market throughout the path of development.

Are you convinced that this search phase and primary market research are essential for launching the business in the right direction? If so, you may have just saved yourself from years of racing toward the wrong finish line.

Errol Arkilic, Ph.D.
National Science Foundation, Founding Program Director
Innovation Corps (I-Corps)
Currently Founder of M34 Capital

Errol Arkilic doesn't back away from a challenge, not even when the Director of the National Science Foundation (NSF) asks for a total redo of its economic development program. Change does not come easy for any organization and perhaps even more so for government organizations with a rich history, like NSF.

Errol and his team's hard work resulted in the formation (in 2013) of the NSF Innovation Corps (I-Corps) program to build a community of researchers and business advisors to provide education toward assessing commercial opportunity around research findings in academic labs. From concept to launch, this program took only 4 months because of support being driven from the top (Director) and from the bottom (Program Directors), which allowed the organization to "clear brush" and quickly initiate the new program. In a way, this is not unlike the process used within I-Corps itself, one that was developed by Steve Blank from Stanford.

The NSF's transformational thinking took the original model of Small Business Innovation Research (SBIR) grants to support commercialization and supplemented it with the education, mentorship, and network needed for a researcher to investigate commercialization potential.

Not all universities were on board with this program and its mission at first. But, less than a year later, there are I-Corps Centers and Nodes in many major universities across the country that serve as educational hubs for academic entrepreneurship. Participants from across the country are learning the fundamentals of Steve Blank's start-up principles on market research and the start-up process. This program lays a critical foundation to shore up best practices across universities in this area, a mission that "only NSF could accomplish."

The process starts with "Opportunity Recognition 101," where you examine your product or service to understand the potential customers, value proposition, revenue model, and capital necessary to get there. Errol and his colleagues wanted to keep the curriculum uniform, even though the projects were quite different—all of this in a community that would serve as a "friendly place to fail."

Failure and/or pivoting in a start-up is part of the process, and Steve Blank has designed a system that uses the familiar scientific method to test and uncover market truths. The process is based on Steve's observation that as researchers thinking about potential customers, we need to get out of the lab. They encourage faculty members to talk with 100 potential customers. "This process allows you to get market-based ground truth to inform the path forward." For the researchers who have participated, the process has been "very easily accepted." Errol and his colleagues have hit on something important, process: whether it's designing an experiment, writing a grant, writing a paper, or starting a company, process is a very helpful framework to guide activity. Hopefully, as we are all educated in this process, we'll become more efficient at coming to a go-no-go decision about a technology for commercialization potential.

While scientists, engineers, and medical doctors are deep domain experts, these independent thinkers sometimes can believe that they are experts in other areas, like market response. Sometimes they "need to be bashed over the head to see straight." Through this process, the market decides the value of the idea. This is one reason why it's critical to the I-Corps process that the lead researcher is involved. The lead researcher on a project after having conversations and getting feedback from the market is best positioned to pivot the technology or potential product, based on the core knowledge that is being exploited. This primary interface between researcher and market need is the foundation of I-Corps.

NSF breaks the process into two stages: search and execute. The search phase (market analysis) must go first because most projects fail because they "execute before being pointed in the right direction." These are expensive and time consuming missteps. The execution phase involves building business, processes, financials, and value proposition (business school talents). If execution begins before search is complete, then the start-up is too encumbered for the search activities. During the transition from search to execution, Errol observes that there are often hurt feelings, pain, and misunderstanding. I-Corps is designed to smooth the transition from search to execute.

Is I-Corps enough to get an academic-based business off the ground? NSF believes that the private sector is responsible for profit activities, not the government agency. The government does not take an equity position in start-ups. But the life cycle might look something like research, I-Corps, SBIR, private investment.

So who is typically successful coming through the I-Corps program? Errol has studied the data and has found that teams that are successful show early indicators for success, in that they do 20–25 interviews in 2 weeks (program requirement is 100 interviews in 7 weeks). Another indication of success comes from teams that are methodical about the specific hypothesis that they are testing in the potential customer interviews (market research). They don't just ask true/false questions. Instead, "is this a top five pain point?" and "how is this paid for now?" This added information may help them to adjust the product to meet this need. "The disruptive perspective is what start-ups do well." And those that fail?

Generally through the search phase, they're trying to sell (force) the product rather than gather information about the market.

The execution phase has its own challenges, but Errol believes that they are not as significant as those of the search phase. "Poor business decisions pale compared to working on a project no one cares about." If Errol has one message for academics considering commercialization, it's to "put the market up front." Spend lots of time getting the market right and then execute.

The Value Proposition

Let's assume that you pass through the market analysis stage and find customers who are interested in your product or service. Now it's time to consider the value proposition of your discovery envisioned as a product. Here's where you may need some help from the business sector. Understanding the value of your product means appreciating not only customer demand but also the importance of your product to their business or lifestyle. Value is different from price but will influence the price that you can demand for your product. Value includes intangible as well as tangible benefits from your product. For example, value for a medical device might mean pain relief for a patient, but intangibles could be reduced continued medical bills from an untreated patient, lost wages from lost work time of the patient, disability costs associated with the lost work time, etc. There may be value to different stakeholders in the chain of the product. That new medical device might mean insurers no longer have to provide lifelong care, which will end up reducing their overall cost. They may be willing to pay more for your device than staying with the current standard of care. All aspects of the benefit of your product or service should be thought through so that a realistic and thoughtful value proposition can be developed.

Once you begin to quantify value and market, you can set a pricing strategy. There are as many pricing strategies as there are businesses, and the pricing field has its own type of creativity and expertise. One model you may consider is a one-time fee. In this model, you buy my company's widget and you use it, and that is the end of the business relationship until you need a new widget, like buying a hammer at the hardware store. Another model offers a subscription where the customer can have your software license for 1 year for a fee, but to use it next year, you'll need to renew the license. There may be add-ons or consumables (razor and razor blade models) that generate revenue. Pharmaceuticals and medical devices as well as health IT all have unique models that are influenced not only by your pricing strategy and market tolerance for the price but potentially also by insurance and government reimbursement rulings (which may differ from country to country, requiring a unique pricing strategy for each nation). These models will be a part of your financial analysis. The considerations of market analysis and value proposition along with pricing will help you to define the financial basis for your company. Creativity in the model may give you a true competitive advantage.

The size of the market, price, and market uptake will determine the revenues predicted for your product or service. The uptake of the product into the marketplace is a major factor in making these predictions over time and is another unknown. The uptake default is typically a hockey stick-shaped curve of revenue generation over some course of time (lower revenues in the early stages but after a key turning point, a sharp upward slope) (Figure 3.3). Market uptake is another source of planning, where you will consider how you will introduce the product to the market. Will you use thought leaders to influence purchase of your product or service? Will you use direct advertising? What is your demographic? Will you go door to door, use social media, or some combinations of the previously mentioned?

Each of these analyses is recognized as predictions of a future that may or may not be where you think it will be as you sit in your lab. List your assumptions and support your market numbers from literature including marketing reports as you would cite a scientific paper. This lends credibility to your analysis for you and your potential investors. The purpose is not to tell a rosy story that savvy investors will see through or to set up expectations that can't possibly be met, leading to disappointment down the line. It is to see if the great idea that you have can be turned into a commercially viable business. Would you invest in you?

The next part of the analysis is predicting how much money it will take to get from where you are today (a research discovery in the lab) to a product or service ready to sell. The product development cycle really ranges by sector. For a health IT app, you might be looking at 3–4 months and $100K before you're ready to launch your minimum viable product (MVP) and earn your first revenues. On the other end of the spectrum are pharmaceuticals, which

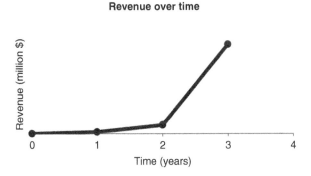

Figure 3.3 Typical market uptake projections for revenue over time for many start-up companies: "hockey stick" curve.

are looking at a 15+-year timeline with $100 M+ investment associated with significant technical risk at each milestone along the way. In the end, the investment needed to get you to your finish line must be justified by the potential revenue of your product for the business to be viable.

Building the business case for translating your discovery into a product needs market analysis and a developed value proposition. The earlier you can analyze these two components of the potential business, the better positioned you will be to address the marketing risk associated with your technology.

Summary

Definition of the market from primary marketing research will serve as a foundation for the analysis of the commercial potential of your innovation. It will help you to translate the innovation into a product that customers will buy. This is a key step in examining the viability of a start-up company based on your technology. The NSF and NIH I-Corps are two federally sponsored programs that can guide you through this process.

Reference

Blank, S. and Dorf, B. (2012) *The Startup Owner's Manual*, The Step-by-Step Guide for Building a Great Company, Pescadero, K&S Ranch Publishing.

4

Friend or Foe: The Tech Transfer Office and Licensing

I'll make him an offer he can't refuse
—Don Corleone, The Godfather

By now you've disclosed your invention to the university and the provisional and maybe non-provisional patent applications have been filed. The patent may or may not have been issued yet (it can take more than 5 years in some sectors to have a reply from the patent office). You've established a market need and may have sufficient data to show a proof of concept.

Let's assume a start-up or an established corporation is interested in licensing the IP. Whether the IP will go to a start-up or an established corporation will depend on the technology, market sector and market need, and competition for such technology. A general rule of thumb is that a one-off product or an improvement to an existing product or process may be licensed to a company that is in the business already. The company may want the IP to advance their current process or product (better, faster, cheaper), or they may want the IP to strategically block others or to expand their own product offerings. The majority (80%) of license agreements from universities go to existing companies (not start-ups) (AUTM, 2012).

What is the investor's role in the negotiations of a license agreement? The American Association of University Professors issued a statement in their June 2014 Bulletin.

The management of university-generated intellectual property is complex and carries significant consequences for those involved in direct negotiations (faculty inventors, companies, university administrators, attorneys, and invention-management agents) as well as those who may be affected (competing companies, the public, patients, and the wider research community). whether ownership of a particular invention resides with the inventors or is assigned by the inventors to a university

Academic Entrepreneurship: How to Bring Your Scientific Discovery to a Successful Commercial Product, First Edition. Michele Marcolongo.
© 2017 John Wiley & Sons, Inc. Published 2017 by John Wiley & Sons, Inc.

technology-transfer office, a university-affiliated foundation, or an independent invention management agency, it is essential that all those involved recognize the distinctive role that inventions arising out of scholarly research should have.

Faculty inventors and investigators retain a vital interest in the disposition of their research inventions and discoveries and should, therefore, retain rights to negotiate the terms of their disposition. The university, or its management agents, should not undertake intellectual property development or take legal actions that directly or indirectly affect a faculty member's research, inventions, instruction, or public service without the faculty member's or inventor's express consent.

AAUP, June 2014 Bulletin

License Agreements with Existing Corporations

The most straightforward path to translating your discovery to commercialization and back to society is to license the technology to an existing company. If Old-Corp wants to license your new algorithm for patient sensing for a hospital room—awesome. The university will likely have a set term sheet and agreement that can be used if Old-Corp and the university agree. If not, there will be negotiations between Old-Corp and the university until the terms are agreed and the language of the agreement is satisfactory to all.

Terms will include payment by Old-Corp of the fees associated with the writing and prosecution of the patent(s), which will go directly to the university budget and potentially the support the IP protection of new university discoveries, continuing to fulfill their academic mission. In addition, Old-Corp might pay a cash fee up front and/or offer royalties based on the gross or net sales of a product associated with your IP. Aside from patent fees, any remuneration to the university by Old-Corp will be shared among the university, college, and inventors in proportion to the stated tech transfer policy at your university. Here is where the inventorship of coinventors on patents will come into play. In many universities, the proceeds of the license will be split among the provost office, the dean of the faculty member's college or school, and the faculty member himself/herself.

Example

Let's assume there was a $100 000 distribution to be made from the licensing agreement, and the provost, dean, and faculty member each get 1/3 of the income according to the university policy. The provost office would get roughly $33K, while the dean's office and the faculty member would each get $33K. Now, let's assume there were three inventors on the patent. The provost office and the dean's office (assuming the faculty members were all in the same college or school) would each get $33K and each faculty member would get $11K, if the faculty members all decided that they would share equally as inventors; if not, there would be a proportional distribution of the faculty members' $33K according to their previously agreed proportions. To reiterate from Chapter 2, this is why it becomes imperative to decide on inventorship proportions at the time of disclosure. This can preempt any ill will that may come among inventors at the time of distribution of IP income to the university.

In addition to your IP, Old-Corp may want access to your continued support to help develop the technology. Independent of the TTO, they may offer you a consulting agreement. Universities often allow their faculty to consult one day/week, and if this is the case and you are interested, then you could accept this offer. In some cases, the consulting agreement can be part of the terms of the license agreement. In other words, Old-Corp may not want your IP unless they also have access to your expertise to help them execute the IP. Similarly, Old-Corp may offer a grant to your lab to continue some of the work or to research along a similar path and expand the basic knowledge in this topic area. Under the terms of the university's sponsored research agreement, this can also be executed at the time of the license agreement and, again, may be a nonnegotiable term in the license agreement in that Old-Corp may not want the technology unless you will help them advance additional research in the area.

Jane Muir
University of Florida
Director of Florida Innovation Hub
Associate Director, Technology Transfer Office
President of AUTM (Association of University Technology Managers),
2014–2015

Jane Muir has built an innovation ecosystem for the Gator Nation. As a long-standing member of a TTO and the current president of the Association of University Technology Managers (AUTM), she can recall a time when no one on campus paid much attention to her office.

But times have changed.

Jane has helped UF faculty start more than 150 companies over the past 15 years and in the past 2 years has spun out 15 companies per year. How does she do it? She believes that the UF Incubation Hub is the "critical piece to getting an increased number of companies." Now faculty recruits want to speak to members of her office before taking a position at UF.

Jane believes that a successful incubator needs good proximity to campus. The incubator at UF is four blocks from campus and six blocks from downtown Gainesville. It helps to integrate the incubator with campus; also helpful is having a Starbucks and a few good restaurants where students and faculty will want to hang out mixed in. This kind of live/work community is attractive to the new generation of "creative class" who do not want a 45 minute commute. They want to walk to work and proximity is important.

Another approach that Jane has taken is matching faculty with a CEO for the company. "Faculty members should not run companies," but they should be involved but matched with experienced entrepreneurs who know the product space. That being said, it's still a challenge to find entrepreneurs to run the spin-out companies. She draws heavily on the Gator Nation, a group of 300 000 alumni as a foundation to identify entrepreneurs looking for their next project. She also tries to match CEOs to spin-outs through connections made by service providers. IP attorneys that UF uses to patent inventions are great connectors between faculty, entrepreneurs, and investors. While she recruits seasoned entrepreneurs, she also works on growing her own through "boot camps." In particular, she's run a camp for women in start-ups and has seen amazing results. These campers already have bachelor degrees or more and now receive training in entrepreneurship.

As if managing all of this is not enough, Jane is also the current president of AUTM. She sees technology transfer as a way to bring discoveries to society and make the world a better place and improve the human condition, not as a cash cow for universities. Profitability for a TTO office is a slow process. She predicts that over the next 10 years universities will have increasing levels of success with commercialization of university technologies, but not every university or faculty member will necessarily rise to a higher level. The process is fraught with so many complexities and misconceptions, and companies always need more time, money, and energy than the team thinks at the beginning. A good TTO cannot have unrealistic expectations. AUTM tries to help universities learn about the process.

Jane has figured it out.

A direct university–corporate license is probably the most straightforward way to translate technology from the lab to commercialization. There is no start-up to finance, there is no inherent conflict between you and the university, and there is no assumption of personal risk, while there is the potential to share in the upside benefit. What then is the risk of licensing your technology to Old-Corp? Old-Corp may want your technology not to offensively promote a new product or service, but may want it to block the competition from doing so. In that case, your discovery will sit on a shelf at Old-Corp and never be realized in a commercial application. This would result in no future royalty back to the university after the initial licensing fee. Or Old-Corp might initially want your IP for product development, but with a management or strategy change, which is quite frequent in major corporations. The drive for commercialization of your IP may wane and, again, your technology can remain on the shelf—or perhaps be sublicensed to a third party. Alternatively, the market demand, which was assessed at the time of license, may change or a competitor may have beaten Old-Corp to the market, and now the motivation to pursue your IP is reduced and the development discontinued. Sometimes the university will put in a contractual clause that will require the IP to be returned to the university if significant progress is not made within a certain time period, which may give you a second chance at commercializing the technology, although at that time the technology may be years older with no additional value added. As you can see, you immediately lose control of the destiny of your IP once you license it to Old-Corp.

Aside from these risks, licensing agreements are great deals for universities. Why, then, don't universities license everything they have this way? There are several possible reasons:

1) *Marketing.* The perfect corporation for your technology may not know that your patent or patent application exists. In many universities, the communication of market need by existing corporations with university TTOs is poor at best. The largest university players in licensing may have major corporations constantly combing university IP inventories, but more often than not, the burden falls to busy tech transfer administrators to market their IP to the major corporations. Within one market segment, let's say energy, that would be hard enough, but performing business development for the wide range of technologies of a university is an expensive and time-consuming task to manage.

2) *Large corporations don't like negotiating with universities.* University TTOs are not living in the fast-paced world of business and are often subject to layers of approval in executing a deal (tech transfer officer, his/her boss, legal, maybe the vice provost of research). This all takes time, and the corporate interest may be reduced or the budget for the next fiscal year changed by the time the agreement is negotiated.

3) *The technology is too "early stage."* When a corporation licenses a technology from a university, they are expecting to do development to make the IP into a viable commercial product. However, if additional research, further proof of concept, prototype development, scale-up feasibility, and the typical development steps are necessary, oftentimes a corporation is not inclined to license the IP, no matter how "promising." This typically happens in high capital sectors with long development cycles like energy and health care. There is a long and risky road to go before a great concept proves out into a viable long-lasting battery or new drug, and depending on the market and competition around that technology, existing corporations may or may not be likely to take that risk with an early-stage license agreement.

There are some potential ways that you can mitigate these risks and make your IP more attractive to a large corporation:

1) *Marketing.* You can market the IP yourself. Oftentimes, we as academics get to know our industry counterparts. Through our interactions in conferences or specific meetings, you can present your IP and drum up interest in the IP with the corporation, and then bring the TTO into the discussion to negotiate a deal. Another way is for the TTO to contract with a business development consultant in your sector that can market the IP on the university's behalf. Some TTOs have budgets for this kind of activity and it may be productive for them.

2) *Large corporations don't like negotiating with universities and the technology is too "early stage."* While a direct license may not be possible for these reasons, there is the option to start your own company where the start-up licenses the technology from the university and then raises some seed money (perhaps from a corporate investment partnership) to expand the proof of concept and de-risk the technology to the point where the large corporation will license, in this case, from the start-up. The rest of the book is devoted to this idea.

University IP Licenses to Start-Ups

Platform technologies and disruptive technologies, creating a solution to a new need or a revolutionary solution to a long unmet or inadequately met need, may be better suited to a start-up (Figure 4.1). For example, a new way to make a highly used polymer that saves on cost or waste could be a license to an existing large-scale manufacturer in that space. The development of a new biocompatible nanoparticle that can be tailored for use in imaging, drug delivery, or gene therapy may be suited to a start-up, where the family of products has the potential to completely disrupt current diagnostic and treatment strategies,

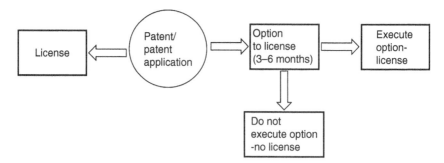

Figure 4.1 Paths to licensing technology to existing or start-up company from a university.

and the $1 billion plus market potential is substantial. Importantly, when a technology has capacity for revolutionary change in numerous separate applications, it gives investors depth: in case the first target area fails, there are others immediately to consider, and if the first target application is successful, other opportunities that can immediately be expanded.

In a license agreement to a start-up or existing corporation, the terms of the agreement must be negotiated through the TTO. Here's where things get tricky. This component of start-up process is unique to academic-based start-ups, or technology transfers from universities, rather than non-academic start-ups. In behalf of the university, the TTO is responsible for securing the best agreement possible for the university. But who is the university? It's the trustees, administrators, staff, faculty, and students. In this case, the TTO is acting in behalf of both the administrators (after all, the members of the TTO are administrators) as well as the faculty and possibly students, if they are inventors. The faculty members and students could be employees or shareholders of the start-up while still being employees or students of the university. This situation has resulted in a conflict of interest for the students and faculty members as they balance their interests in the start-up and the university.

There are many ways that the university tries, through policy, to mitigate and manage these conflicts. In one aspect, the policies might state that the proceeds from the license agreement are shared between the university (layers of administrative offices) and the faculty members and students as they are with licenses to existing corporations. This is an important component of sharing the potential wealth. In many universities, the proceeds of the license will be split among the provost's office, the dean of the faculty member's college or school, and the faculty member himself/herself. If an equity position in a start-up is negotiated in behalf of the university as a term in the agreement between the university and the start-up, then the equity distribution of the inventors' portion may be split according to the same inventorship formula as would be done for cash payments or royalties.

This is straightforward as long as none of the inventors are taking a separate equity position in the start-up. If, however, you choose to serve as, for example, the CTO, CEO, or scientific advisor to the start-up, you may receive founder's shares in the company. These shares or equity position in the start-up company are awarded for your role or position in the company and are separate from your shares in the university component of the agreement (as a university inventor). So, wearing your university inventor hat, it would be in your financial interest for the university to have a large equity position in the start-up. However, from your management position in the start-up, it's in your best financial interest to have the university equity position as small as possible—instant conflict. Some universities have policies about "double dipping" in equity to mitigate this university inventor/founder conflict.

Negotiation is all about coming to a mutually agreeable solution that lets each party feel satisfied with the deal or satisfied enough to sign the deal. The process of this negotiation can be long and contentious, quick and agreeable, or anywhere in between. This depends on many factors including the philosophy and the clarity of the policy of the TTO office and university, respectively, as well as the philosophy of the start-up management. *You may feel be trapped in the middle.*

There are some strategies that help to speed this process along and let it result in a reasonable agreement for both parties, without you ending up feeling like a ping-pong ball...or worse. One way is for the faculty member to completely abstain from the negotiations. If you have decided to be the CEO of the start-up, this strategy is difficult; however, you may be able to use a proxy for negotiations, such as your corporate attorney.

If you are an officer or board member of the company, but not the CEO, this is quite doable. The CEO of the company will represent your interest as a founder and officer, while the TTO will represent your interest as an inventor and also the interests of your coinventors (who may or may not be participating in the start-up). If you choose this path, it will be lesson number one of you giving up control. You give up direct control of the negotiation by not participating; however, you have representation (by the CEO you chose) guiding your interests. You and the CEO will decide if the deal is agreeable for the start-up. You and your CEO in partnership according to your equity positions in the company and by your formal operating agreement will have a foundational procedure by which to decide on terms in behalf of the start-up entity. This strategy could offer an advantage for you as the inventor/professor/start-up officer in that you still have to live in the university after the deal is complete unless you are resigning from your faculty position. Whatever negotiating tactics, collegial or confrontational, may be used, if you are not the one in the room with the TTO official, then you are less likely to get into a situation where you may compromise your internal university relationships. This is not meant to say that all TTO negotiations will be contentious, but after numerous interviews reported here as well as other more informal discussions among faculty entrepreneurs, this happens at least equally as the more collegial and straightforward negotiations. Personalities aside, it is simply due to the internal conflict discussed earlier.

Some universities have predetermined deal structures for start-ups. They specify how much equity, royalties, or other terms are assigned to the university in exchange for an exclusive license of the IP. This makes sense if you agree with the terms (see Figure 4.2 for a sample of terms from five universities in 2016). At least you know what to expect from the agreement and the benchmark for the university. Otherwise, terms can vary from university to university and from deal to deal within one university within and across market sectors. Determining what terms are fair and what terms are typical is

Stephen Fleming
Former Georgia Institute of Technology
Vice President and Executive Director
Enterprise Innovation Institute
Current Founder Boostphase

Stephen Fleming has done a lot of deals: over 100 since he has been walking the halls in search of translatable IP at Georgia Tech. He first joined Georgia Tech in 2005 as the chief technology commercialization officer and is currently vice president and executive director of the Enterprise Innovation Institute (EI^2). Oh, and he's a former venture capitalist with a degree in theoretical physics, among other things.

In the past decade, Stephen has learned that there's a quite a gap between the "aha moment" and a license agreement to get started on the commercialization pathway. This is where EI^2 comes in.

Through EI^2, faculty can receive a small amount of translational research funding early, when there is "low friction." For Stephen, this is critical to test feasibility of a concept and to prepare the technology for a licensing agreement, either with an established company or start-up. "Without a source of translation funds, this is hard to do at scale." One factor that contributes to this is that technology transfer organizations are seldom profitable (or breakeven) on their own in real time. These are long-term investments for the university. They "need a budget line item like everyone else in the university system." However, that being said, his hope is that if a company start-up or license supported by Georgia Tech does very well, the founder will come back to the university with a major gift, as recently occurred with a Georgia Tech entrepreneur's gift of a new building. This strategy keeps deals from getting caught in the weeds of negotiations over equity and royalty positions and optimizes the process for "maximum speed by minimizing friction." EI^2 has worked closely with local law firms to develop standard license agreements that's "good for both sides" to further accelerate translation. While the standard agreement is optional, EI^2 has found that about half of the licensees have chosen to use it.

Central to Stephen's strategy are the faculty members. For a faculty member to license a technology, it's easy: they have to go to class. Through a series of videos on IP, corporation structure, taxes, hiring/firing, and partnering with a major corporation, he's hoping to encourage a cultural change among faculty.

Stephen is also a "Steve Blank disciple." He values the customer discovery process. While it's really difficult for engineering professors and graduate students to do 100 interviews with potential customers to develop a good sense of the market needs, he requires this process. The interviews are not meant for you to "tell or sell or educate or convince. It's an opportunity for professors to listen. After about 30–40 interviews, you run out of friends." You now have to talk to strangers who will give you direct and honest feedback. Through this process,

90% of the time, the original concept will have morphed into something more suitable for the real demands of the marketplace. "Then it's time to go build."

But educating faculty members about business practices is only one side of the coin.

He, like others, believes that a successful start-up out of the university needs a business partner in addition to the faculty's scientific contribution. So among Stephen's many talents, his best may be that of a matchmaker. He and his colleagues have learned that they need to be a "dating service" to essentially put the right management with the right technology, keeping in mind the interpersonal connections that are critical to success as well. EI^2 does this, in part, by hosting networking meetings for mentors and business managers from large or small companies in the Atlanta area. These mentors, many of whom are part of a close alumni network, are shown business deals and in some cases asked to mentor a business through the translational stage. They also run a "management challenge" where they have about 60 people mentoring companies. All volunteers.

How does Georgia Tech support all of these innovative programs? The State of Georgia has committed to translation of university discoveries back to society. There are taxpayer-funded programs, such as the Georgia Research Alliance, that funds six universities in Georgia with translational support in staged phases. These programs are a combination of grants and loans. There is also the Coulter Foundation endowment. Atlanta has a strong angel network. All of this help is enough to position strong and highly marketable technologies in a start-up.

But how about the follow-up funding? Most major venture money is in a few regions of the country (Atlanta not being one of them). He has made a few observations on that front. One is that VC's go-to airports. Georgia Tech's spun-out companies have VC funding from the West Coast, Boston, and Texas. He has found that "a good deal will get funded." He has also observed that by not being in a region with many VCs, funding at this level can take longer and their companies tend to get lower valuations. But he believes that there is also a trade-off: the cost of doing business in a place like Silicon Valley is much higher than Atlanta, making the Atlanta companies attractive on another level.

Stephen Fleming and EI^2 are an outstanding resource for academic entrepreneurs. And if you happen to need any help solving Euler–Lagrange equations....

very difficult because this information is generally not publicly available. This is really an early challenge to the formation of a company out of a university and many just don't get off the starting block because of it. Typically, universities that start many companies each year and have a database on which to draw can get to an agreement much easier than those that only do a few deals each year or are just starting to support this process. The CEO of the company has a challenge to maintain a good relationship through the

Start-up licencing terms	Equity	Liquidation event payment	Royalty rate	Minimum annual payments	Milestone payment	Up-front payment	Patent expenses	Source
UNC-Chapel Hill	No	0.75% of exit	1% for any FDA regulated product; 2% net sales for all others	Starting 3rd anniversary $5–30K		No	Ongoing deferral past fees for 180 days, then min payment; all fees after 1st anniversary	http://oced.unc.edu/files/2016/05/Carolina-Express-User-Guide.pdf
Carnegie Mellon	6% (at closing of $2 million financing)	No	No royalties for 3 years; then 2% royalty	No	No	No	Can be deferred for additional equity	https://www.cmu.edu/cttec/documents/spin-off-guidelines-cmu1.doc
Washington University at St.Louis	No	0.95% of exit	2% with sliding sublicense revenue, no minimum	No			No fee for past patent costs; Ongoing only	https://otm.wustl.edu/for-inventors/quick-start-license/
Yale	No	1% of exit capped at $1 million (reductions to 0.5% for on-time payments during license)	3% net sales; 20% sublicensing revenue and royalties	Starting 2nd anniversary $5–40K (minimum royalty payment)	No	No	Deferment of past patent fees for 2–4 years (1/3 each year); payment new fees	http://ocr.yale.edu/faculty/startup-support/yale-startup-license
Kansas University	No	0.95% "success fee"	2% fixed net sales	No for non-pharmaceutical technologies	No	No	Past patent expenses up to $20K plus ongoing fees	http://kuic.ku.edu/swift-startup-license

Figure 4.2 Exclusive license terms for five universities (2016). *Source:* Adapted from discussions with Johann DeSa and Mike Neidrauer.

negotiations: you may need additional support from the university or may want to license additional IP, and most people want to be good members of the innovation ecosystem community. The CEO also needs to secure the best deal possible in the company's interest while being realistic about the expectations of the university.

Some terms that you might want to consider are patent fees, royalties, equity, cash, reduced overhead for company research done at the university, follow-on patents being assigned to the company and start-up space in a university-owned incubator, and incubator services like legal, accounting, and grant writing. However you decide to negotiate these terms is entirely up to the CEO and management of the start-up. Benchmarks of other similar technologies from similar universities may be important to inform the process.

Most universities will negotiate to reclaim expended patent fees up front or at the time that a certain amount of investment is achieved by the start-up. For example, $125K of legal fees that are accumulated by the university to cover your IP will be paid back to the university upon seed funding of $ 1.5 million. This is simply a cost-flow issue for most universities in that they can only cover new IP as far as their budget will reach, and by reclaiming the expended patent fees for your start-up sooner rather than later, they can support the IP protection of the next best thing. Sometimes universities are more interested in supporting the start-up than collecting the patent fees, and if a start-up runs into financial difficulty, they may let this payment slide. Others are quite strict about the terms and will take the fees out of the start-up, even at the expense of the survival of that start-up. In any event, the university will deduct the expended patent fees before making any dispersion of revenues from IP licensing internal to the university.

Equity may be given to the university in the start-up, which may very well be cash poor. As stated previously, the equity may put the inventor into a conflicted situation between his/her employment by the university and management of the start-up. Aside from this consideration, there are terms in the licensing agreements that most universities have for equity positions where the university is allowed to participate in subsequent rounds of financing the company at the same equity position it was given in the initial company formation. This term (potentially negotiable) allows the university the option to follow its investment of IP with monetary investment to maintain a stronger equity position through dilutive rounds of financing the company. Some universities have and more are initiating venture funding for university start-ups, which is one way that they can execute this option. This may change the complexion of negotiation for those universities. Some universities are now spinning out the start-ups from university IP *and* providing seed funding for the company that may provide the university with a stronger equity position in the start-up and perhaps more control (board seat). Several universities have established venture funds to support university start-ups; however, the vast majority of universities do not have or are not interested in this component of the innovation ecosystem.

An innovative venture capitalist firm, Osage, is exploiting an often over-looked investment option in university license agreements to start-ups. Osage has created a highly profitable fund that executes the university's option for investment in the later rounds of financing a start-up, which is typically part of standard contract language in the licensing agreement. In exchange for this option, Osage provides the member universities with a percentage of the fund's profits. Osage will not be the lead investor, but will play a significant role in the investment rounds. This concept has worked well and is an innovative twist on mitigating risk through investment in a variety of spinouts and allows Osage to review and select the latest and greatest in university spinouts from their partner institutions. This focused investment strategy has allowed Osage to collect data from university spinouts that rivals no other. The longer they do this, the more data they get, which provides insights to guide future investment. Clearly, not all innovation happens in the lab (see box on Bob Adelson, Chapter 9).

Royalties are another term in the license negotiation. The percentage of net or gross profit that is given to the university via royalties can vary from sector to sector. Generally, a royalty of 2–3% to 5–6% may be negotiated. If you are working toward a holistic deal, based on the overall finite value of the technology, more royalties may mean less equity issued from the start-up to the university. Paying the patent fees up front with cash may mean less royalties. Without a set formula, this is an open-ended and nonlinear problem.

Let's consider the process for executing a license agreement from the university to the company. Again, there is no one way of doing this; however, here are some possibilities along the path.

Step one could be an option agreement. An option to license or option is a placeholder on the technology used when a company may not be ready to license the technology, but may not want anyone else to license the technology. This agreement, an option, for a limited period of time, may be issued from the university to the company. The terms of the option may or may not spell out the terms of the potential license agreement. The option may or may not have a cost associated with it. Options are usually given over a finite period of time (e.g., 3 months, 6 months, or 1 year) and may be renewable for an additional fee or for no fee. Options give the start-up or company the option to license the technology during the specified period while precluding any other company from licensing during that period. Options are often used when management teams are building a business plan and testing the waters with investors or when a company is doing due diligence around the technology. It is not necessary to have an option agreement before spinning out your start-up or licensing to an existing company, but it certainly could be part of the process. A license agreement can be made during the terms of the option (no need to wait until the option term is complete before executing the license agreement).

After the terms are negotiated by the start-up management, the start-up's corporate attorney will need to review the agreements to check if the language is consistent with the term sheet and if the language of the agreement is consistent with language that both protects the start-up and will be agreeable to potential investors. As is often the case with contracts, there will be further negotiations around the language of the agreements themselves. All of these will be resolved from passing contracts between your attorney and the university's attorney (either in-house or external). All of this back and forth takes time and expenses that will be billed to the start-up for your attorney and likely billed to the start-up for the university's attorney as well. A poorly worded agreement could hurt you later, so it's important to get the actual language right in the contracts; however, it all adds to your life cycle and cost of getting the company off the ground.

Once the agreement is signed and the company has the license to the technology, there may be further relationships between the university and the start-up or large company. Sometimes there can be some more technical work that will be performed in the university labs with the start-up founder/inventor serving as the principal investigator (PI). This work may be funded from the operating budget of the company (via investment) or through an SBIR or other proof-of-concept grant that subcontracts work to the university lab in behalf of the start-up. The work performed in your lab for your company leaves you again in another conflict of interest. The potential exists for unethical or fraudulent behavior for you to report findings from your lab that benefit the mission of the company, but that may not be accurate. This conflict has been recognized for over a decade now, and many universities have conflict-of-interest policies to address how it is managed. While it is recognized that the conflict exists, the conflict does not preclude the work from being done, only that there may be additional oversight so that any potential unethical behavior can be prevented.

Summary

An early step in translating your discovery toward commercialization will result in an agreement for the (typically) exclusive license for the intellectual property protecting the invention. The intellectual property can be licensed to an existing or a start-up company. The technology transfer office of the university is in charge of the licensing agreements and all negotiations will go through this office. Some universities have fixed terms for the agreement, while others negotiate each deal independently. For the faculty inventor, licensing intellectual property for your own start-up from the university can raise a conflict of interest that will have to be managed by you and by the university.

References

American Association of University Professors (2014). Committee A on Academic Freedom and Tenure. Statement on Intellectual Property. American Association of University Professors Bulletin: 35–37, Washington, DC.

AUTM (2012). AUTM Licensing Activity Survey FY2012 Highlights. https://register.autm.net/detail.aspx?id=2012_SUMMARY (accessed May 30, 2017).

5

Proof-of-Concept Centers: Bridging the Innovation Gap

I've missed more than 9,000 shots in my career. I've lost almost 300 games. 26 times I've been trusted to take the game's winning shot and missed. I've failed over and over and over again in my life and that's why I succeed.
—Michael Jordan, NBA Hall of Famer and Professional Basketball Player

What is the fastest way of getting your academic-based technology out of the "early stage"? This question has been wrestled with by some of the brightest entrepreneurs and academics in the country. While there is not one clear answer and, in fact, the strategies are rapidly evolving, there are some approaches to consider. The evidence that makes a company in early stage has to do with risk. The more the company is de-risked, the more mature it becomes. There are numerous forms of risk to consider:

Technological risk:
- Will the technology work?
- Under what conditions will the technology work? (Patient diagnosis, technology platform and processing speeds, environmental conditions, etc.)
- Is the technology cost-effective for the targeted market?
- Are there scale-up considerations to be addressed?
- Any shelf-life issues?
- How much will it cost to get to launch?
- How strong is the IP?
- Whatever else can an investor think of that will form the basis for a successful technological solution?

Regulatory/reimbursement risk:
- Is there a regulatory body that must be considered in this product or service (FDA, FCC, FAA, etc.), and what is the likelihood of success in achieving regulatory approval in a projected time?

Academic Entrepreneurship: How to Bring Your Scientific Discovery to a Successful Commercial Product, First Edition. Michele Marcolongo.
© 2017 John Wiley & Sons, Inc. Published 2017 by John Wiley & Sons, Inc.

- Are there milestone experiments on the way to full regulatory approval that can de-risk the technology (like animal studies, first-in-human, pilot human, alpha version demonstration, minimum viable product data)?
- Is there reimbursement risk associated with insurance companies or other third parties paying for the future product or service?
- Is there an existing diagnostic code (for a medical condition) and/or reimbursement code (for insurance payment for medical device or pharmaceutical), or will you create a new code? How will you approach that in the United States or globally?

Market risk:
- Who will be your first customer? Does the product fulfill market need?
- How large and robust is the market?
- Is this a disruptive technology in that it will revolutionize the way things are done, or is it an incremental or cost improvement within an existing market?
- Is this a platform technology and does it have the opportunity to pivot or expand into other market segments?
- Is this a consumer- or a business-to-business (b-to-b) product or service? How specialized is this product?
- What is the competitive landscape and how is this technology positioned?
- What does the projected market uptake look like in terms of sales over time? Where is the break-even point?
- What are projected costs associated with sales and marketing strategy?

Management team risk:
- Is the CEO talented and highly capable in leading the technology into a successful company?
- Is the CTO technically and socially excellent in managing development?
- Does the management have the ability to recruit outstanding talent to the company?
- How well do the partners work together?

In Chapter 3, we discussed market risk and ways to assess market potential. That is probably the best first step in tackling risk because if there is not a strong case for market adaption (current or projected), then there is little motivation for translating the technology. Market definition is an iterative process, and the product vision can become clearer as the market information emerges and the feedback loop continues. Market positioning is one of the major obstacles for academic-based technologies. However, it's not the only one. Management team risk is discussed in Chapter 6.

Here, technological risk will be considered. Academic technologies are unique from technologies that are imagined outside of academic institutions because ours are typically discovered as the result of observation from a research question, which is by their nature fundamental. Academics generally don't set out to develop a product in basic research, but the research findings may light a spark of connection that will allow visualization of the discovery into a product, in addition to its scientific interest. Academic-based start-ups can be compared with those outside of academics started by an entrepreneur or company who likely began with a market need and then targeted development of a technology to address that market need.

Because of the more fundamental starting point from which academic-based technologies are grounded, there is often further to go in the technology development toward "proof of concept" (POC). The term POC describes the key technological evidence that convinces investors that the research finding does indeed solve the societal challenge. This is sometimes called the "killer experiment." For the research to translate to a product with a specific function, there needs to be evidence that the technology will work in the given environment. If you show this evidence, the data goes far to de-risk the technology. If it does not work, then you will have to save considerable time and resources either in trying to get investment for the start-up or, if you have investment, in development and scale-up for a concept that will not work. This may mean getting your new chip to interface seamlessly with multiple platforms on specific frequencies without interference or decayed signal intensity. It may mean doing the degenerative or diseased animal model that most closely mimics the clinical condition that you are treating or scaling up your bench process for synthesizing a molecule into a 1 or 10 kg production run—all within a cost structure that won't impede a realistic pricing strategy. The result of the POC is not a finished product but will demonstrate that the technology will perform to given design parameters under conditions of operational use. Designing the POC experiment itself takes some work. Talking to potential investors in a friendly way to assess their impressions of the technical risk (which may be different from yours) as well as discussions with potential users will help to guide the key question(s) that you need to ask about your technology.

RoseAnn Rosenthal
President and CEO
Benjamin Franklin Technology Partners, Southeastern Pennsylvania

"Disciplined focus toward actionable milestones."
  This is how Ben Franklin and specifically RoseAnn Rosenthal help to build companies in Southeastern Pennsylvania.
  RoseAnn leads one of the most successful seed (or even pre-seed) funding organizations in the country, with a portfolio of over 140 companies. In many cases, before a venture capitalist will make an investment in an academic start-up (or nonacademic start-up) they like to see de-risking of the technology and evidence that the management team can deliver. But, how do you get started doing work without an influx of capital?

This is where Ben Franklin comes in. Ben Franklin will invest in "early stage" companies. Often times, they are the first investors into a company along with angels. Because the companies are earlier opportunities and less developed, RoseAnn's team works very closely with them to ensure that there is a "clear path to provide commercial impact." When just getting off the ground, it's often challenging to keep focus on what will bring value to the fledgling company when there are so many tempting tangential paths to explore. The company may still need to pivot, but at least it would be a conscious decision and not because market events are pulling the venture this way and that. "Of course, you can't live with blinders on either." The challenges is balancing decision making in the early stage can be critical to the later success of the company.

RoseAnn doesn't see much difference between the start-ups from academia or industry in her organization. If the technology is good and there are strong commercial prospects, then companies from academic and nonacademic sources can be viable. Often, she does see challenges with inflexible terms of license agreements for technologies out of universities and advises start-ups to thoroughly review all terms and conditions of licensing agreements.

One observation that RoseAnn has made and advice that she would give is to get market feedback as soon as you can. Pick up the phone, find a way to get to the person who lives where you want to be as a company. You may be afraid that someone will steal your idea, but you need that market feedback somehow. Quickly.

Even with early investment from Ben Franklin adding value to the start-ups, RoseAnn still sees a gap in first phase follow-on funding after her investment. She sees the need to develop relationships with venture capitalists from outside the region and investment varies by sector. Through this next stage of investment, Ben Franklin works closely with their companies and continues to provide contacts and support to get the company through the next stage.

How does RoseAnn so successfully manage a highly risky portfolio of start-ups with state-funded resources? She is always ahead of the curve. RoseAnn reads and studies markets, travels and listens, watches for signs and signals in coming new market growth. She is able to react quickly and nimbly to move her organization into the emerging area. "If you love what you're doing, you immerse yourself in it, you love it and live it." Sounds just like an entrepreneur.

Typically, federal research funding is not awarded for feasibility research/development necessary to achieve POC outcomes. Investors are not often interested in sourcing an endeavor without a POC. The start-up lingo around this part of academic entrepreneurship is the "valley of death." Right from the start, you know this is not going to be good. The valley of death is a key factor in the lack of translation of academic research toward commercialization. How will you successfully cross the valley?

Proof-of-Concept Centers (POCCs)

In universities, before a start-up is spun out, there are additional opportunities for POC studies. These are generally set with the goal that Eric Ries puts forth in his book *The Lean Start-Up* as well as numerous other strategists. The idea is that you succeed or "fail fast."

You may be thinking, this is not so easy and my new drug has to go through a multiphase clinical trial before I'll know if it will succeed or fail. That may be true, but what the POC experiment is trying to answer is this: in the closest conditions to the actual condition of product use, does this technology work? Defining that environment and the outcome assessment is entirely up to you. However, at the end of that experiment or study, there should be ample evidence to prove feasibility of the concept toward a product or prove or disprove the feasibility of the concept. It's that simple.

In Silicon Valley, this strategy has been used for years (see box on Roy Rosin, Chapter 3). Roy Rosin, the chief innovation officer at the Perelman School of Medicine of the University of Pennsylvania and former vice president of Innovation at Intuit, speaks about how software platforms do the fail-fast test all the time, that is, rigging up a not-so-polished alpha version software platform and then launching it for a period of time and getting both marketing data (by the number of people to interface with the site or download the software) or by feedback that they collect from user comments. Then, the site is removed and they now have real data to make decisions over feature development, to debug, and to assess target markets.

Some other technologies have different risk from a technological perspective, like power plant design, new manufacturing processes, drugs, or medical devices. No one, not even the shrewdest investor, will expect this whole thing to be finished. However, they will be more receptive to a technology that has been assessed for the potential fatal flaw and found to have passed.

The other opportunity that POC experiments allow is that before millions of dollars are invested in scaling a technology and hiring an outstanding team, this gives the academic research the ability to pivot. If there is a failure in the POC, it may that the technology will work, but under a different set of conditions for a different market or in a different way. This gives opportunity to pivot or change direction and try the POC again. All of this is done under the academic roof, prior to the incorporation a start-up company and prior to investors and maybe even before management consulting is formally brought into the enterprise (Figure 5.1).

Sometimes the failure of the POC experiment provides a straightforward message that this concept will not make it as a product. At all. Ever. This is okay. Not what you're hoping for, but still okay. You are a very busy person and don't want to waste years of your life on a venture doomed to failure for a fundamental technological reason. Failing fast saves you time and allows you to get on to your next big idea in an efficient manner.

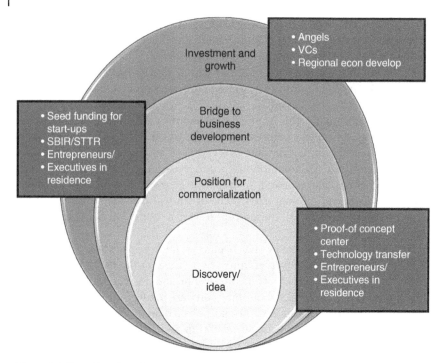

Figure 5.1 Transition from discovery to commercial product has many transitions. Support from university or regional business development community is critical to drive the research discovery forward along the commercialization pathway, which is different from advancing the research and requires different sources of support from research grants.

There are some proof-of-concept centers (POCCs) within universities and some within economic development organizations within a region. There are over 33 university POCCs in the United States as of 2013. The POCC awards are typically small, ranging from $25 to $100K, depending on the market sector. Sometimes, there is follow-on funding available to continue or expand a pilot study. The idea is that with each successful experiment, you are de-risking and building value in the technology. Since there are generally no sales at this point, value is generated from the promise of the technology for tomorrow. The key factors that help build that value at this stage are the IP, data supporting the product in a POC, market assessment, and you, as the lead investigator.

In addition to financial support to do critical experiments, POCCs often provide guidance from advisors in the start-up world. Entrepreneurs in residence help faculty members to frame the potential company with the help of consultants, market analysis and introduction to investors, economic development organizations, and potential corporate partners. This environment creates a community and enhances the social capital of the entrepreneur through the introduction to numerous key players in the innovation ecosystem.

A significant difference from a POC project and a research project is the sheer volume of reporting that can be required. Quarter reports are not unusual along with presentations to various committees for review of your progress. These analyses ensure that you are making progress with your experimentation but are intended to encourage your IP development and your communication with the key people who can help you to translate your innovation.

The Kauffman Foundation has studied the first university POCCs, the von Liebig Center at UCSD (founded in 2001) and the Deshpande Center at MIT (founded in 2002) (Gulbranson and Audretsch, 2008).

Leon Sandler
Executive Director of the Deshpande Center for Technological Innovation
MIT

"Select, direct, connect."

These are the elements that Leon Sander spends his time doing for MIT technologies every day as the Executive Director of the Deshpande Center. Leon's mission is to prepare academic innovations for translation to commercialization. The Deshpande Center is one of the oldest academic POC centers in the country. From 2002 to 2014, Deshpande has supported technologies that have resulted in 28 start-ups (out of about 500 grant applications and 100 funded projects: approximately 30% of funded projects become start-ups). The Deshpande start-ups together have over $500 million in follow-on funding.

How does Leon sift through all of these technologies to support likely successful ventures? Primarily, the supported technologies are ones with a clear market need. Once the market need is defined, the companies target everything toward that end (no detours). He spends time with the faculty members to be able to clearly communicate the technology and detailing specification levels which make the potential product or service competitive to solve the market need. Leon wants to understand "where's the there" and what's the roadmap.

Different sectors have different market needs. For example, a residential or consumer product must be competitive on cost while a NASA customer may be looking primarily for weight or power saving features and the cost consideration is secondary. Even though the academic may have some "cool stuff," the details about the market may result in the technology not being commercially competitive. Sometimes, there may be an interesting idea with early discovery, but you may not be able to get the concept to work reproducibly or at scale. "At times, these difficulties can be engineered around and at other times, the project just gets stopped."

Leon believes in primary market research. Talking with potential customers to fully understand issues that the product is intending to solve or treat. "This defines the solution space and the earlier one can do marketing research, the better."

The most important thing in a start-up company is its customers. You have to have customers to buy your product or service. "Business produces product that someone wants and will pay for."

Consider the agricultural analogy. In agriculture, there is a whole supply chain. From seed providers to seedlings to farming home gardens to plants to harvest to supermarkets. Leon likens the universities as seed providers (the start of the chain). Start-ups are like the home gardening with companies akin to the plants, harvest and supermarket end game. To execute this chain, they key is the farmer, or in the start-up world, the CEO.

"The CEO is one factor that is key to the success of the start-up." Leon suggests finding and partnering with a CEO as a co-founder rather than founding the company and then bringing in the CEO as "hired help," which he has not seen work out. He does not recommend faculty members serve as the CEO.

Even with a good product idea and strong management, raising money for early stage technologies is difficult. This is where Deshpande comes in. With funding from Deshpande, laboratory findings can be de-risked to make the next stage of funding more likely. There is a lot of risk around a new company, including market, regulatory, reimbursement, management and technological risk. The Deshpande POC support is intended to reduce the technological risk associated with getting from a great idea to a viable product concept. Leon thinks that it's less likely for concepts that have a long-term view (naturally, many of the academic ideas being researched today) to draw investment without the support of the Center. While the 28 Deshpande companies have raised over $500 million in follow up funding, the distribution of that funding is skewed: five companies have together raised $250 million, a few have raised $10–12 million while many have raised about $5 million. Of course, the financial need for each company is different (consider the difference between the IT and pharmaceutical or energy sectors), however, raising money for the start-up is always challenging.

With support from Deshpande, MIT is cultivating new companies with amazing innovations that are focused on market need and have strong management. That should keep the supermarkets stocked for years to come.

The von Liebig Center at UCSD's Jacob School of Engineering was founded with a $10 million gift from the William J. von Liebig Foundation. The center's mission is "to accelerate commercialization of UCSD innovations into the marketplace, foster and facilitate the exchange of ideas between the University and industry, and prepare engineering students for the entrepreneurial workplace" (vonliebeg.ucsd.edu). In funding 10–12 projects a year, the funding rate is between 35 and 60% of proposals submitted. A faculty member must be included in the project. The review process is rigorous. From a letter of intent, there is then a collaboration with the applicants and an advisor who jointly prepare a full proposal and presentation to a review committee of five to eight members. The review criteria consider business and technical expertise.

After the grant is awarded, the advisor works with the team to prepare a com-mercialization plan with technical and business milestones and a 12-month budget. The advisors to the program are paid and part-time to the center. The advisors have business expertise and help to guide the business aspects of the project, while the technical aspects are being de-risked. In addition to business mentorship and funding for the POC experiment, the center offers incubation space and meeting locations before licensing, and external investment is achieved. In addition to project support, the center also provides graduate courses to introduce students to the entrepreneurship careers (Gulbranson and Audretsch, 2008).

The Deshpande Center at MIT was founded in the School of Engineering in 2002 from a $17.5 million gift by Jaishree and Gururaj Deshpande. The objective of the center is to increase the impact of MIT technologies. There are two levels of support through the Grant and Catalyst programs up to $250K in stages. They award about 16 grants annually at a funding rate of about 18%. Like the von Liebig Center, there are advisors to support the teams through the business development of the concepts. The Deshpande Center also provides showcases for investors and interaction with the Entrepreneurship Center for graduate students for education in entrepreneurship (Gulbranson and Audretsch, 2008).

Separate from an individual university, the Coulter Foundation has endowed Coulter POCCs in numerous universities ($20 million endowment) across the United States to advance Wallace Coulter's (of Coulter counter fame) vision to help academics translate research toward the bedside for medical devices. The Coulter centers are administered centrally by the foundation but managed locally in each university. Projects follow a similar path as the other POCCs with a letter of intent for application, mentoring through proposal and presen-tation submission, and a multidisciplinary committee to review proposals. The Coulter funding is at $100K/year, renewable with flexibility for pilots and fol-low-on support. As of 2013, the Coulter Foundation awarded 280 projects with at least 1 year of funding. Licenses were issued to 31 medical device companies. There were 60 start-ups, 55 of which received venture capital funding over $900 million dollars (Wallace, 2016).

In addition to university and foundation POCCs, there are regional POCCs such as those supported by the Commonwealth of Pennsylvania including Nanotechnology Institute (NTI), Energy Commercialization Institute, and QED. NTI was created in 2000 with the goal of accelerating commercialization of university research in nanotechnology and addressed these challenges by using the following core principles from Green *et al.* (2011):

1) Core public investment of funds carefully managed by a leadership team that integrates faculty, economic development experts, and university TTO officers at the same administrative level
2) Multi-university participation through a novel, comprehensive IP pooling and revenue-sharing strategy

3) Strategically targeted grants to universities and loans to small businesses that promote faculty–industry collaboration and prioritize university IP with commercial potential
4) Strong emphasis on interdisciplinarity, regional strengths, and high quality research
5) Recruitment of commercialization experts in oversight and program review and solicitation of university technology transfer professionals in prioritizing projects to fund
6) Extensive outreach, networking, information sharing, and marketing efforts

This organization found a way for the TTO's of over 15 universities to agree in terms of operation for universities. The founding members of NTI were Ben Franklin Technology Partners of Southeastern PA, Drexel University, and the University of Pennsylvania. In 2011, the affiliate members included Children's Hospital of Philadelphia, Fox Chase Cancer Center, Harrisburg University of Science and Technology, Lehigh University, Millersville State University, Philadelphia University, Temple University, University of the Sciences, Villanova University, and Widener University (Green *et al.*, 2011). The program support for multi-investigator and multi-institutional projects made awards in the range of $150–300K/year. The projects required progress toward commercialization by moving the funded technology toward licensing or forming the basis for a start-up company. In an analysis of productivity of the multifaceted program, the outcome from 2008 to 2011 exceeded the cumulative activity of the previous 7 years, showing that education of the entire ecosystem, learning by doing among the participating institutions, had a long learning curve but then was able to see major benefit from the program.

So how do POCCs perform? From an analysis of the UCSD von Liebig Center, the MIT Deshpande Center and the NTI for the State of Pennsylvania, outcomes showed that of the roughly 80 projects funded through each POCC, there was follow-on grant support of $4.6, $11 and $16.7 million, respectively. Again, there were 6, 20, and 48 licenses generated and 26, 23, and 31 start-up companies, respectively (Green *et al.*, 2011). The POCC concept has demonstrated success in helping to foster innovations to commercialization.

If your university does not have a POCC itself or belong to one, there are still options for you to consider. Small Business Innovation Research (SBIR)/Small Business Technology Transfer (STTR) programs may be the best way to go. The federal programs are helpful, with the potential of even more follow-on funding than the typical POCC, but the application process will likely move more slowly because of the longer grant review process. You may also be able to encourage an angel investor to support your POC (see Chapter 9). Either way, adding this data to the technology assessment will further your understanding of the potential product and help you to position the product for your investors, building your bridge and allowing you to successfully cross the valley of death.

SBIR/STTR Programs

Traditionally and still today, once a company is founded, SBIR funding from federal agencies (NSF, NIH, DoD, DOE, and NASA) can be granted to the company, which can then be subcontracted to a fixed percentage with the academic institution in order to de-risk the technology. The SBIR program was initiated through the Small Business Innovation Development Act in 1982. The SBIR program is aimed to support investment of federal research funds. An assessment of the SBIR programs across agencies was reported by the National Academies in 2008 (Wessner, 2008). Their findings showed the following:

- *Generating multiple knowledge outputs.* SBIR projects yield a variety of knowledge outputs. These contributions to knowledge are embodied in data, scientific and engineering publications, patents and licenses of patents, presentations, analytical models, algorithms, new research equipment, reference samples, prototypes products and processes, spin-off companies, and new "human capital" (enhanced know-how, expertise, and sharing of knowledge).
  - Over a third of respondents to the NRC surveys reported university involvement in their SBIR project. Among those reporting university involvement,
    - More than two-thirds of companies reported that at least one founder was previously an academic.
    - About one-third of founders were most recently employed as academics before founding the company.
    - 27% of projects had university faculty as contractors on the project, 17% used universities themselves as subcontractors, and 15% employed graduate students.
  - Small technology companies use SBIR awards to advance projects, develop firm-specific capabilities, and ultimately create and market new commercial products and services.
    - *Company creation:* Just over 20% of companies responding to the NRC Firm Survey indicated that they were founded entirely or partly because of a prospective SBIR award.
    - *The decision to initiate research:* Companies responding to the NRC Phase II Survey reported that over two-thirds of SBIR projects would not have taken place without SBIR funding.
    - *Providing alternative development paths:* Companies often use SBIR to fund alternate development strategies, exploring technological options in parallel with other activities.
    - *Reaching the market:* Although the data vary by agency, respondents to the NRC Phase II Survey indicate that just under half of the projects do

reach the marketplace. Given the very early stage of SBIR investments, and the high degree of technical risk involved (reflected in risk assessment scores developed during some agency selection procedures), the fact that a high proportion of projects reach the marketplace in some form is significant, even impressive.
  – As with investments made in early-stage companies by angel investors or venture capitalists, SBIR awards result in sales numbers that are highly skewed. A small percentage of projects will likely achieve large growth and significant sales revenues—that is, becoming commercial "home runs." Meanwhile, many small successes together will continue to meet agency research needs and comprise a potentially important contribution to the nation's innovative capability.

The SBIR grants are typically on the order of $100–300K for a Phase I grant over 6–12 months. The real beauty of this program is that the money comes in as a grant (no cost) to the start-up, rather than a loan or investment. The SBIR program has been successful in supporting the launch of numerous start-ups within and outside of academia. SBIR Phase I awards totaled $534 million in 2012 (sbir.gov).

A Phase II SBIR is where this program has much higher impact. For the Phase II program, grants by law (1992) can be a maximum of $750K. However, for some agencies (NIH), this maximum can be adjusted to the higher end of the million dollar range. For a start-up, one million free dollars can be highly significant and so there is tremendous competition for this funding. There was $990 million in Phase II federal funding in 2012 (sbir.gov). As academics, we are uniquely poised to compete for this type of funding because we are used to writing grants, and we have the institutional resources to accomplish the research/development projects.

There are also SBIR Phase III Awards, which are not subject to further competition and can be awarded by the funding agency to awardees of Phase I or II SBIRs. The Phase III program is targeted exclusively at commercialization.

Before applying for an SBIR, the start-up (with all of the official EIN and incorporation documentation) has to register your company and wait for about 6 weeks to gain official approval to compete for the award. Eligibility for the SBIR program are as follows (acq.osd.mil):
  For SBIR:

- A small business with 500 or fewer employees
- Independently owned, operated, and organized for profit
- Must have its principal place of business in the United States
- At least 51% owned by US citizens or lawfully admitted permanent resident aliens

In addition:

- Work must be performed in the United States.
- The principal investigator must spend more than one-half of the time employed by the proposing firm.
- A minimum of two-thirds of the research work must be performed by the proposing firm in Phase I and one-half in Phase II.

A similar program, STTR, is also available across federal agencies. A primary difference between the SBIR and STTR programs is the amount of research that must be performed in the company itself. For the SBIR and STTR programs, minima of two-thirds and 40% of the work must be performed by the company, respectively. The STTR allows for more work to be performed at the university, if desired. (acq.osd.mil): http://www.acq.osd.mil/osbp/sbir/sb/eligibility.shtml

For STTR:

- A firm must be a US for-profit small business of 500 or fewer employees; there is no size limit on the research institution.
- Research institution must be a US college or university, federally funded research and development center, or nonprofit research institution.
- Work must be performed in the United States.
- The small business must perform a minimum of 40% of the work and the research institution a minimum of 30% of the work in both Phase I and Phase II.
- The small business must manage and control the STTR funding agreement.
- The principal investigator may be employed at the small business or research institution.

The advantage of the SBIR and STTR programs is the free money that can come into a start-up or academic lab to work toward a POC with or without product development. The challenge is the tremendous amount of competition for the awards as well as the long lead times for the review (and potentially revision) processes. In some cases, your technology may not fit with the mission of the federal granting agency and not be considered. In others, if they like the technology, they may create a special call for proposal just for you.

When writing an SBIR/STTR, you need to change your perspective from a researcher who is trying to forge a new scientific ground to a company that is trying to prove or disprove that a technology will make a viable product. This change in focus in writing style confounds the success rate of academics, and the research detailed in the title of the program confounds many nonacademic start-ups. To increase chances for success, some universities, incubators, and economic development programs offer SBIR grant writing workshops and consulting. You can hire an SBIR grant writer to write the grant for/with you, and the good ones will greatly increase your chance of success in winning the award. There are numerous local programs that will pay for the grant-writer to work with you. It helps to seek out these services for your region or within your university. The TTO should be able to guide you in this direction.

Summary

POC is a critical component to developing a viable business from your innovation. Designing an experiment (or more than one experiment) that will enable you to assess the technical viability of your discovery is an important component of the process. So is testing it. When research funding does not allow for the types of POC testing that you need to do, POCC- or SBIR/STTR-funded testing may be able to fill that gap. The result of the POC testing should be an evidence to significantly de-risk the technical aspect of your innovation on the way to becoming a viable product.

References

Green, A. P., Chen, E., Pourrezaei, K., Marcolongo, M., and Carpick R. W. (2011), "Accelerating innovation: The Nanotechnology Institute." *Nanotechnology Law and Business*, **8**: 176–193.

Gulbranson, C. A. and Audretsch, D. B. (2008), "Proof-of-concept centers: Accelerating the commercialization of University Innovation." *The Journal of Technology Transfer* **33**(3): 249–258.

Wallace, H. (2016), Coulter Foundation, whcf.org. http://whcf.org/coulter-foundation-programs/translational-research/coulter-translational-partnership-tp-and-research-awards-ctra/coulter-translational-research-awards-ctra/ (accessed May 29, 2017).

Wessner, C. W. and T. Committee on Capitalizing on Science, and Innovation, National Research Council, Eds. (2008), *An Assessment of the SBIR Program*. Washington, DC, National Academies Press.

6

Start-Up Management: You've Got to Kiss a Lot of Frogs...

Keep away from people who try to belittle your ambitions. Small people always do that, but the really great make you feel that you, too, can become great.

—Mark Twain

You have IP and know-how, have checked out the market opportunity, and done a key proof-of-concept experiment, and things are looking good. By now you know how much time and expertise this kind of endeavor takes. One of the best ways to leverage your time and use your expertise to its greatest advantage is to partner with a colleague who has demonstrated leadership in the business world.

The start-up CEO world is quite a bit different from the investment banker or corporate type of business leader. They need skills to gain investment in a potential business with nothing more substantial than an idea and some IP. They need to be broad in terms of business skills including market analysis and making markets, pricing strategies, valuations, financing, manufacturing, packaging, regulatory, sales, and marketing. Start-up CEOs have to be able to recruit outstanding people and motivate them to work tirelessly toward the start-up's mission. They have to foster a good working relationship with the cofounder: you. The CEOs need to have and to continue to develop wide networks on which to draw expertise at different times during the start-up process. They need to have a high degree of integrity and ethics. There is a small and tight-knit start-up community and reputation is extremely important. This is not an easy position and an outstanding CEO is critical in driving the success of your start-up.

Who are these talented people? Do you want a recent MBA graduate with half a year's experience? Maybe or maybe not. While recent grads may be highly driven, their network can be limited initially, and it may take some time

Academic Entrepreneurship: How to Bring Your Scientific Discovery to a Successful Commercial Product, First Edition. Michele Marcolongo.

for them to learn to navigate the entrepreneurship ecosystem. Do you want a successful entrepreneur with a proven track record, who has had an excellent prior exit? This person may have all the necessary skills, and investors tend to like CEOs who have prior start-up experience, but is he or she still hungry enough to drive the business? There are as many possible CEO types as there are start-ups. A few personal characteristics that a strong CEO may exhibit:

- High degree of integrity and ethics
- Honesty
- Innovative thinking
- Charisma and strong presence
- Risk-taker, but with measured risk
- Personable
- Strong work ethic, not a procrastinator

Mostly, you need to believe that this person can run the start-up and lead it to success. One of the hardest things to do when you have conceived of a technology and nurtured it along through an already long cycle (generating the concept, writing grants, securing funding, training students, doing the research, writing the patent, doing market analysis, and proof-of-concept experiments). You needed to have ownership of this process or it would have remained a laboratory discovery and would not be turning into a viable commercial product. But now that you are taking in a partner, you need to be able to encourage that partner, your new CEO, to have ownership of the start-up. This is the step one of the founder: being able to trust in the leadership of the company (this is where integrity and ethics become critical). The CEO will start to take over day-to-day operations that are not technical at first, but later, may also influence the technical product development. You need to be able to trust and work with this person. While you can't just let go of the technology and move on to the next big thing, you will have to relinquish some control for the success of the start-up. This is a stumbling block for many academics. While we are experts in a technologically specific area, we will rely on others to add additional dimensions to the business. This takes a certain amount of humility and trust. You will teach the CEO everything you know, then you'll need to back away and give the CEO space to internalize the information so that the CEO can further develop the story with such conviction that when presenting to investors, recruiting consultants, advisors, employees, and others, the CEO can secure the support that is needed for the company. The skills and time that your business partner will bring to the company are exactly what it needs. So, by you stepping back a bit, you are making a major contribution toward helping the company succeed. This can be difficult: you may need to leave your ego in the lab.

One key question is where to find a highly talented CEO? This is the most difficult part of the process in many academic centers across the country and the one discussed often and at length by academic entrepreneurs. The entrepreneurial network that you have developed up to this point is a great place to start. If your institution is more sophisticated in assisting academic start-ups, then the TTO, POCC director, or university venture investment group may be helpful in matchmaking. Patent and contract attorneys also have good networks of business entrepreneurs as well as investors and may be a good resource. In fact, when interviewing attorneys to work with your start-up, the attorney's network is often a major criterion for selection. Local economic development groups have supported entrepreneurs in the past and many entrepreneurs check in with them when they're looking for a new business opportunity.

The following are some organizations/people who can help you to find a strong business partner/CEO:

- TTO
- POCC directors
- University venture investment group
- Attorneys
- Local economic development organizations
- Incubator/accelerator directors
- Other faculty who have started companies
- Consultants that you may have used
- Industry contacts that you might have
- Alumni organization from your institution or alma maters
- Venture capitalist/investor friends
- Meetings where seedling start-ups present to investors

You need to work this and it may take quite a bit of time. While a strong CEO may be hard to find, this is well worth the time.

Sometimes, in the absence of a good business partner, academics will engage their postdoc or graduate student who will assume the CEO role in a start-up. This alternate strategy has worked with exceptionally talented students who are interested in and quickly pick up the business side of start-ups. However, this strategy will generally result in a start-up that moves at a slower pace as the student develops the business, network, and entrepreneurial skills. This approach may have a reduced opportunity for success because investors generally feel comfortable with business people, and it will take some strong convincing to the investors that the student is capable of managing all aspects of the start-up. According to Bob Adelson, as his venture group, Osage, has invested in 350 out of the 2700 university start-ups each year, companies that use postdocs or professors as the management team (CEOs) typically fail.

Students not involved in the business management but in the operations of the start-up are a great way to transition the technology from the lab to the start-up and are a major asset to the technical management of the company. The students often know the technology extremely well and can help in expanding it to the next level of development. Many times, they are passionate about the technology, since they participated in its development. In other cases, the professor is not interested in the start-up, but the postdoc or student is. In this case, the student can be the cofounder and professor can be on the scientific advisory board, for example, or not participate at all (see Chapter 7).

While this can be extremely beneficial for the company, there is another source of potential conflict between the student and the faculty member. If the student is currently still undergoing training and has not yet received a degree (current student), there is obvious conflict between an advisor who is responsible for supervision and the student, who needs to satisfy the degree requirements under the faculty member's supervision. The degree requirements and company requirements may be widely divergent, leading to a source of conflict in the relationship between faculty and current student. If however, the student or postdoc has completed mentoring under the professor, then the relationship has less conflict. There is still the need to distinguish the research goals from the company objectives, but these details can be worked out. Over time, the student will gain more responsibility for the technical management of the company, and the professor may again need to step back in order to allow the former student to develop into a leader in the start-up.

Bob Langer, cofounder of 23 start-ups from his Chemical Engineering lab at MIT (at the time of this writing, but probably outdated already), says that it's hard for him to spot an outstanding CEO, but he knows right away when there is a poor one. Every academic entrepreneur that was interviewed for this book as well as those in casual conversation have said that finding a strong CEO is the most critical and difficult part of this process.

Kathryn Uhrich, Ph.D.
Rutgers University
Professor, Chemistry and Chemical Biology

Kathryn Uhrich is an amazing person all around. When you first meet her, she immediately exhibits intellect, honesty, and integrity.

It's no surprise, then, that in addition to her academic responsibilities as faculty and as administrator being the dean of Mathematical and Physical Sciences, Kathryn made time to become an academic entrepreneur.

Polymerization of drugs and controlled release of those drugs have been the topics of ongoing innovative research in Kathryn's lab at Rutgers. Since the start of her first company, Polymerix, in 2000, Kathryn has been an academic entrepreneur.

When Polymerix first spun out of the lab, she was offered the opportunity to leave Rutgers with enough capital to run the company herself. But Kathryn chose to remain an academic and instead, with the help of Rutgers, found a business partner to be the CEO of the company. This model has worked for Kathryn through her subsequent (4–5, but who's counting?) start-ups.

Because she chose to remain an active faculty member (and administrator), Kathryn took a more hands-off approach to her first company. When she founded Polymerix, she admittedly had no first-hand experience with the start-up world, like the majority of academics. Working with an experienced CEO and president, she often defaulted to them when there was a disagreement over a business decision, thinking that they must know best. But as time progressed and Kathryn learned more about the business of technology start-ups, she developed a different and, she believes, more effective approach. She and any new CEO are equal partners. "You can't just make stuff and hand it off. There is a relationship and a good bit of back and forth needed." Kathryn is more comfortable with this integrated partnership model. "You have to have confidence in yourself as a successful academic. Be engaged in important issues, challenge decisions, and pick good partners."

Kathryn chooses a CEO for her company in the same way she chooses an academic collaborator. She looks for someone with a good track record who is solid. She values someone who understands science and business development. "It's a bit like dating—you have to find the right partner."

But how does she manage to be involved in her start-ups and direct an active research program and hold administrative positions? Kathryn has a strict and thoughtful approach to control the inherent conflict between her academic responsibilities and her start-ups. She does not do technology development in her academic lab. There are no students working on her company business development. She does train the employees from the start-ups on how to synthesize polymers, but the employees don't work in her lab. Kathryn's strategy is to get early financing for the company, start a separate facility outside of the university, and hire people specifically to work in the company. As founder, she takes a corporate position as a consultant and chair of the Scientific Board. She even controls the time of the week and number of hours that she spends on the start-up. With a rigorous compartmentalization of her time, she again is able to manage the inherent conflicts.

What does Kathryn like most about her start-up experience? She feels that this is another challenging learning experience where she is thinking, inventing, and doing science, but with a practical focus. She wants to help humanity and this is where the business comes in: the business is a conduit to the patient. "It's a fascinating process, making discoveries from the lab into a product." Dozens of people are alive because of the drug eluting stents that she has developed through one of her start-ups. Developing disruptive and life-saving products to treat patients? That's something to like.

What if you can't find a strong CEO in your backyard? There is always opportunity to recruit from another region. Sectors tend to concentrate in certain regions of the country as of this time: Silicon Valley and New York for digital technology; Boston, San Diego, and Philadelphia for biotech; or Nashville for behavioral health, to name a few. Entrepreneurs tend to congregate regionally because the venture capitalists are congregated regionally and in many cases the VCs like to have the start-ups nearby. So in your sector, there may be opportunity to find a CEO in the region of greatest investment. You can easily track this down with year-end venture investment reports that are targeted to your market sector.

Once you have a few names and start to initiate dialog with possible CEOs, really think of this as an interview. Your objective is to put your technology into hands that will shepherd it to a mutually agreed end goal. You need to understand the potential CEO's competencies in terms of business. And you need to be able to work with this person. The following are some "interview" questions to consider:

- For your last start-up, tell me about a challenging event that you successfully managed. One that you unsuccessfully managed and how would you approach it differently?
- How do you approach investment strategy? Debt financing or equity? Tranches or full rounds? What would be best for our start-up? Which investors have you worked with in the past? Describe that experience.
- What is your experience in recruiting talent? How do you ensure the best and brightest will work for you? How do you retain them?
- What type of culture do you want in the start-up? How do you facilitate that culture?
- How do you approach a start-up partnership with a cofounder? Some things that have worked for you in the past (and some that didn't)?
- Try to get a sense of their network breadth: do they have good relationships with investors, attorneys (patent and contract), consultants in key areas, and other entrepreneurs?
- For personal traits, try to assess their confidence and humility
- What are three things about this technology and market that draw you to the business opportunity? What are three things that will keep you up at night?

Let's say that you've gotten to the point where you would like to go forward with a potential business relationship. Before you run off to set up your operating agreement and deal out equity positions, it might be good to work toward the business plan together for a month or two. This does a couple of things. It lets you see how the partnership will be on a day-to-day basis. How is the communication and mutual respect? Is the CEO able to explain why different approaches are being used and explain all of the business terms (contractual, legal, regulatory, pricing, marketing) to you? Is the CEO able to understand all of the technical subtleties that you explain back? Is there a curiosity and a keen work ethic? Is the CEO an effective decision-maker?

You may click with the first CEO that you engage. After a month or two, you may be ready to progress to a formal agreement and begin to move the company along together. It's not something to rush into immediately because many academic start-ups will take years (maybe 10 years) to fully mature. This partnership has been likened to a marriage of sorts and lots of entrepreneurs (academic and business think of it this way). You may have "love at first sight" and develop a strong and lasting relationship. Or, you may need to date a while to realize that your potential partner "leaves the cap off the toothpaste" and just won't work between you. Some uncommitted time together will allow both your and the CEO's real personalities and working styles to come through so that you can both decide if it's a good match. This approach may potentially save you a lot of time and frustration if you can succeed in achieving a business relationship based on trust and mutual objectives with a comradery and respectful partnership.

The risk for you in jumping in too early with an operating agreement and assigning equity is that once the equity has vested, even if you need to part ways with the CEO, the CEO retains the equity. That is less equity you will have to draw in a new CEO or to share among other key members of the team.

Once you have agreed to go forward with your CEO, you are ready to take the next steps. There are some detailed agreements that must be executed to make your start-up official.

Step one is incorporation of your start-up. This can be done through a contract attorney or with a do-it-yourself incorporation online. While the contract attorney will cost some money, sometimes start-up attorneys are willing to work with you to delay billing until you have some seed investment. You need to determine what type of entity the start-up will be. There are limited liability corporations (LLCs), C-Corps, or S-corps to choose from. Your attorney will guide you through this process. Today, some start-ups choose begin as an LLC and don't transition to a C-corp until necessary with a series A round of investment.

C-Corp:

- Legally, C-Corps separate entities from their owners.
- Income is taxed at the corporate level and is taxed again when it is distributed to owners,
- Can reinvest profits at a lower corporate tax rate,
- Most corporations are C-corps,

S-Corps:

- So-called because it falls under the IRS subchapter S code.
- Must be small business (less than 100 shareholders).
- Protects shareholders, but profits are not taxed at corporate level, only shareholder level.

LLCs:

- Shareholders are from company liabilities.
- Crossover between corporation and partnership.
- Partners are taxed personally, no corporate tax.
- Cannot be used if the company plans to go public (must be C-corp).
- Dissolved under death or bankruptcy of member.

Now the fun part—naming your new baby. After you have a list of a few names, it's a good idea to do a search to see if the name is available for use in your sector. The same name of a corporation can be used in different markets, but if you don't want to overlap, you'll need to search around a bit. While you're searching for naming, you may also consider trademarking the name and securing the domain name for a future website. As of now, as soon as you incorporate, trolls can jump in and buy the domain rights for your company name. If you want to obtain those rights from them, they will charge a greatly inflated price. So, it's a good practice to check and align all of this at the same time. The attorney can help guide you through this process or you can do it yourself.

Once you incorporate, you can then apply online (or the attorney can do it) for an employee ID number (EIN; see IRS website). This will be your tax identification number for the corporation, needed when you acquire financing or even to apply for SBIR eligibility.

When you incorporate, you will also need to execute an operating agreement. This is a contract among the founders (you, the CEO, and any other colleagues included in your start-up). The purpose is to define the rules of engagement among the partners in the operations of the company. The operating agreement is where you define the equity positions of each member of the company. You may also define a salary and bonus structure for the CEO or other founders. If/when you have a board, the criteria and rules for operations of the board will be included in this agreement. Here is your first lesson in contracts. You'll need to read the operation agreement closely, have input to the terms, and have conversations with your partners over equity, salary, voting rights, and so on. Once again, the attorney can guide you through this process. The operating agreement can be revised when necessary, according to rules that you lay out in the agreement. For example, when you bring in board members, the voting rights change from votes by equity to tallied votes by each board member with a defined majority securing the vote, or if you want to issue additional shares, you need to amend the operating agreement. This is your rule book and it's important for you to completely understand the rules from the start. This will preclude any miscommunications in the operations of your new company.

As an academic founder, you will need to decide on your level of active participation in the start-up going forward. The first question to ask yourself is if you will keep your academic position or go full time into the start-up. There are as many options for your participation in the start-up as you would like to consider and to which your partner(s) will agree. The following are some more common options:

1) *Leave your academic position* and do full-time management in the company. This is perhaps the most aggressive and risky decision for an academia to make. You've likely spent a good chunk of your career developing your academic credentials. Completely leaving academia, while always an option, is not to be considered lightly. Even with the excitement of starting a company, so many things can go in an unexpected way. Before leaving your job, an exercise you might consider is thinking through what your career path will look like in the event that the start-up fails in some way. Will you still be happy to be without your faculty position? The approach of leaving academia to start your company is not that common today. Academic entrepreneurs are more likely to follow Bob Langer's model of spinning out a company and then going back to the lab to come up with the next big thing and then continuing the process. That being said, this may be right for you and then you should follow your passion.

2) *Keep your academic position* and serve as a C-level position in the company (e.g., chief technology officer or chief medical officer) and devote 1 day/ week (or another time partition that may be acceptable to your university) for management of the start-up. Your ability to participate in the start-up of the company and keep your day job as a faculty member may work, while you get the company off the ground. Initially, you will be key in recruiting talented people to work with the company, as employees, advisors, or consultants; you will participate in decision-making of the start-up; and you will likely play a major role in the technical development of the commercial product. As the company grows, there may be a need for a full-time CTO and you may transition your role to head of the scientific advisory board or other similar position. To maintain some control, negotiating a board seat from the beginning would be one way to keep involved and participate in the direction of the company through the company life cycle. This approach also helps you to stay in the lab, keep investigating new directions that may expand the current company through your new research or just come up with completely new directions that may be the seed for another start-up in the future.

3) *Keep your academic position*, hold a board seat on the start-up, and consult on technical guidance and management. This approach is a step down in control from that of a C-level position in the company, but with the compromise that you are still involved in the start-up in an advisory capacity and still hold a board seat to participate in financial, strategic, and technical decision-making. This may be a realistic approach considering the expectations of

your time with your academic position and its time commitments. The time expectations cannot be underestimated in a start-up. If the CEO's expectation is that you will be available whenever needed, but you have classes to teach and grants to write, it's better to discuss the amount of time that you can participate and set up expectations that are realistic so that no one feels frustrated.

4) *Keep your academic position*, take an equity position, but do not participate in daily activities of the start-up. Some faculty members are happy to see their technology going forward but have little interest in the commercialization process. Typically in this type of situation, a student will be participating in the start-up and will be responsible for the translation of the research. You may be given equity and a potential of royalties in accordance with the university's policy and terms of the IP license for your technology. For this option, that would end your involvement with the company, and you would maintain your academic position and only hear from the company when a significant event occurs and the university is notified. This approach allows the technology to go toward commercialization, but in other people's hands, so that you can continue with the academic work that you enjoy without distraction.

There are tax considerations associated with taking equity after the "founders shares" are issued, so now is the time to make these decisions for both you and your partners. Often, if you are bringing in management, like a CEO, it is common not to assign all of the equity at execution of the operating agreement but to hold some in reserve for future investors and/or other key personnel that you might like to incentivize with equity. Equity for the CEO can be vested over time or over milestone events (like funding rounds, first sale, regulatory hurdle, etc.). This again is part of a negotiation between you and your CEO. In addition, the total percentages of equity will need to be addressed, which can be a more challenging discussion. There are no real guidelines, but some strategies can be considered: all partners have an equal amount of equity and everything else.

There are many reasons for you to decide not to equally divide the equity among the founders. Considerations relate to the previous discussion as to your role in the company. Ownership in companies is largely based on your value to the company. The CEO brings management expertise and the ability to raise capital. You are brining technical know-how to the company. The institution where you work is bringing IP (you may be the inventor, but the university controls the IP), and so the institution may require an equity position as you transfer the IP from the institution to the start-up. You may also be technically necessary to advance the technology toward the commercial application and therefore bring value in those skills going forward. Depending on how much you agree to participate in the company, your equity position may be adjusted. It is more common for academic founders who keep their faculty positions not to take a salary, but to take an equity position and perhaps have a paid consulting agreement as the company gains investment. You may personally invest in the start-up and that may have an influence on your equity position. Remember that these are starting equity positions and that this will all change after investors come into the picture after which all of the founders will likely be diluted in their equity position with each round of investment. So, your equity is not likely to increase as the start-up evolves (unless you invest yourself), but be reduced to some degree in proportion to your founder's shares.

In your company there may be common stock, preferred stock, and options. Founder's shares are typically granted as common stock. Some definitions and uses for these types of stocks (Investopedia.com):

- Common stock
  - A security that represents ownership in a corporation.
  - Holders of common stock exercise control by electing a board of directors and voting on corporate policy.
  - Common stockholders are at the bottom of the priority ladder for ownership structure. In the event of liquidation, common shareholders have rights to a company's assets only after bondholders, preferred shareholders, and other debtholders have been paid in full.
  - If the company goes bankrupt, the common stockholders will not receive their money until the creditors and preferred shareholders have received their respective share of the leftover assets.
  - This makes common stock riskier than debt or preferred shares.
- Preferred stock
  - A class of ownership in a corporation that has a higher claim on the assets and earnings than common stock.
  - Generally has a dividend that must be paid out before dividends to common stockholders and the shares usually do not have voting rights.
  - Preferred shareholders have priority over common stockholders on earnings and assets in the event of liquidation and they have a fixed dividend (paid before common stockholders).
- Options
  - A financial derivative that represents a contract sold by one party (option writer) to another party (option holder).
  - The contract offers the buyer the right, but not the obligation, to buy or sell a security or other financial asset at an agreed-upon price (the strike price) during a certain period of time or on a specific date (exercise date).

The CEO's compensation may be in equity as well as salary and bonus as investment is raised. The salary may be deferred until a larger raise of investment or a sale occurs, and there may be interest accrued over that period of delayed time. A student may not only work for some equity but also draw a salary right away.

Each founder must be able to articulate his/her plans for active participation in the start-up. These plans should be in keeping with any university policies if the academic founder is taking a position in the start-up and keeping an academic position. Be as realistic as possible in these scenarios because you need to keep agreeable relationships among the founders and one quick way to tarnish those relationships is by overpromising what each plans to deliver.

In addition to potential financial gains that may be realized by an equity position, there are control issues at stake as well. If you have a business CEO, you've already decided to give up some control of your endeavor in order to gain business expertise for the start-up. The equity positions, by the operating agreement, will typically allow decision-making based on equity positions. In a good management team, you won't be voting against each other all of the time. Hopefully you'll be working toward a consensus to best develop value in the company. But still there may be times when the vote will go according to equity position or board vote, depending on your operating agreement.

Example

Mary and Emma have a research collaboration that focuses on a new tissue scaffold to grow liver tissue in the laboratory. They make a major discovery. They write a disclosure to the university as equal coinventors and the university decides to pursue a provisional patent application based on the work. Mary and Emma work together and submit the provisional patent application. They are granted university proof-of-concept funds to do the "killer experiment" and demonstrate that the technology has huge potential. They decide to investigate the possibility of a start-up to spin the technology out of the university and start a company to commercialize the technology.

Emma is really interested in entrepreneurship, but Mary wants to get back to her lab to work on more basic research. Mary is supportive, but does not want to participate heavily in the start-up. They agree that Emma will do the work to formulate plans for the start-up, which they will call RegenLive. First, Emma enrolls in the NIH I-Corps program and does primary market research to see if the concept is viable from a business perspective. She learns about the market, competition, regulatory pathway, reimbursement strategies, and competition for tissue engineering through discussion with companies, consultants, and attorneys in the sector and emerges from that experience with a vision for a commercially viable product based on the IP that she and Mary filed. Emma then works her network until she finds a great candidate to be the CEO, Sarah. She works with the CEO candidate for 3 months, taking the concept from the laboratory data into what looks like it could be a great platform technology and together they develop a 15-page slide deck that is the foundation of their business plan. They run the pitch by a few friendly investors to gage interest, get reasonable feedback, and revise the plan accordingly. At this point, Emma decides to move forward with Sarah and Sarah is very interested to take the technology toward commercialization and agrees to serve as the CEO of RegenLive. All of this happens before RegenLive has been formally formed.

Emma and her university colleague, Mary, meet with Sarah to discuss their roles in the start-up. Emma is quite interested in the start-up and would like to keep her university position but play an active role in the company as CTO. She will work with RegenLive to translate the technology from the lab toward the commercial realization of a product. Mary still wants to get back to her academic work and does not want participation in a start-up to distract her from her research mission. She does not want a management role in the start-up or a seat on the board. Sarah, the CEO, will manage day-to-day operations of the RegenLive and will be responsible to work, with Emma, toward securing investment in the company. With the roles and interests of the primary stakeholders openly addressed, the discussion turns to compensation. Sarah (CEO) would like to have a salary ($75K/year) and cash bonus structure ($50K/year) based on milestone targets with the first being close of a seed round of $1.5 million in 6 months. She would like an equity position of 30%. They agree that Sarah will have 5% equity vest immediately and then 2% vest/month until all 30% is fully vested. Through discussions with the university and through their option agreement to license the relevant IP, they have negotiated that the university will take 10% of the equity in RegenLive. Of this 10%, the inventors (Mary and Emma) will together receive 5% according to university policy. Mary decides that she will take the university portion allotted to her and no further equity or responsibilities in the start-up. Together, they decide that 20% of the equity will be reserved for future incentives. That leaves Emma with 40% of the company. She is the main shareholder. Because Emma has a significant share of RegenLive, she forgoes her university portion of equity from the license of the IP, and so Mary ends up with 5% total equity in RegenLive (Emma's 2.5% and Mary's 2.5%), which will be distributed through the university portion. All equity will be issued as common stock. If you're doing the math...

Founder's Term Sheet for RegenLive

- Sarah (CEO, cofounder)
  - 30% equity
  - 5% vested immediately and 2% vested monthly until the 30% equity is realized
  - $75K salary plus cash bonus of $50K after milestone of securing $1.5 million investment into RegenLive
- University
  - 10% equity vested upon transfer of the IP from the university to RegenLive, non-voting stock.

- All patent fees to date to be collected after $500K is raised in RegenLive.
- 2% royalty on net sales of RegenLive for 10 years from first sale.
- Mary (inventor with no further participation in the RegenLive).
  - o 5% equity that is realized through her portion of the university equity position (Emma has forfeited her university portion because she has a significant interest in RegenLive separate from the university interest).
- Reserve
- Hold 20% equity aside for future incentives and investors.
- Emma (inventor, cofounder, and CTO)
- 40% equity vested immediately
- No university portion of equity
- No salary

This may or may not be your story, but you can begin to see how the proportions and equity negotiation may go forward. In this case, Emma has control over the company with 40% equity for now. One thing to keep in mind is that some attorneys will not recommend 50–50 equity positions because of the difficulty in resolving tie votes, which may need to go to expensive arbitration. The key to a successful start is that each member who receives founder's shares or a starting equity position is reasonably happy with the arrangement. If one key stakeholder feels slighted or out of balance at the start, then there may be serious repercussions as the start-up progresses. The truth is that if you end up taking venture capital investment, the VC will come in and reorganize the equity positions according to the value that each member is bringing to the start-up at the time. There will be dilution of equity as a minimum as the investors enter the picture (see Chapter 9).

However, each member of the team must be incentivized to meet the many demands necessary to move the company forward. If this occurs, then the group will gel, and the team will work together for the greater mission with a feeling of fair compensation and financial motivation.

What if you can't come to terms with each member of the team for founding equity positions? This may be a deal-breaker. The academic founder may have to rethink his/her position and role and also the decision to take on this particular CEO. Sometimes this negotiation is quite straightforward and at the other extreme this first negotiation will terminate the business. Keeping in mind good negotiating skills, you may try to "get to yes." You all want the same thing, a successful company that brings your discovery toward use by society. You all also want to have a reasonable share in the financial rewards of the endeavor (this is a business after all). The key unifying objectives and your envisioned role will help to guide you as you negotiate the founders' equity positions. Thinking through some scenarios and rationale for your decision and then being able to articulate your thinking to your partners is also helpful to resolving "fair" equity positions for all.

Kathleen M. Shay
Partner
Duane Morris LLP

Kate Shay is not your typical attorney. She's been listed in *Smart CEO's* Leading Lawyers, *Best Lawyers in America*, and is the recipient of the *The Philadelphia Business Journal's* Life Science Award for Best Consultant (Early Stage).

Kate talks start-up corporate structure, partnership, and operating agreements like she's ordering a latte at Starbucks.

It all began with Interspect, a medical ultrasound company that was an emerging business that Kate shepherded through an IPO. Venture capitalists came to her next. The network grew and Kate developed a reputation for providing outstanding legal advice to the start-up community.

Kate also works with technology transfer offices across the country. She sees that "TTOs with experience and methods that have been modified over the years can make a deal. Others start by being difficult. They don't see all sides of things." Size and the number of deals help universities to refine their licensing philosophy. She believes universities could be more flexible in their deal structures, but they look at others and with the small volumes they see, it's hard to know enough to make good judgments with their business partners. "The type of deal often depends on the university policy and if they are trying to get deals done, make money or manage conflict."

Sometimes in the university environment, she sees that there is no agreement within the university. The M.D. and Ph.D. can't agree with the TTO or the university wants non-dilutive stock, while everyone else can be diluted. Part of the challenge is that no one knows the value of the IP early on. After a deal is negotiated and executed, it can be renegotiated when an investor or major corporation enters the picture.

Kate has some advice for academics founding a start-up. She suggests that you find out what to expect with the process. Usually (75% of the time) academics do not leave the university to go with the company. She suggests that you get a good business partner to negotiate on the start-up's behalf. Kate finds that TTOs like to negotiate with the business partner and not with attorneys. It is essential that you need a business partner that you can trust.

Even with a business partner, the academic should go through the operating agreement when he/she forms a company. The academic should also understand the licensing terms from the university. Consideration should be made as to whether the company should be an LLC or a C-corp. Once the company has formed and has secured the IP, she suggests that the company retain corporate counsel. At some time, you may also need a personal counsel to represent you for negotiations with the company.

As for investment, the academic should do what he/she can to retain personal value in the company. However, there's only so much you can do to protect dilution, especially in highly capitalized markets like biotech and medical devices. "In the end, you can own 50% of nothing or 5% of millions." The best way to keep equity is to get preferred stock by putting cash into the business yourself. Regardless of whether you invest yourself or have external investors, "still, you don't have to take every deal."

Setting up a corporation with all of the legal documentation and agreements among partners can be daunting for a novice academic entrepreneur. Attorneys like Kate are critical to lay the legal framework for the company and to best ensure that there are no misunderstandings among the partners from the start.

Management Structure

Additional parts of the management team include directors, advisors, consultants, subcontractors, and employees. There are numerous people your executive team needs to recruit (and retain). Every person counts in a start-up.

Directors (Board of Directors)

Initially, when your start-up is formed, it will be run under the voting authority of the major equity holders, who will vote with their shares, as you would define in the founding operating agreement. While the start-up is organizing and soliciting investment, the same operating agreement will hold. However, after some level of seed investment, depending on your investors, there may be a need to have a board of directors to oversee the major decision-making of the company. A board of directors is (Investopedia, 2016):

> Board of Directors: Group of individuals that are elected as, or elected to act as, representatives of the stockholders to establish corporate management related policies and to make decisions on major company issues. Every public company mch shave a board of directors. Some private and nonprofit companies have a board of directors as well.

The role of the board member is outlined in amendments to the original operating agreement, where control was with voting shares of equity holders, as executed by your corporate attorney. The amended operating agreement will continue to provide operations guidelines for the company.

A board of directors consists of "inside" and "outside" members (Investopedia, 2016).

> Inside Board Members: "Have the interest of major shareholders, officers, and employees in mind and whose expertise in their business and their market adds value to the board". There is no compensation for

inside members, for whom board duties are a component of their job responsibilities. These can be C-level executives or major shareholders, including a founder.

Outside Board Members Or "Independent Board Members": These members are "not involved in the inner workings of the company and bring experience from working with other businesses". The idea is that outside board members provide an outside or objective perspective on company strategic decisions and conflict resolution including resolving disputes. Outside board members are compensated for their time serving on the board. This compensation can be around 1% equity (negotiable).

There is a wide range of advice on how to compose a board of directors. Some entrepreneurs recommend starting one early, before you get major investment so that you can leverage the management strengths in your C-suite and have a sounding board for strategic decisions as you launch the company and its direction. Others recommend not having a board until you absolutely are forced into one by your investors. The rationale for this strategy is that it keeps the start-up more nimble in early days and allows the equity holders themselves to drive decision-making (typically the founders).

When you construct the board, one thing to consider is the number of directors. It is typical to select an odd number of directors, so that disputes and decisions put to a vote can avoid ties. (Although, your operating agreement could outline what a majority is and what percentage of votes are needed to pass.) Start-ups can have as many board members as you like, although the more directors, the more cumbersome meeting organization and communication will be. Also, this advice is not free consideration of the cost of outside board members is significant (about 1% equity, typically). Start-ups typically have three to five directors, inside and outside.

Board members have a role to oversee the CEO. They will set targets and determine compensation for the CEO. They will also potentially decide to replace the CEO as necessary. Founders can have a board seat, and Bob Langer recommends that you do in order to keep current with the business and have a say in its direction, including financing and exits. Sometimes, even though the founder may have been the catalyst to the formation of the company, there is resistance to assigning the founder as a director. This has often been a battle, especially after investment in the company is made. Not a minor point, if your operating agreement states that the board governs the company and you are not part of the board, even if you have a significant equity position, you will have little or actually no control over the decision-making for the company that you founded. To gain and maintain a director position, you will likely need to show your value to the board, which can be in many ways. Sometimes, just having your name associated with the board will help drive investment.

Sometimes, the technical/regulatory development is so closely tied to you that you are needed to manage the development and therefore bring value. You may have a C-level position in the start-up. You may have contacts in business or government that make you useful to the board.

Choosing the board members will be voted by equity shareholders. If it's just you and the CEO who hold equity, then whoever holds more equity will be making the decision, in accordance with the voting process documented your operating agreement.

Let's say you decide on a five-member board. You and the CEO have discussed the board and decided that both you (the founder) and the CEO will serve as directors (inside directors). Now, you both need to select three other directors for the board, although the major equity holder will make the final decision. Assuming you are still in the seed stage of funding, you may not need to put an investor on the board. You may, however choose a director that would be an investor representative, literally representing the interest of all of your investors (friends, family, economic development funds, angels, and/or corporate partners). Regardless, the selection of directors should bring value to the management of your business. Included may be another CEO who has start-up experience and ties to the investment community or corporations. Or it could be a CFO type who will help in planning and monitoring finances, burn rates, sales projections and compensation, and other expenses, possibly a marketing and sales strategist, attorney, or regulatory strategist. Generally, business and not technical guidance is the focus of the board of directors.

If your board is convened early in the start-up process, before major investment, then you may choose the option to allow major financial decision around financing or exit to remain with the shareholder vote and not be controlled by the board, who will make other major decisions. This strategy allows oversight of the CEO and strategic decisions to be governed by the board but keeps financial control in the shareholders. Otherwise, the directors will control the financial decisions of the company along with strategy and other oversight. Regardless of the control that you give to the board of directors, the general governance of the board is documented in the operating agreement.

With the governance of the board, you can see how your control is diluted (e.g., now one vote out of five, rather than voting your shares). Selection of directors is crucial for the success of your company. You will need to spend time candidates to see if you can have a good working relationship with them. You may need to talk to references and see how they have performed on other boards or in their positions. If the CEO nominates three board members and you simply agree, you may have just stacked the board completely toward the CEO's benefit should conflict between you arise. While the board offers numerous benefits, the change in control is a significant consideration for founders and should be taken very seriously.

Chairperson of the board is a role of facilitator for the board. The chair may call votes, determine agendas for board meetings, and serve as advisory to the CEO. In early start-ups, the CEO may also serve as chairperson of the board; however, one of the outside directors typically serves as chairperson in an effort to balance the control with the CEO.

Board of Advisors

In addition to a board of directors, a company may have a board of advisors. Advisors are simply that and do not control the company. There may be a scientific advisory board or a clinical advisory board. An advisory board is a group of people who has expertise in a focus area and who will provide insights and guidance to the tasks at hand. For a scientific advisory board, the members may help to guide manufacturing scale-up or regulatory issues or testing strategies. They may review development plans and offer suggestions for strategy or offer critiques on experimental or testing results. These advisors may be chosen for expertise and insights into the area of interest. Advisory board members can be more fluid than directors.

Sometimes advisory boards can serve the broader mission of financing, human resources, marketing, or strategic advising, more like a board of directors but without the control or the cost. A general advisory board may be a good option for early start-ups who need insight but want to still be nimble in decision-making among founders and major equity holders.

As part of the management team, the advisors can also help to attract investment in the start-up. If Dr. Q is on the clinical advisory board, that might be another seal of approval that the investor needs. Some start-ups are highly strategic about selection of advisors because of the clout that can bring the new company.

Regardless of the focus area (broad or specific) of the advisory board(s), there should be documentation as to the rules governing the board and the mission/ objective of the board. There may be terms for the appointment members. The members should clearly understand the expectations, time commitment, and compensation for their time and efforts. The size of the advisory board should be adequate to obtain input, but not too large to make discussion and fruitful input difficult. Advisory boards can be useful strategies in getting detailed feedback from a range of interested and talented people in the targeted area.

Consultants

Consultants can be a great resource for your start-up. Business consultants can help in domain-specific areas, especially those that are not in your expertise. Consultants exist in almost every business niche that you might be able to imagine. They will work with you and help you in whatever task you need.

For their expertise, consultants, of course, come with a price. This may be completely worthwhile for, say, a regulatory consultant for your medical device or a business development consultant in your specific sector who can help you get the lay of the land. Before you decide to work with consultants, you can ask for their CVs, ask for references, and see who they've worked with in the past and what kinds of projects they've done for the start-up or other company. Before you discuss your business and needs, first execute an NDA. Then, have discussions with the consultant about mutually agreeable milestones and fee structure (can be hourly or by the project). Communication about objectives, timing, and costs are critical to ensure that you actually benefit in the way that you hope to benefit from your working with a consultant. Depending on what type of consultants, you can ask about their insurance. When you execute the contract with any consultant, engage your legal counsel who will likely insist that you own any IP that might come of the engagement among other contractual concerns.

As you engage more and more with the entrepreneurial ecosystem, you'll find that there are a plethora of consultants available to work with you. You will be approach, unsolicited, by many who are looking to build their own businesses. You and your team will need to judiciously decide what types of activities from which you can best benefit through the use of a consultant. The relationship will need to be managed and followed closely to ensure timing and content are meeting your needs and the terms outlined in the contract.

Subcontractors

Aside from advice and information that you might receive from a consultant, you may sometimes need to outsource projects or tasks such as experiments, manufacturing, prototyping, marketing analysis, sales distribution, or others. For these a subcontractor engagement may be appropriate. For example, if you need to run a GLP animal experiment on your medical device and don't have that capability, you could chose to contract with a lab that specializes in GLP where you know that the results of the study would be acceptable to FDA when you are ready to meet with them. You may need to scale up manufacturing from your batch size in the lab and want to subcontract with a manufacturer to make kilogram size batches. You may need a HIPAA-compliant cloud to interface with your health IT app. Depending on your sector, product development can be complex. You'll need to decide what you do in house (inside your company with your employees) versus what you subcontract out. Part of this decision process will depend on your corporate philosophy. Will you be a virtual company or a bricks-and-mortar company or somewhere in between:

Virtual company: A virtual company is one where the employees or most of the employees do not locate in the same space. The company functions through remote communications with employees generally working from a noncentral office location. Communications within the company are done through numerous online systems. In addition, a virtual company could be one that essentially subcontracts the majority of its tasks and therefore does very limited hiring of employees. A central office could be $500\,\text{ft}^2$ in an incubator or home office. Both models are intended to reduce costs while accelerating progress.

Bricks-and-mortar company: The more classical bricks-and-mortar company is formed in a physical space. Employees generally work for the company in that space, which may include office, conferencing, and lab space. Funds are raised to support the physical space needs that the company will have, and as the company grows, the space needs may change from an incubator-like start to a stand-alone building. In a bricks-and-mortar company, the classical approach is to develop the product primarily in house, thus growing unique and competitive know-how in their domain to give them competitive advantage in the marketplace.

Hybrid company: There is no right answer to this part of business strategy and few companies are fully virtual (subcontracting every task and having all remote employees) or bricks and mortar (physical space with everyone working at the office 100% of the time). How much a company subcontracts out or how much a company has employees work remotely will depend on the product, sector, business strategy, financing, culture, and vision of the company.

Chuck Cohn founded and served as CEO of Varsity Tutors, an online tutoring matching service for college students. It started when Chuck was an undergraduate; he had limited financing initially. Chuck built Varsity Tutors on the virtual business model (Cohn, 2014). While the business was ultimately successful, Chuck talks about some advantages and disadvantages of a virtual company from his perspective. The advantages Chuck lists are as follows:

- Low overhead versus bricks and mortar, leading to a competitive advantage on cost
- Can draw from a wider pool of talent because you are not geographically constrained (to a physical office)
- Better retention of employees because of work conditions that do not include commute or constrained physical location.
- Exceptional technology development because to operate virtually you must be expert at your data management and this may lead to a technical advantage for your business.

While these advantages are excellent for a competitive businesses costs and employee satisfaction in working from home or remotely from anywhere with an Internet connection, Chuck also found some disadvantages or challenges with his virtual company that he shares:

- Weak communication among employees, leading to misunderstandings.
- Difficulties in coordinating tasks.
- Corporate culture was hard to cultivate.
- Everyone cannot work effectively in a virtual company, therefore, he must hire for intrinsically motivated and self-disciplined workers.

Through trial and error, Chuck found ways to optimize the work environment in his virtual company. Seeing each other through Skype or other platforms helps quite a bit. So did employees getting to know each other, leading to a more enjoyable (and productive) workplace for everyone.

So, whether you decide to follow a virtual, bricks and mortar, or hybrid structure, you will likely have subcontractors. Managing subcontractors is similar to managing consultants, except subcontractors will typically be stand-alone businesses with their own corporate structure and internal processes. A major advantage of subcontracting is that you do not have to develop the capabilities in house. This may be more cost-effective and timely for some tasks or projects that you have that serves to your advantage.

There are some considerations in subcontracting, however. Aside from the normal governance of confidentiality, contract negotiations, and legal contract review, there is the management of the subcontract project. For many of your projects, the milestones will be more important to your start-up than to the subcontractor (who may already be a large business entity). The subcontractor will have numerous customers like your start-up and will have to manage priority within their business. Your job will be to manage the subcontractor so that you get the priority, attention to detail, correct service, and timely review that you need. Subcontractors are not typically turnkey, where you ask for the service and get it back at the due date. To avoid significant delays on your internal time line, proactive subcontractor management is essential. You may have more than one subcontract at a time, so organization and attention to all projects will be essential to maintaining your promises to investors. This is a risk, although a moderate risk if managed effectively from the start.

Employees

Employee management is a critical responsibility of the start-up leadership. The CEO and C-level managers will recruit, hire, manage, and retain and fire employees in the start-up. There are numerous books, scholarly articles, and strategies on hiring and management of employees. From all of this advice, one approach is to set the tone or culture of your company and then bring on the most highly talented people you can find that fit the culture you are trying to develop. Motivate those hires and have them help to set the tone for the next set of hires you bring in. Both the management and the peers will contribute to the start-up's culture. The following are some considerations when setting the culture:

- Innovation—big thinking
- Domain expertise
- Target accomplishments—attention to detail
- Every day matters—sense of dedication to mission

- Flexibility—tolerance to uncertainty
- Respect—collaboration
- Hardworking
- Effective communication
- Risk taking
- Diversity of backgrounds and thinking

Management sets the initial culture and must work to develop and sustain it. As a founder, you decide on the weight or emphasis of the cultural traits that you want for your business. If you are able to focus on this from the start, then you can target new hires who will fit with your philosophy and who will contribute with domain excellence so that you can recruit and develop a talented, effective team.

Initial hiring needs may be highly technical. Start-ups from university labs often recruit postdocs or graduate students as early employees in the spinout. This is logical in that the students are likely very close to the technology and dedicated to the project turned business. It is likely that the students will be adaptable to the culture that you are setting for the start-up; however, a discussion about the expectations for the start-up versus the university lab might serve to clarify expectations from the beginning. There must be a transition from the laboratory project to the start-up business, and other employees with prior industrial background may help to facilitate this transition, especially if the student has not worked in a corporate setting previously.

All employees will need to be compensated to take on the risk and potential benefit associated with working at a start-up. While you may not be able to offer a Wall Street starting salary, consideration of a comprehensive offer is necessary to recruit and keep the brightest talent. You may consider a combination of salary, benefits (insurance, vacation, etc.), and some amount of vested equity. Many employees join start-ups for additional reasons, including the opportunity to be part of something big and important, which you have to offer.

Interviewing new employees for a start-up includes discerning their degree of technical know-how in addition to their capabilities to thrive and lead to the areas that you have highlighted for your corporate culture. In addition to filling the needs in the technical development area, manufacturing, development, sales, and marketing, as the team grows organizational dynamics, will come into play. Considering the classical (but controversial) Myers–Briggs personality preferences, you may consider a diversity of personality preferences in your employees with some visionary thinkers to keep the dream alive and to imagine potential. Some detail-driven experts who will run experiments or prototyping fifteen times until the results are acceptable, some data-driven decision makers and some who are more on the feeling side, and some may be more planners, while others are doing their best work only for a deadline. It may be difficult to balance your team for peak performance, but thinking about these components of team dynamics may help in your selection of team members.

Assembling a world-class team facilitated by outstanding leadership and a motivating and supportive corporate culture will likely help your start-up drive success including investment, product launch, and sales. Each employee, especially early on, will be critical to your mission. What happens on the off chance that one of your team does not fit, or is disruptive to the rest, or does not produce or is careless is some significant way? What if you need to lay off a group of employees because of funding difficulties? Firing employees is tough medicine to maintain the health of a young company. Ben Horowitz was the cofounder, president, and CEO of Opsware, which was acquired by Hewlett-Packard for $1.6 billion in 2007 and current partner in the VC firm, Andreessen Horowitz. In his book, *The Hard Thing About Hard Things*, Ben discusses laying off of employees and firing executives, which unfortunately were part of his experiences at Opsware (Horowitz, 2014). He suggests firing should not be taken lightly; it is sometimes necessary and should be done quickly and professionally. When he needed to fire executives, Ben talked to the employee one-on-one with a short conversation about the termination and terms. For the layoffs, the hiring manager of the employee talked with the employee directly about the state of the company and about the resources and not performance issues that went into the decision. While this part of business is not enjoyable for anyone, it sometimes is necessary for the health and current reality of the company.

Summary

Building a management team is a critical step for your start-up. Recruiting a business partner takes relationship building and time. When you bring on partners, you will employ an operating agreement that will be the rules of engagement for the company. In this agreement, you will also divide equity among the founders and sequester equity for future investors and/or key employees. You'll need to decide if you will keep your academic position and if so will need to decide on your level of participation in the start-up, keeping in mind your university policies. Communication with your partner(s), attorney, and university administration is necessary to enable you to set up an agreeable foundation for the start-up. Executives will set the tone for culture in the start-up and is worth discussion as you start to do your earliest hiring and assemble your board of directors.

References

Cohn, C. (2014), "Lessons Learned the Hard Way about Running a Virtual Company," *Forbes*, August 11.

Horowitz, B. (2014), *The Hard Thing About Hard Things*, New York, Harper Collins Press.

Investopedia (2016), http://www.investopedia.com/terms/b/boardofdirectors.asp (accessed May 29, 2017).

7

Graduate Students and Postdocs, Start Up Your Career

Tell me and I forget, teach me and I may remember, involve me and I learn.
—Benjamin Franklin

Introduction

As a graduate student or postdoc, you are the one person most familiar with the details of your thesis or research project. You have spent countless hours in the lab experimenting with conditions and doing run after run to investigate your research questions. You have studied the literature and are up on all of the past and latest findings in your thesis/project area. You know who is doing what across the world on your topic. And with all of this effort, guided by your advisor, together you have made a very intriguing discovery or designed a promising new approach that you think may have far-reaching benefit as a commercial product. Like the faculty entrepreneurs addressed through this book, you should be congratulated for your significant accomplishments.

Graduate students or postdoctoral students (hereafter referred to as *students*) play a key role in the translation of research into commercialization (Figure 7.1). In an analysis of 46 university start-ups, 77% had a student involved. Of those, a third (11 start-ups) had student involvement but *no faculty participation* (Boh *et al.*, 2016). Graduate students have been shown to play a significant role in the early stages of university start-ups, often acting as the catalyst for the start of the venture by convincing the faculty to start the company and serving in venture leadership to get the company off the ground (Boh *et al.*, 2016; Hayter *et al.*, 2016). In many cases, the faculty in these studies noted that the start-up would not exist without the commitment of the student who served as the CEO or co-founder.

According to the Hayter study, student participants in university start-ups were found to have both the technical expertise to solve problems and guide

Academic Entrepreneurship: How to Bring Your Scientific Discovery to a Successful Commercial Product, First Edition. Michele Marcolongo.
© 2017 John Wiley & Sons, Inc. Published 2017 by John Wiley & Sons, Inc.

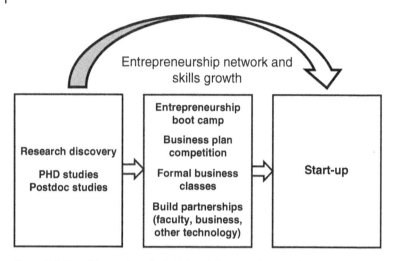

Figure 7.1 Transition options for building skills going from graduate or postdoctoral student to start-up.

development and the time to provide leadership in getting the company started. However, the students did not generally have the "knowledge or networks needed to accelerate spinoff development." This is not surprising, in that the same is true for faculty starting along the same path for the first time. Students to this point in their careers have typically been in high school, college, and graduate school and have not had too much opportunity to explore the entrepreneurial ecosystems in their regions. Here, we would like to harness the technical expertise, motivation, energy, time, and leadership ability of students to drive university start-ups by providing guidance on how to approach the business of starting a company from your university research. The objective is for you to quickly and efficiently build the networks you need to propel your company forward while managing the important relationships with your university administration, co-founders, and thesis or postdoctoral advisor. This last part differentiates you from your entrepreneur peers who are starting companies outside the university setting and so deserves special consideration as you begin this exciting journey.

Why Do It?

Why should you participate in or lead a university start-up? There are several motivators that might resonate with you. The most altruistic of them is that you believe that you have a significant contribution to make to the field or sector with a product or service from your university innovation. That passion will go a very long way toward driving you through the long days and the ups and downs of start-up reality. But there could be different or additional motivators. You may want to make some serious money and/or seek fame and recognition and/or learn entrepreneurship and business skills. None of these motivators is mutually exclusive. There is no right or wrong to your motivation. It does help, however, if you stop for a few minutes and consider your personal motivation. This motivation may help to guide some of the decisions that you will make along the process. Be honest with yourself. Because the average time for a sale or public offering for a university spinout is about 8–10 years, you will need to have some significant motivation to sustain you through this process if you intend to go the distance. The potential benefit to starting a company is multi-faceted, in that you may very well deliver a great product or market need, obtain fortune and fame, and develop a great reputation that may allow you to do it all again. You will gain skills in business, interpersonal relationships, management, and more. In addition, you will explore a career as an entrepreneur. You may find that you fall in love with the process of making something from nothing. This might be a career direction for you. Even if you decide that you'd rather not have a career in entrepreneurship, the skills that you will have added to your considerable technical talents and training will translate to any other career path that you will choose.

However, there is also the consideration of what the business school calls an opportunity cost. This is the cost of lost opportunities that you potentially forgo by choosing to work on the start-up and not doing that something else. For a graduating doctoral student or postdoc, this may mean a potential faculty position, corporate job, next postdoc, or other potential position. Is this an affordable cost based on the potential gain? Again, taking some time to assess these options will allow you to enter the start-up with a thoughtful commitment, rather than making an impulsive decision. This is your first risk/benefit analysis around the start-up and, in this case, your personal risk/benefit. That being said, if you're still reading, you're probably all in.

Who are the types of students who participate in start-ups? While studies of the characteristics of entrepreneurs and faculty entrepreneurs have been documented (see Chapter 1), there is little consideration in the business literature to student entrepreneurs and maybe none at all to graduate students and postdoctoral researchers who take an entrepreneurial path. You may see overlap with some of the faculty entrepreneur traits with your own. A study of students in Turkey showed that student entrepreneurs showed a statistically higher prevalence than their non-entrepreneurial counterparts in (Gurol and Atsan, 2006):

- Risk-taking propensity
- Internal locus of control
- Need for achievement
- Innovativeness

The same characteristics could be said of many graduate students, along with high intellect and grit (to get through all those tough experiments). It's no wonder, then, that students are great assets for start-ups out of the university.

Challenges and Opportunities Spinning Out from the University for Students

The exciting business opportunity springing from your research under the supervision of your advisor brings with it some unique situations for conflict compared with start-ups that do not initiate from university research. For you, like for faculty members starting companies, there is the potential for conflict with the technology transfer office as you negotiate the terms of the license agreement around IP. Please refer to Chapter 4 for some considerations during this negotiation.

Aside from the potential conflict with the university administration that you may need to manage, as a student, you may have additional potential conflict with your advisor. Studies of advisor/student relations through starting a company based on research done by the student under the supervision of the advisor have been varied. Hayter *et al.* (2016) studied eight companies from MIT that were started by students from university labs. Their findings conclude the following:

- Graduate students, not faculty, played the *lead* role in initial setup and launch of all eight start-ups in the cohort.
- Graduate students played a *critical role in the continued development* of the start-up through positioning the start-up for commercialization.
- Graduate students were often faced with multiple conflicts with faculty and other students associated with the start-up and experienced tension between their start-up and academic roles and responsibilities.

In all but one of the eight ventures, the conflicts were managed to a successful conclusion. Conflict with the outlier failed due to a disagreement between the faculty member and student, which resulted in each starting a separate company around the same technology. Both companies failed. The article states that it is important in the early phase of start-up exploration to clearly define the roles and relationships between the faculty members and student entrepreneurs. This is a great advice, but much easier said than done.

There are considerations of power and authority between the faculty and student in the advisor/mentee role through the doctoral thesis process and through the postdoctoral mentoring period. The faculty member has considerable influence over the student in supporting progression of the thesis toward successful defense as well as access to the academic network that relies heavily on personal recommendations. The faculty member can also influence the internal reputation of the student within the university. The student's leverage is quite different. The student typically has in-depth knowledge about the discovery and all of the technical or experimental details behind it. The student also has time and energy to devote to the monumental task of starting a successful company. Where does that leave the advisor/student relationship? In the start-up, the roles could be reversed, where the student has "authority" over the faculty member in the decision-making of the start-up based on equity position or role in the company (e.g., student CEO and faculty scientific advisor). This is tricky to manage, to say the least.

In discussions and negotiations around the start-up, what are your common motivators? It may be that each of you would like to see successful commercialization of the discovery. If that is true, then you have a great mutual starting point in your negotiations. Both the faculty member and student need to realistically consider how this start-up will function organizationally. Each of you is acutely aware that there will be significant time commitments necessary for finding a business partner, developing the entrepreneurship network (different from the academic network), putting together a business plan, advancing the discovery through proof of concept, and, of course, raising funds. The faculty member may want to be in control, closely involved, or more distantly involved in the start-up management and operation.

Research assessing university start-ups from eight US universities (Boh *et al.*, 2016) showed that both faculty and students are most heavily involved in the earliest phases of the technology commercialization process. They describe the initial stages as

1) Idea generation
2) Commercialization decision
3) Prototype generation and establishment of commercial and technical viability
4) Founding team formation
5) Strategy and commercialization process determination
6) Fundraising to sustain activities

For this analysis, they interviewed 130 individuals from those 8 universities about their participation level in the university start-ups. They determined that there were four strategies that were employed by the early start-ups (Figure 7.2):

Model A: Partnership with experienced entrepreneur (23% cases)
- Faculty
- Experienced entrepreneur
- No student

Model B: Partnership with PhD/postdoctoral researcher (41% cases)
- Faculty
- PhD/postdoc student

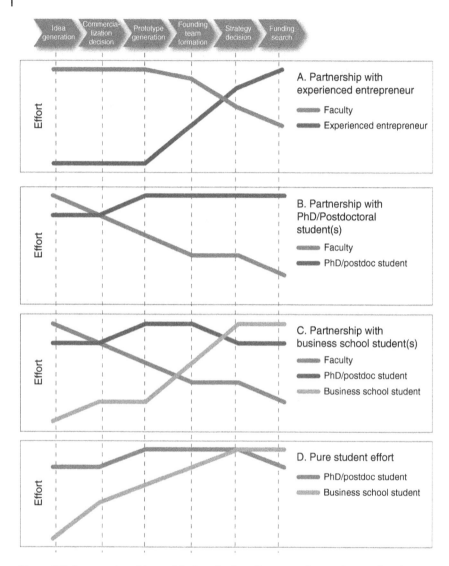

Figure 7.2 Some partnership models describe founding teams for translation of academic research among faculty and students. *Source*: Boh *et al.* (2016). Reproduced with permission of Springer.

Model C: Partnership with business school students (13% cases)

- Faculty
- PhD/postdoc student
- Business school student

Model D: Pure student effort (23% cases)
- Phd/postdoc student
- Business school student
- No faculty

For each model, Boh *et al.* describe the level of effort for each member of the start-up. For Models A–C, the faculty member starts off as quite active through the founding team formation stage and then decreases the level of effort. For Models B and C, where faculty and graduate students or postdocs are involved, the faculty effort is reduced much earlier in the process, while the student effort starts high and is maintained through all six stages of early commercialization. For Model D, where there is a graduate student or postdoc and a business student, the grad student or postdoc level of effort is sustained throughout all six stages, while the business student effort gradually ramps up to the same level, only by stage 5.

Faculty Member Participation

If the faculty member would like to be in control of the start-up, then you are looking at something more like Models A–C. In these scenarios, the faculty member would be participating in stages 1–6, but if the graduate student/postdoc is involved with the faculty member (Models B–C), the faculty member will generally have a greatly reduced participation as the stages progress and the participation will fall more on the grad student or postdoc. A frank discussion with the faculty member about the realistic time commitment and role necessary to advance the start-up is necessary before you get started in stages 1 or 2. Some points of discussion are as follows:

- What are the roles that both the faculty and student will take in the start-up?
  - CEO
  - CTO
  - Scientific advisor
  - Senior scientist
  - Board member (eventually)
  - Other
- What will be the equity position for the faculty and student in the start-up?
  - 50–50
  - Anything else

It's impossible to gage even typical equity splits for faculty/student start-ups from business literature to date, which makes benchmarking difficult for you. You want to end up with a deal that you feel is reasonable and that provides sufficient motivation for you to work as hard as you will need to work to advance

Charles Cohen, Ph.D.
Chief Technology Officer
Polymerix Corporation

Charles (Chuck) Cohen is a serial entrepreneur. Now in the management team of his third company, Chuck was part of his first start-up while finishing his Ph.D. in Biomedical Engineering at the University of Pennsylvania. When Chuck was getting to the end of his dissertation and considering the paths that lay before him, he knew that he was not interested in becoming a university professor. However, a corporate R&D position did not seem all that appealing either. Chuck thought he might be interested in starting his own company. He started taking classes at Wharton while writing his doctoral thesis, ending up with a management degree where he learned market development, finance, accounting, and management from the entrepreneurially focused Wharton faculty. Serendipitously, Chuck's doctoral advisor, Paul Ducheyne, was interested in starting a company out of some work in the lab. Together Chuck and Paul founded Orthovita, a bone regeneration company. Chuck successfully defended his thesis and at the same time negotiated with the university for licensing rights for Paul's patents and wrote the business plan for the start-up. Talk about multitasking.

Chuck was willing to take the risk of starting a company with his advisor right out of graduate school after considering the risk/benefit. "I thought this will only be harder to do 5–10 years from now" and jumped into the start-up. "The timing for everything was great and at that time I did not have a lot of family or financial pressures." Chuck thinks that the time period right after graduation is the best time to start a company. However, he points out that even though you have the "freedom to start a business" at that period of your life, you have little to no experience.

Chuck had and continues to have a good relationship with his Ph.D. advisor. This helped when Paul and Chuck needed to negotiate equity positions in the start-up. After some difficult conversations, they struck an agreement and the company moved forward. "Students are generally not sure of their worth and the right amount to ask for." Paul decided to keep his position as a professor at Penn and Chuck's full time job was to write the business plan and get the company off the ground. Chuck drew from his Wharton management education (which was occurring in real time to the writing of the plan). He also was instrumental in early fundraising efforts with angel investors. The company nucleated in the lab until, under advice from their attorneys, Orthovita brought in a seasoned entrepreneur to lead the company. This led to a significant investment that helped to catalyze the angels that Chuck had been courting and the company was funded and became independent of the university. With the new CEO, Chuck took on the role of product manager, which included everything from developing to launching the product, developing packaging, preparing sales and marketing information, and running numerous post-FDA clinical studies.

Orthovita eventually had an IPO and was later sold to the leading dental implant company. What did Chuck think of his 9 years with a university start-up? It was completely worth it. On the job, Chuck learned what it takes to start and manage a successful venture. He used his technical and business training to promote the company technology and, at the same time, built his entrepreneurial networks, including investors. Since that exit, Chuck cofounded another medical device company and is currently Chief Technology Officer in his third.

While Chuck had lots of opportunities before him at the time of his graduation, his sense that he wanted to start a company motivated his path and the serendipity of his advisor having the same drive at the same time was a win–win. Chuck never looked back. He has thrived in the demanding and often uncertain world of entrepreneurship. All three of the start-ups that Chuck has founded or worked with have been spun out of university discoveries. Chuck has become an expert in the business of bringing a research discovery to the market and it all started for him as a young graduate student in the lab.

the start-up. That is a personal decision and will be different from one start-up to another and from one person to another. Some universities have policies that preclude faculty members from holding an officer position in the start-up. For this case, the student is often made CEO and the faculty member is a scientific advisor. Most universities allow faculty members to hold significant equity positions in the start-up. In addition, some faculty members may want to keep control a major equity position, while others may not be that interested and may instead want to be a scientific advisor and let you take control of the company. Each of these scenarios has happened. It's interesting that in over half of university start-ups, the faculty and student start the company together.

Keep in mind that you will likely be working full time on the start-up, while your advisor will likely be keeping a day job. In addition to equity, you will need to consider your compensation as far as salary, benefits, and perhaps bonus. This is simply a point of negotiation (please read *Getting to Yes* or equivalent book on negotiating). If these talks go well between you and your advisor and you are in agreement about roles, corresponding equity positions and salary, then you and your advisor will be walking into this venture smiling, shaking hands, and with the optimism and teamwork necessary for start-up success. However, if there is disagreement, then you are in the more challenging position of negotiating with your advisor, who has so far had authority over you. You can work through this negotiation amicably using standard negotiating strategies and maintaining a good working relationship if you approach it with a good strategy and a calm, professional demeanor.

If you are a graduate student and have not yet completed your doctoral defense and graduated, this could be a more delicate situation. Negotiation is a discussion to get to a common agreement between parties. However, upon occasion, for one reason or another, negotiations can result in the feeling that one side does not appreciate the other or has taken advantage of the other, leading to a compromised relationship between the parties. As a student, you are in a generally lower power position than your advisor concerning your academic degree requirements. You want to avoid the start-up work interfering with your academic work as much as possible. If you still need to graduate, in addition to getting the company started, you may experience this conflict. This may be a point of consideration in the timing of the start-up, where a possibility is to delay the founding of the company until you complete your degree requirements. If you'd really like to seize the opportunity now, your university may have a policy around this situation to guide you through starting a company with your advisor. If so, understand this policy before your discussions with your advisor. If not, you can look on other university's websites to see how they handle this. If there is no university policy, a department head or member of the TTO or Office of Research may be able to advise you on conflict management and resolution while you are a student and entrepreneur, at the earliest possible stages of the process.

Most people are reasonable, and if you are considering entering a business relationship with your advisor, that is likely the case. However, contracts and agreements and well-understood negotiating strategies are all standard business practices for a reason. Talk things through, use contracts and agreements to document your discussions, and then work like crazy to make your business a success.

Faculty Member Not Participating

In about a quarter of university start-ups, the faculty member does not participate at all (Model D). The faculty member may not be interested in pursuing a start-up but does not stand in the way of the student taking the technology forward with a venture. Another reason for a faculty advisor not participating in a graduate student or postdoc university spin-off can occur when the student partners with a business student in an entrepreneurship, design, or other student-only class or program to develop their own concepts. In either case, the students will have control over the start-up. In student-only start-ups, negotiation will occur between the grad student or postdoc and the business student. The same negotiating principles hold for these relationships. Recognize each other's strengths and potential contributions and negotiate in good faith, preserving the business relationship while representing your interests. In some ways, this is a more straightforward discussion because there is little overlap with your individual expertise in that a graduate student or postdoc will have the scientific expertise, while the business student will provide the sales/marketing, business strategy, and financing side of the start-up.

None of the Above

Models A–D are generalized in the framework based on Boh's analysis of 46 companies spun out of universities. The part of innovation beyond the lab lies in innovating business structure and partnerships. There is no single formula for putting together a successful business. A hybrid model that blends faculty, student, and experienced entrepreneur could be used. There may be two or more graduate students or postdocs from the same or different disciplines that start the company. These frameworks are only intended to allow you some starting points as you consider the specific needs for your venture.

Formal Education

However you decide to set up your business relationships, there will be a lot for you to learn as an emerging entrepreneur. You've already been in school a long time (as parents, friends, and partners may have had occasion to point out to you). After completing high school, college, graduate school, and maybe a postdoc or two, most of your formal education to date has been on the technical side of things. Even though you are an accomplished researcher, starting a new venture places a demand on additional skill sets within the framework of starting and growing a company.

You need to get up to speed quickly on how entrepreneurship works. That is why you're reading this right now. While this book is an overview of the start-up process for a university technology, there are so many opportunities for you to learn about business practices that will help you to navigate the start-up world. Universities are adding entrepreneurship programs to their educational offerings more and more each year. Classes where graduate students/postdocs and business or law students collaborate through business plan writing or design strategies are abundant. From Boh's study, almost half of the start-ups had founding members who took these classes. In addition to these classes, which are informative and interesting, some additional business principles will be necessary for you to put in your tool box as you begin this adventure.

Graduate student and postdoc entrepreneurs described two key challenges, moving their ventures from technology to commercialization of a product (Hayter *et al.*, 2016):

1) Managing the composition of their staff and management
2) Managing the transition to different funding sources

Management of staff includes hiring, firing, setting goals, and motivating staff and management. Knowing how to hire, what to look for in a start-up employee, what kind of skill sets you need, and when are difficult for the most seasoned business executive, so it is no surprise that student entrepreneurs share this challenge. First, you have to decide on the job description and then be able to compete for talent and put together a good package that will draw the best talent you can. You need to run this through an attorney (for legal and potential tax issues) and perhaps your board. Of course, you need some resources to pay these employees. What level of employee will get equity or options? Additional importance is the culture that you're creating in your organization and so you, along with the early hires, will set the tone of the company. This includes the work ethic, the opportunity to innovate and to fail, and the collaborative relationships. You will consider diversity of thought, backgrounds, and talent. How will you assemble, manage, and retain this critical team? We can all wing it to some degree, but management articles, books, and classes may help you to de-risk this process to get you higher chances of success from your hiring. Mentors and advisors are extremely helpful with specific challenges as they come up. But what if you hire poorly? For whatever reason, what if the new employee just doesn't fit or work out or contribute in ways that you need? You may need to fire that person. Entrepreneurs who find themselves in this situation, and it happens to most despite the best intentions and judgment, have only one regret—they didn't fire the poor employee sooner. Waiting too long to see if the employee will turn around or get with the program has been a major liability for start-ups where every employee counts. It is not easy to fire someone. Once again, management strategies can help to guide your decision-making and give you a philosophy and strategy to help guide your actions.

The second challenge from Hayter's analysis among graduate students and postdoc entrepreneurs was managing the transition from a grant or angel investor company, where the management team had most control to larger venture funding when boards of directors are established. You need to learn all of the financing options and trade-offs for those options. There is management of the investors and the investors' management of you. Learning how to navigate through investors between rounds as the company is progressing can be challenging for any entrepreneur. Students needed to manage through this uncertainty, tension among investors, and potential staff cuts between rounds of financing. Some formal education in finance, along with mentors and advisors, can help you to get up to speed on burn rates and stretching a budget through transitions. If you have a business partner, either a student or experienced serial entrepreneur, that can certainly help. However, there is every reason that you should educate yourself in this area. You need to understand fully the ramifications of the business decisions that you and your partners make. Some formal classes, boot camp, and one-on-one mentoring from senior business advisors can help you to come up to speed in critical business aspects of the company.

Business Plan Competitions…Not Just for Undergrads

Business plan competitions are prevalent on most college campuses with PhD programs (research universities) but can be found on numerous non-research campuses as well. These competitions allow students (both undergrads and graduate students) the opportunity for mentoring and feedback around the planning of a foundation for a business venture. The prize is typically a cash award (which can vary widely, but is usually in the range of $10K–$100K). While the cash award may be modest, the opportunities for mentoring, feedback, and contacts from the program are intangible but significant benefits. Students from the University of San Francisco International Business Plan Competition cited the following reasons they participated in the business plan competition (Roldan *et al.*, 2005):

1) Potential funding from investors
2) Feedback from investors and executives
3) Overall learning experience
4) Prize money

Business plan competitions can be run through the university's business school, engineering college, or other organizations on campus. In addition, there are competitions that are regional or national. The larger competitions typically accept candidates who have previously won at a local (university) level.

For most business plan competitions, the team of students writes an actual business plan according to the requirements specified by the sponsor. This is like the plan covered in Chapter 9 of this book or those described in numerous other texts (see Suggested Reading). Briefly, the innovation is presented along with the market need, market potential and marketing data from search phase, value proposition, growth potential, intellectual property, finance and sales projections along with break-even point, plan for execution with milestones, and team including company advisors. In addition to a written plan, there will be a pitch competition where your team presents the plan to the judges (including a demo, model, or data if relevant to your business idea). There may be a preliminary and final round to the competition. The judges are generally members from the entrepreneurship ecosystem and may include technology transfer officers, angel investors, economic development administrators, venture capitalists, attorneys, corporate executives, and more senior entrepreneurs.

The thing to remember about business plans is that it is not a presentation of your research. It is a presentation about the market potential for a product or service that comes from your innovation. So the innovation or discovery itself is not the only part or may not even be the most important part of the plan. It takes some broadening of thinking to frame your innovation into a potential business. If you are a STEM graduate student, postdoc, or med student, you may not have training how to do this and is likely why you're reading this book. Courses on many campuses exist to teach you some of these skills, but if you don't have time to take one, you may consider partnering with a business student for the competition.

Because you are serious about building a business from your discovery or concept, the experience of the business plan competition can be useful to guide your start-up proposition. When eight graduate students who led ventures from MIT were interviewed about how they started companies from their academic labs and thesis projects, six of the eight students had participated in at least one business plan competition. There was a perspective by these new entrepreneurs that the business plan competition was a good way to test their venture ideas. One of the MIT graduate student founders relayed that the business plan competition was an important tool for both refining the business concept and building his confidence. The competition enabled this graduate student founder to convince himself that his concept was "commercially feasible" and that he was going to start a company with his research "no matter what" (Hayter *et al.*, 2016). Of course, the business plan process could also help you to come to the realization that your concept needs significant restructuring and the feedback about this is also helpful to get before you start to present to investors and others outside the university system.

Another potential advantage of a business plan competition is the credibility and publicity that you may achieve. When a business is at the earliest stage, it is perhaps one of the biggest hurdles to convince the very first investor to commit to your company. For almost every start-up, this is the first big mountain to climb. Any validation of your venture is one more step up the mountain. Winning your university's business plan competition or a regional or national competition is a step toward vetting your plan and team. It can give you credibility among the entrepreneurship community. The publicity that comes along with the potential win could give you even more visibility from investors and others in the system that is key to your success. You can use this to open doors.

So, while you may join a business plan competition for the win, and you should compete that way, even a loss could be beneficial for your growth as an entrepreneur and in meeting people in the ecosystem.

Conclusion

If you are an innovative, talented researcher with a great education, your future is bright. By choosing to expand your skill set by starting a company based on your research discovery will be the experience of a lifetime and may turn into an entirely new career path for you. In the early stages of setting up your start-up, have honest discussions within your university and with your faculty advisor. Manage any potential conflicts that arise in a professional manner. Build a great team of partners that you trust and that are as motivated as you are to bring the technology to commercialization, and consider the use of business plan competitions as a source of feedback and networking for your venture concept. This is going to be a great adventure.

References

Boh, W. F., U. De-Hann, and R. Strom (2016), "University technology transfer through entrepreneurship: Faculty and students in spinoffs." *The Journal of Technology Transfer* **41**(4): 661–669.

Gurol, Y., N. Atsan (2006), "Entrepreneurial characteristics amongst university students: Some insights for entrepreneurship education and training in Turkey." *Education and Training* **48**(1): 25–38.

Hayter, C. S., R. Lubynsky, and S. Maroulis (2016), "Who is the academic entrepreneur? The role of graduate students in the development of university spinoffs." *The Journal of Technology Transfer* 1–18.

Roldan, M., A. Osland, M. Solt, B. V. Dean, and M. V. Cannice (2005), "Business plan Competitions: Vehicles for Learning Entrepreneurship" in Wankel, C. and R. DeFillippi, eds. *Educating Managers through Real World Projects*. Greenwich, Information Age Publishing, pp. 309–331.

8

Incubators and Accelerators: It's Time to Move Out

Screw it. Let's do it.
—Richard Branson, Virgin Airlines

When you're ready to move your innovation out of the lab and into an independent space, there are many options. Incubators and accelerators are two options that cater to the start-up company. In addition to providing real estate for rent or investment, they can bring additional services necessary to propel the company forward. While incubators and accelerators have a similar mission, in actuality the two are quite different (Figure 8.1).

Incubators are typically *nonprofit* organizations and are often associated with universities. They are intended to provide office and/or lab space to early-stage companies for the start-ups that they support. Many incubators focus on local start-ups and can be motivated by creating economic development in a region. Incubators do not generally invest in start-ups. In practice, incubators have traditionally been more of a real estate venture, sometimes supplying additional business and legal services or connecting start-ups with additional service providers and advice around business and legal services. The incubator concept is well established, and some incubators have been supporting start-ups since 1959.

Accelerators have been emerging in great numbers across the country since 2001. They are typically *for-profit* corporations that provide funding, common space, and business mentoring to start-ups in exchange for an equity position in the company. They are typically for a short, fixed term (commonly 3–6 months). Accelerators can target local or national/international start-ups and bring them to the accelerator's physical space. They do not typically differentiate between university-based start-ups and nonuniversity start-ups, unless specifically associated with a particular university.

In either case, the idea of having your university-based start-up in a physical space with like-minded entrepreneurs can provide community from which to

Academic Entrepreneurship: How to Bring Your Scientific Discovery to a Successful Commercial Product, First Edition. Michele Marcolongo.
© 2017 John Wiley & Sons, Inc. Published 2017 by John Wiley & Sons, Inc.

Two approaches to physically moving start-up out of University Research Lab

Accelerator	Incubator
Short term (3–6 months)	Long term (1–5 years)
Equity for investment	Space for rent (no equity or investment)
Common space among cohort of like start-ups	All start-ups may or may not have sector selectivity
Succeed or fail fast	Office and lab shared facilities
Business mentoring and shared business services and network	Business mentoring and shared business services and network

Figure 8.1 When a start-up is ready to move out of the lab, there are options with accelerators and incubators.

learn as each company progresses along the path toward building a sustainable and profitable business (Figure 8.2).

Incubators

Incubators provide a place where you can move your discovery and research from the university lab to the development in an office/lab external to the university. They are typically nonprofit organizations. Incubators support early-stage high-growth businesses and ideas. Often located near campuses, 73% of about 1200 incubators in the United States in 2014 are affiliated with universities, economic development agencies, or government entities (Isis Report, 2014).

Incubators provide real estate for start-up companies, usually at reasonable rates and with flexible leases. In more recent years, incubators have evolved to also provide experienced business people to advise start-ups and give them an office space for them to work and grow the business and access to business equipment and technology support services. These services can be described as three types of intellectual capital: human, structural, and relational capital (Calza *et al.*, 2014). Human capital is the leadership experience within the incubator or the advisors who will help to guide your start-up and help you

Characteristics	Incubators	Accelerators
Clients	All kinds, including science-based businesses (biotech, medical devices, nanotechnology, clean energy, etc.) and nontechnology; all ages and genders; those with previous experience in an industry or sector	Web-based, mobile apps, social networking, gaming, cloud-based, software, and so on; firms that do not require significant immediate investment or proof of concept; primarily youthful, often male technology enthusiasts, gamers, and hackers
Selection process	Competitive selection, mostly from the local community	Competitive selection of firms from wide regions or even nationally (or globally)
Terms of assistance	1–5 or more years (33 months on average)	Generally 1- to 3-month boot camps
Services	Offers access to management and other consulting, specialized intellectual property and networks of experienced entrepreneurs; helps businesses mature to self-sustaining or high-growth stage; helps entrepreneurs round out skills, develops a management team, and, often, obtains external financing	"Fast-test" validation of ideas; opportunities to create a functioning beta and find initial customers; linkage of entrepreneurs to business consulting and experienced entrepreneurs in the web or mobile apps space; assistance in preparing pitches to try to obtain follow-up investment
Investment	Usually does not have funds to invest directly in the company; more frequently than not, does not take equity	Invests $18 000 to $100 000 in teams of co-founders; takes equity in every investee (usually 4–8%)

Figure 8.2 Characteristics of incubator and accelerators. *Source*: Dempwolf *et al.* (2014) and Adkins (2011). Reproduced with permission of www.sba.gov.

navigate the fits and turns of your new business. Structural capital is the real estate holdings of the incubator: the office space, laboratory space, or shared facilities available to the members of the incubator. The relational capital is the network of contacts to resources that the incubator can provide to your business. These three components taken together have been shown to support start-ups through the early stages of development and are intended to save you time by facilitating support in each area. The idea of having multiple start-ups under one roof, so to speak, enhances the leverage of the incubator in developing high level and potentially helpful advisors, making it a win for the ecosystem at large as well as for the start-up itself.

Some services offered by incubators include the following:

- Office space
- Laboratory space
- Shared equipment (laboratory, Internet, office)

- Business planning and advising
- Connection to stable potential business partners
- CFO/accounting consulting
- SBIR grant writing
- Legal advice (IP and general contract)
- Angel and VC networks
- Marketing research

Incubators can have a competitive selection process, depending on the timing and the market need for start-up real estate. For competitions, the start-up presents its technology and business model to a panel of incubator advisors including incubator administrators, technical experts, industry representatives, and investors who judge the team and their business proposition based on the realities of the market, the growth potential of the company, and the team members with their likelihood of success. Most start-ups in an incubator are local from the community, have some ties to the region, or want to start the company in that region. The length of stay for a start-up in an incubator is 1–5 years (33-month average) (Adkins, 2011). Incubators are often motivated in economic development, where the successful incubator graduates have the potential to "create more jobs, revitalize neighborhoods, commercialize new technologies, and strengthen regional economies" (Dempwolf *et al.*, 2014).

Start-ups using incubators have greater success than those that have not received assistance with those using incubators, having an 85% chance of business success after 5 years compared with the 30% for those not using an incubator (Bollingtoft and Ulhoi, 2005; Hoffman and Radojevich-Kelley, 2012; Isabelle, 2013; Isis Report, 2014). Typically, incubators cross various industries and are not sector specific. They provide resources to help move entrepreneurs toward self-sustaining, mature businesses. Incubators generally do not financially invest in their start-ups.

University incubators when compared with nonuniversity incubators were shown to have higher job growth rates both pre- and post-graduation from the incubator (Lasrado *et al.*, 2016). University incubators also showed increased sales rates as well as overall sales pre- and post-graduation compared with nonuniversity incubators (Lasrado *et al.*, 2016). So while all incubators are not created equally, in general those associated with universities have better outcomes in terms of job creation and sales than the nonuniversity counterparts.

One example of a university incubator is Georgia Tech's VentureLab. Founded in 2001, the VentureLab has helped Georgia Tech faculty researchers and students to found more than 150 companies. Those start-ups have raised over $1.1 billion in nonuniversity capital. They are currently hosting about 100 start-ups in a wide range of sectors. Computer science and Internet-based companies are 20% of their portfolio, but engineering-based start-ups in materials and electronics are the bulk of the focus of the technologies for VentureLab.

They are ranked among the top ten in the world for economic enhancement, job creation, performance of incubator graduates, and post-incubation valuation (Georgia Tech Newsletters, 2013, 2014). How do they make the magic happen? They offer ever-evolving services including access to physical resources, financial resources, start-up support, networks, and entrepreneurial training. Having this resource has grown symbiotically with the culture of entrepreneurship at Georgia Tech among faculty and students. This celebratory culture of entrepreneurship along with the real estate and services provided by VentureLab and the other services in the Georgia Tech system has made this an academic innovation ecosystem that works.

Even with this great track record for university incubators, it's still worth doing your homework to determine if the incubator at your university is strong in the key services provided previously. The following are some points of consideration prior to signing up with an incubator:

- What are the square footage rental rates? What office space size is available? Conferencing space access? Video conferencing? Does the incubator have lab space that suits your needs (hoods, power, benches, sinks, etc.)? Is there a differential cost for lab space versus office space? How long is the lease? How flexible is the lease? Tour the exact space that you are considering renting.
- Ask for a list of the current tenants in the incubator. Is there a pattern by sector or technology? Does this suit your start-up? Can you somehow leverage knowledge or partner with the other members of the incubator?
- Review the graduates of the incubator; ask recent graduate company management how the incubator helped them develop their business.
- Get a list of all of the services offered by the incubator and who the service providers are. Is this an A-team? How often do you have access to different advisors (per week or month)?
- What type of shared equipment is available and at any additional cost? How often can you access the equipment? Are there technicians or experts that maintain, service, certify, or calibrate the equipment?
- How often does the incubator hold seminar/networking sessions? Ask for a calendar of the prior year's activities; maybe attend a couple as a visitor to determine the activity of the group.
- Ask which investors have invested in the incubator's start-ups. Is there a connection between the start-ups and active investors locally, regionally, and nationally? Is the incubator tied into the local economic development agencies that might be a resource for the start-up?

With an incubator, you are interviewing them. You will be paying for the incubator in your rental fees per square foot and, in return, will be receiving office and/or lab space and access to business and office services and equipment. Make sure it's a good deal for your company with your needs at the time. This solid footing will serve as home base for you through your critical early years. For academic start-ups, an incubator can be a nice way to transition from university research to independent start-up company in a location that is close to your university office and lab.

Like with most real estate, location is key. If you can easily go between the university and the incubator, there is less of a geographical barrier for communication during this transition phase. If you have an agreement with the university to use university resources and equipment, you can easily accomplish this if you are geographically close. The university will have a strong desire to continue to help your start-up mature, and the power of a university for additional connections through the main academic unit or the incubator may serve you well in the early stages. Limiting the running back and forth between the university and incubator is a huge savings of your most valuable resource: your time.

You may be asking yourself, "How do I get the initial money to pay the rent at an incubator?" This is the start-up chicken and the egg. You need some "walking-around money" to help you get started. This can be from investing yourself, friends and family, or other angels or by an SBIR/STTR grant or an economic development seed stage investment or grant. Maybe the university has a competition to award you rent for a period of time while you work this out. Please refer to Chapter 9 on financing your start-up to see more details on getting started financially. If you are not yet ready to move into an incubator, you may instead want to consider an accelerator.

Stephen S. Tang, Ph.D., MBA
University City Science Center
President and CEO

Steve Tang thinks that we live in a state of "just-in-time" entrepreneurship. He would like to change that.

Through Steve's position in running Philadelphia's University City Science Center, as well as his own experience as a founder who took his company through IPO, he knows a few things about starting companies.

The Science Center is the country's oldest and largest urban research park. It has graduated over 350 organizations since its founding in 1963. Currently 15 000 people are employed by the 93 graduate companies in the Philadelphia region. Specifically, the Science Center is built around the biotech industry and is now expanding to medical devices and the emerging healthcare–IT sector. How does the Science Center do it? They offer lab and office space for start-ups and growing and established companies in addition to support services and education for entrepreneurs.

As an experienced connector among the entrepreneurship community in Philadelphia, Steve has been able to compare companies that start out of university labs to those that are started elsewhere. The main difference that he has observed is that universities are hindered by a lack of urgency and therefore are much slower in getting to a deal. He describes two polar behaviors in technology transfer organizations among the 31 colleges, universities, hospitals, and research institutions that are affiliated with the Science Center. One approach is not to spend any money on tech transfer, where there are not even efficient patent disclosures and technology rarely translates from the lab. The opposing approach is when tech transfer organizations always want to get a "home run," they don't want to give anything away and are so worried that they won't make the right deal, that they often end up not making a deal at all, instead getting, "100% of nothing."

Steve sees another challenge to universities. Until "tenure is informed by invention disclosures, the disclosures will not have much value in the university environment." "MIT and Stanford both include invention in their tenure reviews." If more universities encourage and measure invention, then there will be more value to it and academics would participate more actively.

To propel university discoveries, Steve has created a highly innovative program called QED. "QED is an outside force that can independently validate a university concept for the market." Using a "low barrier to entry," academics submit a one-page white paper about the concept. Everyone gets feedback. For the next step, Steve enlists business advisors who shepherd the project through the early-stage questions that each product needs to answer toward a final pitch, which is given to economic development leaders, businesses, and investors. Oftentimes, there is a match between the business advisor and the technical lead at the end of the QED process, which can result in a management structure in place for a new start-up. How is QED doing? After 5 years, 6 of 16 projects have progressed to licenses and start-ups. The remaining ones are still in the pipeline. The objective of this program is to "retire technical risk" and position the technology for investment.

So what about the significant downturn in venture funding for biotech and medical device companies in recent years? "In sectors which are capital intensive and highly regulated, innovations from academic institutions do well." In these industries "good businesses come from good science." In life sciences, university start-ups are still highly regarded. With the current economy in the Philadelphia region including the downturn of the large pharmaceutical industry, start-ups can leverage expertise that is now readily available. Essentially, "we can arbitrage the economic downturn." "While there is less capital in biotech today, capital has to be smart and there are more sophisticated investors." In addition, Steve believes the emerging healthcare–IT sector uses technology that will do well with an academic foundation.

To promote start-ups, Steve sees regional economic resources as the answer. Mission, not just financial return, is important in the structure of those resources. Patient and low cost capital are needed (like those from a nonprofit). This could be accomplished with scalable foundations and/or local government.

Steve Tang is connecting academics to the business community while instilling entrepreneurship in everyone along the way.

Accelerators

Accelerators work with start-ups and generally admit primarily high-growth potential, for-profit start-ups into the program. Typically there is a highly selective process that likely includes business plan evaluation, start-up presentations to board of advisors for the accelerator, and perhaps follow-up interviews with the start-up management. The accelerator leadership is looking for both a winning concept with a large market potential and a start-up management team that they believe are capable of launching a successful company. Both the business and technical leadership will be critical to this evaluation. Depending on the size of the accelerator, there may be 7–10 start-ups in a "class."

An accelerator is first and foremost a for-profit business. It exists to make money for its investors. Their business model is to invest money in early-stage start-ups for an equity position in the company. If the start-up is eventually successful, the accelerator will enjoy financial success as well, through their equity position in the company. Typical investment was reported in 2011 as $25 000 for equity up to about 8% (Adkins, 2011). Y Combinator, one of the most established and successful accelerators, provides $120K for 7% equity in companies at an early stage, before Series A investment in 2016. These absolute values will be different for different accelerators; however, the general principle is similar across accelerators. The terms for the equity investment will need to be clearly understood by the management team before participation. For example, if a valuation is needed at this early stage, will that potentially hurt later financing? If a valuation is needed, how is this typically determined?

Because the success of the accelerator is directly dependent on the success of the start-ups, the accelerator will typically provide the start-ups with education, mentorship, and introductions to the innovation ecosystem including follow-up investors. They will provide a gathering place for the start-ups, but not necessarily offices or labs. Each of the start-ups in the cohort or class is expected to work in the space provided for a fixed period of time. Typical accelerator time frames are 3 months. The accelerator is designed to move start-ups quickly from the initial phase through follow-up funding or failure. Sometimes this immersive process is referred to as "boot camp." The cohort or class concept serves to provide a healthy competition for progress among start-ups in the accelerator. Participating start-ups also serve as peer mentors for each other. If one start-up finds a great patent attorney, they may share that with another start-up in their group. The exchange among companies is encouraged, and having others going through the same process at the same time helps the start-up teams have extra support outside of their own small company. The start-up teams in the class will serve as a foundation in the development of contacts in the larger start-up world. Often, prior class members will mentor current classes of start-ups furthering yet again the innovation network of the young companies. This is like an alumni network of a university where prior graduates help the current students and can have a very powerful effect.

Accelerators started, and in fact most are still primarily focused, on software and mobile app platform companies. The idea is that if you are a two-person company, for example, a CEO and CTO, and you join the accelerator, you will move to the location of the accelerator and live there for 3 months. For an equity position in your business, the accelerator will give you some money to live on, space to work, and mentor you relatively quickly through the steps of testing your business model. At the end of 3 months, the accelerator will host a demo day where you present your company's minimum viable product (MVP) that you developed or advanced during your time at the accelerator as well as the business case for your product or service. Along with the technical development at the accelerator, you will test the market for your product, learn key business concepts and strategies, and meet with potential investors and business and technical advisors who will all help to mentor you toward the demo day. Demo day is the culmination of your hard work, and the presentation will be made to influential members of the investor and start-up community. The intent is that if you have an investable business strategy at this point or if you don't, you get the feedback on why.

In a report commissioned by the Small Business Administration in 2014, there were 60 accelerators listed in the United States (Dempwolf *et al.*, 2014). The most established of these include the following:

- Capital factory   Austin, TX
- DreamIT ventures   Philadelphia, PA
- Techstars   Boston, MA and Boulder, CO
- Y Combinator   Mountain View, CA

Y Combinator is one of the oldest accelerators, staring in Silicon Valley around 2005. From programming, the term Y Combinator is a program that runs a program. It is a company that helps start companies. This impressive organization has evolved its own business model through the years initially giving about $20K in debt financing of the start-up with a 3-month stay at the accelerator. The initial focus was on software and mobile app companies. In 2016 the deal was about $120K for about 6 months of living expenses for two start-up team members for 7% equity in the start-up company. Y Combinator has broadened the scope of sectors to include biotech, hardware and edtech, and the more traditional software and mobile app focus. They accept companies at all stages from concept to product, but before Series A financing. It's hard to argue with their success rate. Airbnb, Dropbox, and Reddit are graduates of Y Combinator. According to Y Combinator President Sam Altman, the 2015 statistics on Y Combinator show the following:

- Total valuation of all Y Combinator companies was $65 billion.
- Y Combinator companies raised $7 billion.
- 8 Y Combinator companies were worth more than $1 billion.
- 40 Y Combinator companies were worth more than $100 million.
- Y Combinator has started 940 companies, and 177 have closed (outperforming start-up averages at an impressive 81% success rate).

Even fairly well-funded companies (at the seed stage) will join Y Combinator because of the access to their business advisory and investing network. Putting the Y Combinator graduate seal on a start-up now brings a level of vetting and quality that start-ups use to open doors. Continued success has been built on earlier successes for Y Combinator. They now choose from the best start-ups in the country, and this opportunity at selectivity further enhances their wins and those of their cohort of start-ups.

In addition to for-profit accelerators, there are also corporate and university accelerators. Corporate accelerators give seed capital as well as mentoring, networking, and facilities to start-up teams in order to contribute to the specific objectives of the parent corporation through seeding start-ups in those areas. They hope to gain a competitive advantage by assembling the next-generation products in their industry. Oftentimes, the accelerator is able to drive innovation at a faster rate than can be done "internally" in the corporation, which then receives the benefit of quick innovation in their target area, while the start-ups gain industry insights and a potential built-in market for their product or service. Some corporate accelerators include the following (CorpVenturing, 2014):

- Siemens Technology Accelerator
- Nike + Accelerator
- Citrix Startup Accelerator
- Media Camp Accelerator (Turner Broadcasting and Warner Bros.)
- Microsoft Accelerator (Techstars)
- Volkswagen Electronics Research Lab Technology Accelerator
- Kaplan EdTech Accelerator (Techstars)

University-based accelerators are educational nonprofits. They provide seed *grants* to support the development of business concepts, so they *do not* take an equity position in the start-up. These accelerators may fund student-driven start-ups and possibly those from faculty and alumni. University accelerators mimic the structure of the for-profit accelerators by providing similar services, space, network introductions, and demo day.

Stanford's StartX Accelerator is available for those with a Stanford affiliation as a current or former undergraduate, graduate, professional student, or current or former faculty or staff. The Stanford affiliate should have a significant equity position in the company. StartX graduates go through the typical accelerator process and present on demo day. In addition, they have the opportunity for investment in the Stanford StartX fund, which has invested $71 million in 159 StartX companies as of 2015. The Stanford StartX fund invests 10% of a minimum $500K round where 30% of the investment must be from professional investors.

Does your university have an accelerator with potential follow-up funding? You can begin to see how a university or for-profit accelerator can help you to propel your start-up forward. The key is deciding if you'd like to use an accelerator and, if so, which one may be an important component to the success of your start-up. The following are some things to consider before you join an accelerator:

- *Cost:* How much equity for how much investment? What are the valuation terms for the equity position, and is there a market cap? You want to make sure that an early equity investment won't harm subsequent investment from follow-on funding or give you a premature valuation. You also want to make sure that the price that you're paying (in equity) is worth the value that the particular accelerator could potentially bring to your company by way of funds and introductions to the innovation ecosystem including early-stage investors.
- *Community:* Are there other start-ups in a sector where you might gain contacts and learn from each other? If you are the only biotech in an IT accelerator, will the accelerator have the right investors and mentors to guide your business forward?
- *Location:* You will need to live in the area where the accelerator is located for a period of time (typically 3 months). Can you afford to do this? Where will you live and do they help you find a place? Do you want to move for 3 months? Will this affect other aspects of your business (say, if one partner can't move with you) or other ongoing work that you might have?
- *Success rate*: Ask what the success rate of the accelerator has been in the past (see previous Y Combinator metrics for an idea). Of course, keeping in mind that the rates of success are low for all start-ups, it's still a good idea to compare rates across accelerators and then choose one that has a great reputation for supporting their companies and has the depth of connections to mentor the business and connect it with investors to really launch the business. Sector will be an important consideration here. You could talk with graduates of the program to ask about their experiences.
- *Risk analysis*: Like with any business decision, there is a risk–benefit to joining an accelerator. If you are new to the start-up world and don't have an extensive network, need space to work that is not your apartment or a coffee shop, then an accelerator might be a great fit, but it will cost you. In equity.

Try to ascertain if the benefit in potential growth of the value of your company is worth both your time in the accelerator and the cost in dilution of your equity position in the company.

Accelerators have been shown to be highly selective and short-term and survive or fail fast models for exploring business opportunities. The advantages of the best of them are numerous connections to the start-up ecosystem from market development through prototyping through investment. You work with a cohort of like-minded companies in a supportive, open environment. This can be a game changer. The cost to your business is valuable equity. The equity costs of up to 8% are highly significant. The short- and long-term effects of this deal must be well understood before you sign the agreement. But the opportunity cost of not joining an accelerator could be that you keep that 8%, but with a very small valuation where 8% of zero is zero. Definitely some trade-offs for your consideration.

Summary

When you are ready to move your new venture out of the university (or your basement), there are lots of options for places to physically locate. Incubators are for-rent office/lab space that houses only start-up ventures for the first 1–5 years of the life of the company. They may provide the services in addition to rental space and the comradery and potential shared resources among peer start-ups. Accelerators are another option. Mostly started for technology businesses, such as software and app development, they provide a short (typically 3 months) term in the accelerator with some seed investment along with business boot camp and mentoring in exchange for equity for a cohort of companies. The 3-month product of the accelerator-supported start-up is a demo day where you pitch your product and business model to investors. Very quickly through this process, the intent is for the start-up to secure follow-on funding for the business or perhaps failure or significant pivoting of the business model. You could complete an accelerator program and then go on to an incubator; the two are not mutually exclusive. The rates of success for start-ups are higher if they are associated with either an incubator or an accelerator.

References

Adkins, D. (2011), "What are the new seed or venture accelerators?." NBIA Review. Retrieved June 5, 2014 from nbia.org (accessed May 31, 2017).
Bollingtoft, A. and J. Ulhoi (2005), "The networked business incubator-leveraging entrepreneurial agency?." *Journal of Business Venturing* **20**: 265–290.

Calza, F., L. Dezi, F. Schiavone and M. Simoni (2014). "The intellectual capital of business incubators." *Journal of Intellectual Capital* 15(4): 597–610.

CorpVenturing (2014), Corporate Accelerators webpage. Corpventuring.com/services-corporate-accelerators.html (accessed May 9, 2017).

Dempwolf, C. S., J. Auer, and M. D'Ippolito (2014), Innovation accelerators: defining characteristics among startup assistance organizations, College Park, Optimal Solutions Group LLC for Small Business Administration.

Georgia Tech Newsletter (2013), news.gatech.edu/2013/07/15/Georgia-tech (accessed May 9, 2017).

Georgia Tech Newsletter (2014), rh.gatech.edu/news/305231 (accessed May 9, 2017).

Hoffman, D. L. and N. Radojevich-Kelley (2012), "Analysis of accelerator companies: An exploratory case study of their programs, processes, and early results." *Small Business Institute Journal* 8(2): 54–70.

Isabelle, D. (2013), "Key factors affecting a technology entrepreneur's choice of incubator or accelerator." *Technology Innovation Management Review*. Retrieved August 11, 2014 from timereview.caIsis Innovation, 2014.

Isis Report (2014), How to set up a successful university startup incubator, Isis, Oxford University Innovation 2014 Report.

Lasrado, V., S. Sivo, C. Ford, T. O'Neal, I Garibay (2016), "Do graduated university incubator firms benefit from their relationship with university incubators?." *Journal of Technology Transfer* 41: 205–219.

9

Do You Believe in Angels? Financing Your Company

In the business world, the rearview mirror is always clearer than the windshield.

—Warren Buffett, Businessman

You will be asking investors to give money to a concept that may someday become a valuable asset or business. There is little to offer now but the potential for greatness is yet to come. No sales, no profit, but lots of promise. Investors are an innovative bunch themselves and bold yet measured risk takers. Your job at this point is to convince them that your team running this venture is a good bet. An investor will bet on a management team rather than on a technology or market. Part of convincing an investor that your team is outstanding is the plan for developing your business.

Business Plan

Before you start on the investment presentation circuit, some thoughtful planning needs to be done. There are numerous texts and guides on writing business plans (see Suggested Reading for a few), and your CEO will likely have an experience on writing them. Because these have been covered so well elsewhere, here is only a summary of the bones of a business plan, which may include the following components:

- Product or service short description
- Market need
- Market size
- Product solution and differentiation in marketplace
- IP
- Competition

Academic Entrepreneurship: How to Bring Your Scientific Discovery to a Successful Commercial Product, First Edition. Michele Marcolongo.
© 2017 John Wiley & Sons, Inc. Published 2017 by John Wiley & Sons, Inc.

- Value proposition
- Regulatory and/or reimbursement strategy (if needed)
- Pricing strategy
- Sales projections and break-even analysis
- Next markets to develop (if platform technology)
- Financing plan (investment needs/round, milestones, and timeline)
- Space and facility considerations
- Exit strategy
- Team

If you review this general list, you'll quickly realize that only two items talk about the technology and IP from your lab. The rest is the business proposition.

The business plan can take on different forms for different stages of pitching the company to potential investors including the following:

- *One–two-page executive summary text document* that summarizes the business plan and opportunity. This can be used to send a quick email to see if there is any general interest that can progress toward a call or in-person meeting. In addition to the written executive summary, you should formulate a short (about 1 min) elevator pitch or succinct summary or sales pitch for your company that you can use when you meet people and tell them about your business very quickly.
- *Short slide deck* (about 15 slides) that you can use in an initial phone or face-to-face meeting to convey a little more detail to the business plan.
- *Long slide deck* (about 45 slides) when you are getting closer to a deal and the investor wants to do a deep dive into the details of the plan. This will have justification and detailed assumptions of each section.
- *Written business plan document* that will put the slide deck into a text format. This more formal version is not always required but is good to have ready for your investors. It's also a good tool to think through all of the details of the strategy.

The key to the business plan is to have a document with the appropriate level of detail for the type of investor communication or meeting that you're having. You may create more documents as you begin to develop detailed strategies in a specific area or if these are requested by your potential investors. Each assumption that you make should be noted and the data that you quote should be referenced. In general, you should be as quantitative as possible in defining markets and primary market research.

Product definition is the short description of the product that you intend to offer, which will be the basis of your business. This is not necessarily the same discovery from your lab, but the envisioned commercial entity that can be sold. A picture of a prototype or image explaining the product or service can be included.

Market need is the commercial placement of the product or service and defines why your product is in demand now and how the need is projected to grow in the future. This is the "so what" portion of the plan. With the opening statement of the plan, you set the tone for the whole start-up and need to be convincing, exciting the investor.

Market size comes next behind statistics from a respectable marketing research company and/or your primary marketing research (say, from your I-Corps experience or similar discussions with potential customers). The data here should define the overall market sector (e.g., all cancer drugs) and then drill down to your particular market segment (cancer drugs delivered via targeted nanoparticles). You can describe the number of patients in the United States and internationally/year and duration of treatment and costs of some current treatments if available. Is this a billion-dollar market? If not, can you justify the investment necessary to get to a product from start to finish? Does this platform enable other families of drugs to be delivered, which would further expand the market in the future? Quantitative data from your primary marketing research can be inserted here including how many people you surveyed, ratings of the idea (e.g., scale of 1–10), likelihood that they would purchase, and price they would be willing to pay, to name a few.

Product solution and differentiation in the marketplace are critical to assess the unique niche in the market as compared with other products currently being sold or developed. How are you distinguished from the others? Who are your competitors and where are they in the development process? What are their advantages and limitations? Do you disrupt the current standard of care? Will you create a whole new treatment platform that will have quantifiable advantages to the current approach? You can use a table with competitors versus approach and key features including outcomes, price, adaption uptake (sales), ease of use, or whatever features that best fit your application. A visually quick way to assess all of this data is best with text that further documents details available in a written version of the plan. Again, all assumptions should be stated and all data referenced.

Intellectual property should list your patent portfolio including title, inventors, assignee, issued application data (in provisional or non-provisional), US and/or PCT patent, and which countries have been or are planned to be pursued. For key patents that have not yet been granted (not uncommon, given the patent offices' time to review today), you may be asked for a patentability opinion. This is a formal letter from an attorney that includes a patent search around your patent application that tries to mimic the search that the patent examiner will do to uncover any close IP or papers that have similar disclosures. After this analysis, the patent attorney will write an opinion as to the patentability of your key patent application. While this is not a guarantee that the patent will be granted as is, this may serve to de-risk the patentability question for the investors. You may provide this as part of your plan documentation or investors may request this as part of their due diligence. Later, as your product gets closer to commercialization, you may also need to perform a freedom to operate (FTO). While the patent offers you a protected coverage of your product, the FTO tells you that your product is not infringing on any other IP. Patent attorneys also perform this analysis. This is a pricey endeavor, but if you believe that you need to understand the IP in a crowded marketplace, this may save you an expensive legal battle after generating millions in sales. It will further de-risk your business opportunity and let you know if you have FTO or if there is some IP that will be in your way. If a patent turns up that is assigned to another company that you believe that you may be infringing, you have several possible paths forward. Among the possibilities are that you could ignore it for now, try to alter your product so that it no longer infringes, or try to license the patent from the assignee. Again, this is not typically put into the business plan because the product is not finally defined at this time. However, you may be asked about competing IP and it is good to have a general background, even informally by your own doing, to minimize your risk of infringement.

In addition to documenting the patentability opinion, you may need to provide opinions from experts on the *regulatory and/or reimbursement pathways*. For drugs, biologics, medical devices, some health IT, nuclear, and many other industries, the regulatory process must be well understood, along with associated costs. With any regulatory pathway, an opinion from an expert, unless obvious and well-documented previously, is necessary to convey in the plan. With ever-changing regulatory policies, this can be a moving target and, again, a source of risk for the start-up. The same is true for reimbursement strategies for medically related products. If there is not a current reimbursement code (you can search these online) for your product, then you'll have to describe your reimbursement strategy for obtaining a code and agreement of insurance companies like Medicare to pay for your product or service. There are regulatory and reimbursement attorneys that can provide opinions for these as well as sector-specific consultant groups that provide them.

Value proposition is what your product brings to stakeholders. While that is quite vague, you'll need to think through who will be interested in your product and why. The value that you bring may apply to one or numerous stakeholders. For example, for a health IT product, you may pose the product to a hospital administrator, but insurance companies may find value in it as well as patients. The value of your product is not only to the patient but also to all key stakeholders involved in the process or treatment or payment for that treatment. Thinking through the value of the product to each of the stakeholders allows you to conceive the pricing strategy.

Setting a *pricing strategy* for a disruptive technology can be challenging if no other similar product or service has been commercialized previously. Will you follow a subscription service for an IT product or are you restricted by a reimbursement code for a medical device? There are many pricing strategies that you can conceive, but they should all take the value proposition into account. You'll need to define the customer (doctor or hospital administrator for your health IT product...or key corporations for a business-to-business solution like an improved chemical synthesis strategy for an existing polymer). Your strategy should be checked with potential customers to get a sense of the price tolerance. Is $100 too much for a sports betting app? Will the hospital pay a subscription fee of $75K/year with a 3-year minimum contract? How you define the pricing strategy will impact your revenue projections along with your prediction of market uptake.

The *break-even analysis* will relate the costs associated with the start-up getting to enough sales to cover the costs. The break-even point is estimated with investment costs and running costs while in production with sales as projected by your uptake (sales/time). The classic hockey stick curve is often used as an estimate of sales projections with a slower start (lower slope) for some estimated period of time based on your market size and sales cycle as well as your projected sales force and with an inflection point (higher slope) with much quicker accumulation of sales. The devil is in the details in this analysis. You need to make projections with assumptions that can be justified. It's challenging to make all of these projections as a promise of your plan with limited data and realizing that there are ever-changing market conditions. The process of thinking all of this through may help you to reimagine the product or price or costs once you lay it all out. In addition to your CEO, there are business consultants that can help with the pricing and sales strategy.

Investors can be intrigued by platform technologies that may be applicable not only to your specific target market but also to additional markets in other sectors. While the rule of thumb is to focus on a particular product for a specific target market, it is an interesting business proposition that there could be follow-on markets to expand the future sales or contingent products or applications if the first one fails for whatever reason. You should concisely outline additional applications or markets but are not expected to do detailed analyses of these markets as you have for your primary target. It is a good idea to explain why you chose your first market opportunity out of all of the options. Is it the quickest regulatory pathway, even though it's a small market? Is this a niche market where you can make a quick and significant impact? Is it the major market that will prove out the concept so that later markets can follow? All of these helps to bring more potential value to the start-up and can make this a more attractive investment.

The *financing plan* outlines your proposed detailed budget and milestones by financing round. When defining your milestones, keep in mind two main objectives: (1) de-risk the technology and (2) build value in the start-up. For the seed round you should consider all of the possible expenses in detail. All quotes should be documented and up to date. The hiring strategy and projected compensation plan including benefits should be outlined. Costs of facilities and equipment with quotes, supplies, and an administrative reserve could be considered. This is like writing a budget for a grant. More important is the strategy that you use in your financing plan. Will you be a "real" or "virtual" company? Start-ups that are virtual and use other products or services to de-risk and add value to the company can use less capital and lower burn rate (monthly expenditures) to meet their objectives. A virtual company is one that is primarily run by founders and maybe another key hire out of someone's basement or an incubator (or the lab). In this model, the company outsources prototyping, programming, animal experiments, packaging, or whatever the product demands. Here costs are low, but you rely on your subcontractors and the work you do yourselves to advance the business. This can be compared with a real company that has a physical lab (outside of the university), makes several hires, develops a manufacturing capability, acquires its own servers, and so on. There may be a point of transition for a virtual company that starts to build its own infrastructure and ramps up hiring employees. The less capital you accept, the more equity will be left for the founders. This balance needs to be managed so that you are not under or over-capitalized and can make significant progress with the resources you are requesting.

In addition to detailed planning of the seed round, there should be general *milestones and a projected budget* for the subsequent financing rounds (series A, B, etc., if necessary). At a glance, the investor should be able to see the key milestones and associated costs and timeline for your product to get to market and develop sales.

How do you consider *where* to start the company? There are lots of options. To contain costs, you may be able to use the university resources to start the company in your lab. Each university has a different view about this and managing the conflict associated with doing the start-up research work in your lab. However, it's a possibility and should be discussed with the TTO or other authoritative administrator in your institution. Doing this for a short period may enable key technical experiments to be performed without significant early investment in equipment and laboratory resources (hoods, specialized processing equipment, etc.) during start-up. However, there may quickly come a time when it will be necessary to start a lab or facility outside of the university. Some universities have an incubator space that is available to university or other start-ups and provides common meeting rooms, lab and office space, entrepreneurs in residence for advice and connections, and perhaps resources like legal or accounting support for your rental fee. Some will take an equity position in your start-up in addition to monthly fees. Incubators can be short term (couple of months) to longer term (several years). An advantage of an incubator, rather than renting in a suburban office park, is that the incubator would likely be filled with other entrepreneurs getting businesses off the ground. This could be a supportive and to some degree collaborative environment for a fledgling business. The incubator may help with connections of investors and larger companies. How much *space* you will grow into and how quickly will depend on the nature and growth of your business and how much you staff up the business versus following a virtual model. Aside from the more formal incubators and office/lab rental spaces, many businesses use the founder's home basement or garage as an office and the local Starbuck's as a conference room. The lean approach will work for a while until it will become painfully obvious that something more formal will need to be done.

Some start-ups do not plan to become a self-standing corporation with an extensive sales force. You may want to take your start-up through commercialization of the product and then sell the company. You may want to get into phase I clinical trials and sell or partner with another company. There are a numerous strategies for your exit plan and before you take your first investment, you should decide your exit strategy. You will likely be asked about your *exit strategy* in the initial meeting with an investor, at least with the given information you have today. This is a serious discussion that you should have as you are selecting your CEO. The management will need to be on the same page regarding the exit, as best and as sincerely as you can predict at this time. Unplanned opportunities for exit may arise depending on your tremendous success or emerging market opportunities where a feeding frenzy for acquisitions may occur. The board will consider these as they are presented, but the strategic exit plan is something that you should state clearly and work on.

Everything in your business plan will lead investors to a decision about the opportunity of supporting your venture. However, *your team* may be the most important part of the business at this point. Investors invest in people. Both the IP and the plan are important, but execution is the most important consideration for many investors. They bet on people. Describing your backgrounds in the plan and why you are suited to start this company and lead it to a successful outcome is critical. It's difficult to convey this in a document, but your passion and enthusiasm and your dedication to the mission of the start-up will come through in your discussions with investors.

Finding Investors

For your first round of financing, the seed round, you will refine your presentation and begin to meet with potential early investors. These investors can come from any source, but some common sources are

- Friends
- Family
- Local incubators/accelerators
- Economic development organizations
- Individual angels

- Angel investor groups
- Corporate partnerships
- Crowdfunding
- Venture capitalists

Friends and Family

Friends and family are the support systems of our lives. These relationships are very deep and important for how you are today as well as how you will live your life. It's natural to go to the people that you trust most in the world to help you with the idea that you are so passionate about, your new start-up. This is how most new businesses get off the ground. Someone has to be the first investor and in lots of times this comes from those friends and family who believe in you.

This is an obligation that you should not enter into lightly. Here you are with your start-up based on some great data from your lab taking hard-earned money from your friends or parents or siblings to put into your business. It will immediately change the dynamics of your relationships. Remember, successful academic start-ups typically go for 10 years or more before a sale or IPO, so this is a long-term financial arrangement with your friends and family. In addition, this supportive group may not be certified angel investors who do this regularly. They will need to fully understand the risks associated with investment in your company. Being as forthright as possible during these discussions is critical for any type of sustained relationship. The next time you go running with your investor/buddy, think about how the conversations may change. The same for family meals at holidays. Friends and family are a great foundation for a start-up from people who care about you and want to help you succeed while hoping to profit themselves. Friends and family investment really personalizes the abstract "investor" concept.

Local Incubators/Accelerators

As we discussed previously, incubators and accelerators can be nonprofit or for profit, but either way may be able to provide resources for your start-up through a small grant or equity position in the company. Typically, for these programs some residence time in the physical space is required. Accelerators, for example, will have 3–6 month stays with an educational boot camp for entrepreneurs, introductions to other investors and members of the entrepreneurial ecosystem, and a culminating demo day presentation. The general idea is that through the accelerator process, you succeed (secure seed funding) or fail fast, which will let you regroup and decide on your next strategy. One consideration for accelerators who provide resources for equity is setting the valuation of your start-up quite early in the process (see in the following).

Economic Development Organizations

Many universities have strong ties with local economic development organizations. Universities typically train the workforces for the region, supporting companies who employ them and state government agencies interested in advancing economic security for the region. Economic development organizations across the country are excellent resources for early-stage investment. While providing seed funding, typically with a fair cost, they also can be connectors with additional investors, corporations, and other components of the ecosystem. The ties to universities can offer the economic development organization a longer-term focus that is necessary for some academic-based start-ups. Additionally, when there is steep competition for investment from economic development organizations, the vetting process itself can be valuable to the company, just as it can be from a highly competitive accelerator.

Individual Angels

Like friends and family, individual angels can independently invest in your company. These are generally people who invest part of their wealth regularly and are a "qualified" angel investor. To be a qualified angel, you must have $1 million in assets, other than your primary residence, or $200 000/year income over the past 2 years (or $300 000 combined income over the past 2 years if married). The Securities and Exchange Commission (SEC) has special rules for angel investors, Rules 506(b) and 506 (c), that exempt angel investors from those who are publically offered the opportunity to invest in a company (like buying shares of GE). Because of the private offer from you to the investor, they fall outside of the general reporting rules and structure to the special rules. This prevents you, as the business owner, from needing to report all of your angel investments to the SEC, like you would if you were offering investment broadly.

Angel investors on average have a net worth of $5–100 million and invest on average $25–50 000 per company, although this can vary from $10 to 100 000. Typically, angels will come in on a seed round of funding with the same terms as other angels in the round. The seed round terms may be negotiated between the start-up and the lead angel investor. Any other angels who would like to participate in the round must agree to the set terms. This allows the start-up, for example, to have a $1 million seed round where perhaps 20 angels invest, all with the same terms, saving you from negotiating with each angel and providing potentially different deals for different investors in the same round. The SEC rules for angels are ever-changing, especially with the prevalence of crowdfunding (Figure 9.1). Your attorney should be completely current with the implications of angel investment and the regulations surrounding the start-up's responsibility in investment reporting.

Common crowdfunding platform models

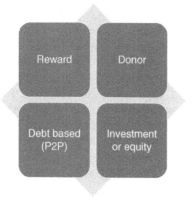

Figure 9.1 Different crowdfunding platforms.

Why do angels invest in risky start-ups? With an average of 50% of angel investment start-ups failing, why do angels take the risk? For some, they are interested in balancing their investment portfolios with high risk, but potentially high reward investments, like those of a start-up. They may invest 10–20% of their portfolio in hopes of having a major return, investing in up to 20 companies at a time. Others like to be in on the next big thing. They like forward-looking investments that are going to catapult a new market and being the one who saw the potential when the company was just a "sketch on a napkin." Some others are committed to solving a focused societal challenge through a personal interest. For example, a parent who lost a child due to cancer will invest in a new start-up with an immunotherapy that has the potential to save the lives of other children. Others are successful entrepreneurs who want to give a start to help new good business ideas get off the ground, having been there before.

While all investing is personal, angels may take more or less of an active interest in the start-up. In some cases, the angels will have a single representative on the board of the start-up who will vote on behalf of all of the investors. In addition, you may give the investors updates as you hit milestones or other significant events. Part of start-up management is management of the investors and this should be built into your system of communications. With many angels invested in a round, there is not time for too much one-on-one communication, but some updates will keep you on good relations with them.

An additional advantage of angels is the connections that they may bring to other investors and to resources that you might need as you progress the development of the start-up. Your investors have your best interest at heart, in great part because their investment success is tied to your start-up success.

Angel Investor Groups or Networks

Sometimes angels flock together. Angel groups are popular for the combined buying power offered from joining investments to many individual investors or a group that invests by majority vote where they may be able to offer a more substantial investment. It also allows comradery among the angels who otherwise might be more on their own in investment decision-making. There are numerous angel groups who tend to invest locally or regionally. The interactions with angel networks can be quite formal with scheduled presentations back to back among those seeking funding to the group. This is Shark Tank style, with 15–20 min presentations followed by 10 min of questions. In some cases the presentations are in person and sometimes by conference call or video.

The Angel Capital Association is a group that compiles information about angel networks and angel investing in the United States including lists of angel networks by region. One component of the angel research is the Halo report, published by the Angel Resource Institute of Willamette University and PitchBook, a compiler of start-up data. The 2015 3Q HALO report showed the following:

- Seed stage valuations rose from 2010 to 2015 to an all-time high of $4 million.
- Median round size of angel only deals more than doubled from 2014 to 2015 to $725 000.
- The most capital invested by region was in California (19.7%), New England (15.5%), and the Great Lakes region (14.5%).
- A number of deals were highest for software, followed by healthcare.

While this data is outdated from the minute you read it, the data shows how sophisticated tracking and analysis of angel investing is becoming. PitchBook is one resource for information about investors and deals for high impact start-ups and another strong resource for you to consider. All of this points to targeting your audience. With angel networks, knowing about past investment preferences may save you time when you are pounding the pavements for investment dollars. Some angel groups focus on specific industries or sectors. Others might focus on investing in a certain demographic of entrepreneurs by ethnicity or gender. With this information, you'll be able to increase your chances of success. As an example, if you are a female entrepreneur with a C-level position in your start-up (one of the 10% in high technology companies), then you may look at Golden Seeds who only funds start-ups like yours. As with all investments, an introduction to a member of the group can go a long way toward consideration of even getting in front of the room to do your pitch.

Another advantage of angel networks is follow-on funding. Some angel networks are developing venture funds to increase their investment in promising start-ups in their portfolios. This opportunity helps to provide a path toward a series A round of financing with investors that you know already.

Corporate Investors

Corporate venture funds or investments are a separate source of start-up funds. If you have relationships with corporations or you know of a corporation's potential interest in your product or service, you may approach them (or they may approach you) about investment in the start-up. Your university may be helpful in facilitating preliminary meetings for your start-up through the TTO, corporate relations office, or incubator/accelerator. A corporation may be interested in investing along the lines of an angel amount (up to or around $100 000) to have a look at how you develop the business. They may have a strategic interest in the business you are developing and want to keep a close eye on yours. They may want to help you or partner with you to develop the business together. They may want to watch you and if you are successful, buy the start-up at some point of its life cycle. Corporate investment will also have terms associated with it, like any investment. If you are in a seed round when approached, the corporation will have to agree to the seed terms or you may need to consider renegotiating terms with each of your current investors, which could be difficult. An advantage to a corporate partner is that it is one more validation for your start-up. If Google is an investor, then maybe others would be more willing to follow. But just as every angel will have to be managed, so will the relationship with the corporation, which means the people in decision-making positions at the corporation. These are people who will influence or control your deals with the corporation, but, like in every corporation, are subject to change. Keeping a good relationship with several people in the corporation is necessary to provide continuity through these inevitable shifts in decision-makers. There is a risk that your start-up is a key piece of strategy for business development for one vice president, but when he or she moves on and the new one comes in, you may be yesterday's priority. Another risk when a major corporation approaches your start-up is that they are fishing for information to try to get a pulse on what is happening in the marketplace and they may not actually be interested in investing in your start-up at this point or ever. Just be smart, use an NDA to talk with them so that you're covered and be cautious about divulging too much at once. That being said, the benefits of validity and potential future investment, partnership, or acquisition may outweigh the risks of working with a major corporation.

In addition to an angel-like investment, some corporations have venture funds for investment in start-ups. These funds have their own terms and the corporation may be lead or be a minority investor in a series A round for your start-up. Corporations with venture funds are across sectors, but typically with major corporations. They run formally, like any venture fund, with their own internal criteria and terms.

Crowdfunding

Crowdfunding platforms had $16 billion investment in 2014 and are estimated to be $90 billion by 2020. This is in comparison with the angel investments at $20 billion and venture capital investments at $30 billion annually. Crowdfunding is something that an entrepreneur can't afford to ignore. The growth rate of crowdfunding has been greatly increasing, in part, due to the JOBS Act, which allows nonqualified investors to participate in equity crowdfunding.

Major crowdfunding web platforms began with Indiegogo (2009) and Kickstarter (2010). Indiegogo was originated for generating financial resources for arts and music, although its focus has broadened in recent years. Kickstarter facilitates funding for projects proposed by entrepreneurs or artists. In general, the project initiator proposes the project, describes it, usually with an interesting project description, and makes a request for a certain amount of funding to work on the project. Anyone can view the project and make a "pledge." The platform itself takes a percentage of the total amount of money collected and serves to facilitate the transfer of funds between investors and the project initiators. What do the investors get in return for their pledges? That depends on what type of crowdfunding platform it is and what the project initiator proposes. This could be a music download if the project from a band that is an initiator or use of software or an app for developer-initiated projects or a new toaster for a designer initiated project. These examples of crowdfunding fall into the "rewards crowdfunding" category, where the entrepreneur offers supporter acknowledgement on their website or in a book or could offer a product or service from the business, often depending on the amount pledged to the project. For the entrepreneur, there is no debt incurred or equity exchanged. In addition to products or services, sometimes scientific research and civic projects are funding using reward-based crowdfunding. The reward there is the knowledge gained by the sharing of information from the projects.

In addition to the obvious gain in financial resources through crowdfunding, other intangibles are often achieved. The crowdfunding pledgers believe in the project and are happy to spread the word about how great it is to all of their networks. This can really get the buzz going for start-up sales to start and publicity to take hold for a new project. It's a multiple on the marketing budget. The crowd also provides feedback along the way. It's a way to interact with a good segment of your market relatively easily. With feedback so important to the development phase of a project, this is invaluable information.

Crowdfunding is not without its risks. Intellectual property protection is one of them. Crowdfunding platforms currently do not support intellectual property protection. There are no NDAs, so prior to a request for funding, the IP must be protected by the project initiator. This is critical for most businesses, who post their ideas openly to the population, including potential competitors.

Another risk is failure to reach your target financial goal. Overall, about 50% of projects fail to reach their financial target. The time frame for the request and uptake in investing is critical to get a campaign going. Often, the product initiators have friends and family lined up to make the first pledges to get the campaign off and running early. They are working their social and business networks to promote the campaign. The initial buzz helps to draw in other investors to consider the project. The successful projects get funding within a given window of time (can be weeks). However, some projects fail due to donor exhaustion if the uptake is too slow. After a period of time, those that don't reach their targets can be terminated (all-or-nothing model) or the project initiators can keep the funding that has been committed (keep-it-all model) even if the full funding target was not reached. The all-or-nothing models are more successful in that they are more likely to be funded. This model removes some risks for supporters. If the project initiator takes the funding, but does not have enough resources to achieve the goals, then there is a chance that the project will be fated to fail from the start. In addition, supporters worry about scams and with the all-or-nothing model, scams are all less likely (Weisul, 2014). In addition to rewards crowdfunding, there are also debt-based crowdfunding and equity crowdfunding.

Debt-based crowdfunding is often called "peer to peer" or P2P. More nomenclature is "marketplace lending." This type of crowdfunding started in 2006 in the United States with the launch of Lending Club in San Francisco. Essentially, borrowers can request unsecured (no collateral) loans from the crowd. The borrowers get the loan and pay back with interest. The platform gets a one-time percentage of the loan amount from the borrower and a loan servicing fee, either fixed annual or one-time percentage of loan) from investors (Freedman and Nutting, 2014–2015). The investors earn interest on each load or bundle of loans if the borrowers make timely payments. The model has been successful. The loans are simpler, cheaper, and quicker than a bank loan, primarily due to lower servicing costs due to automation. In 2013, Lending Club made 200 000 loans totaling $2.7 billion, resulting in an average loan size of $13 490. Returns on less risky loans have been between 5 and 6%, while riskier loans (with higher interest) have resulted in 9.2% returns. Since 2013, institutional investors including Google, insurance companies, and pension funds have become investors in debt crowdsourcing, taking the P2P out of the equation and now resulting in the change to "marketplace lending." This additional sector of crowdfunding is strong, with Lending Club's 2014 IPO resulting in a $1 billion raise and $9 billion valuation (Freedman and Nutting, 2014–2015). The power of the crowd for sure.

Equity Crowdfunding

One form of crowdfunding that may be most relevant to the academic entrepreneur is equity crowdfunding. This segment of crowdfunding is intended to match start-ups (issuers of equity or issuers) with angel investors. The idea is that through an equity crowdfunding platform, issuers can disclose information about the company and terms of the deal. One result of equity crowdfunding is that it can rapidly accelerate the investment process from a typical 8–12 months for the in-person angel raise to weeks or days or even hours from the platform's network of angels. It was reported (Barnett, 2015) that equity crowdfunding resulted in $1 billion investment in 2014–2015. Laws around equity crowdfunding are evolving in synch with the use of the platforms. To understand the value to your business, it's worth understanding the recent and evolving landscape of equity crowdsourcing. This has been succinctly analyzed and summarized by Freedman and Nutting (2014–2015).

As discussed previously, there are rules that govern who can be a qualified angel investor. These rules are intended to ensure that only those with enough assets will be able to make risky investments in start-ups, potentially saving those without from potential financial ruin. But recent changes in legislation have modified the prior limitations on angel investing. In a series of legislation between 2011 and 2015 under amendments to the Securities Act of 1933 and the JOBS Act, increasingly, nonaccredited investors can participate in equity offerings of private companies like yours. This is estimated to enlarge the pool of angels considerably.

Regulation D (Reg D) to the Securities Act of 1933 enabled equity offering platforms. Prior to Reg D, start-ups could not offer investment in their companies broadly, to the public, in the same way, for example, that you could buy shares of a publically traded company. Start-ups were only permitted to advertise their offerings quietly to qualified investors (angels). Under Reg D, issuers can raise unlimited capital in each offering and can sell equity through Reg D platforms but only to accredited investors and not to the "crowd."

Soon after Reg D was passed, new equity crowdfunding platforms were launched including MicroVentures in 2011, based on tech companies and CircleUp in 2012, which focuses on consumer products and retail. Soon after Reg D law was enacted, the JOBS Act was passed.

In 2012, the JOBS Act (effective in late 2013) had legislature that further impacted equity crowdfunding. In Title II of the JOBS Act, there are two specific rules that changed how start-ups are marketed to investors and started to redefine the definition of investors for equity crowdsourcing.

Rule 506(b)
- Unlimited number of accredited investors and up to 35 nonaccredited investors can participate in offering.
- Cannot solicit the general "crowd."

- Considered "quiet deals."
- Accredited investors can self-certify, meaning they do not have to provide evidence that they meet the standards of accreditation.

Rule 506(c)

- Limits offering to accredited investors only, but can have general solicitation to them through the platform.
- Issuers must take "reasonable steps" to verify every investor's accreditation status.
- Investors have to "prove" their accreditation through documentation of their assets and income to the start-up.

The start-up needs to decide which one of these models to follow before soliciting equity crowdfunding. Another consideration is whether the investors in the platform are structured to have direct or indirect investment (Freedman and Nutting, 2014–2015). For direct investment, as it sounds, the investors are directly linked to the start-up and, as such, for an equity position or debt financing, need to be added to the cap table (list of all investors and amounts of equity or investment that they've made). It is the obligation of the start-up to maintain these records and with a crowdsourcing strategy, the number of investors may be considerable. For indirect investment, the platform pools the investor money into a single entity LLC. The LLC is then able to purchase shares or finance debt as a single investor, simplifying the tracking for the start-up considerable. Even in the indirect investment structure, the investors are still able to independently select which companies in which they invest. But more changes opened the equity crowdfunding gates further.

The JOBS Act Title III, issued in 2015 and active in April 2016, opened equity crowdfunding to nonaccredited and accredited investors. This changes the entire paradigm on angel investing, where about eight million investors were participating prior to Title III, now that investment is open to tens of millions. GameChanger. Title III altered the Securities Act of 1933 with a new Section 4(a) (6), more broadly enabling equity crowdfunding. To understand the implications of this regulation, Freedman and Nutting describe its effect on issuers (the start-up companies), investors, and platforms. A simplified summary of some changes in effect from Title III include the following (not comprehensive):

Effect on initiators:

1) Must be a private company in the United States.
2) Investment companies cannot raise capital with crowdfunding platforms.
3) Start-ups can raise up to $1 million in any twelve-month period through SEC and FINRA registered crowdfunding portals.
4) *Issuers may sell shares to unlimited number of accredited and/or nonaccredited investors in deal for up to $1 million.*

5) Issuers are permitted to publish a notice advertising details of terms and direction to the crowdfunding platform where the terms are offered. *General solicitation is now allowed.*
6) Issuers who raise
   a) <$100 000: Have tax returns (if any) and financial statements certified by the chief officer of the start-up.
   b) $100 000–$1 million: Provide financial statements reviewed by independent accountant.
   c) $500 000 more than once: Financial statements must be audited by a CPA.

Effect on investors:
1) The following are qualifications for individual net worth, excluding primary residence:
   a) <$100 000: Investment can be made at a *cap of $2 000/year* or 5% of income, whichever is greater, or 5% of net worth, whichever is less.
   b) $100 000+: Investment can be made at 10% of income or net worth (whichever is less) *but not more than $100 000 annually.*
2) Investors may self-certify.
3) When registering on funding portal, they must demonstrate that they understand the risk of the investment.
4) Investors must hold shares at least 1 year after purchasing them via equity crowdfunding, with few exceptions (can see shares back to issuer or to an accredited investor).

Effect on platforms:
1) Registered funding portals cannot give advice to investors or direct them to particular opportunities (unless they are a broker–dealer).
2) Platforms may "curate" their offerings by industry or region, for example, and can have undisclosed selection criteria for hosting the offering.
3) Platform cannot pool investors' funds into single investing entity (like a VC does).
4) Must provide investor education about risk.
5) Must conduct background checks on officers, directors, and 20% equity holders of the start-up. Disqualifications might be convicted felon, restraining order, financial injunctions, and SEC disciplinary actions of a "bad actor."

While the federal government has been issuing regulations around crowdfunding, so have many states. There are intrastate rules for equity crowdfunding in states (29 at the time of this writing with four additional states pending), allowing residents within those states to invest in companies headquartered in the same states (Figure 9.2). The legislation for the states differs from the federal legislation and in some cases precedes the federal legislation. With that

Alabama	Alaska	Arizona
Colorado	District of Columbia	Florida
Georgia	Idaho	Illinois
Indiana	Iowa	Kansas
Kentucky	Maine	Maryland
Massachusetts	Michigan	Minnesota
Mississippi	Montana	Nebraska
New Jersey	Oregon	South Carolina
Tennessee	Texas	Vermont
Virginia	Washington	West Virginia
Wisconsin	Wyoming	

Figure 9.2 Intrastate crowdfunding: states allowing investment by nonqualified investors. *Source*: http://nasaa.cdn.s3.amazonaws.com/wp-content/uploads/2014/12/NASAA-Intrastate-Crowdfunding-Update-111616.pdf

being said, a new Title IV is currently in congress, which again proposes changes to equity crowdsourcing law. While the regulators are likely to provide adjustments as the market continues to develop and lessons are learned, it is likely that start-up leaders will need to stay on top of the rules so it is best to use them to their advantage.

These changes to equity crowdfunding have a potential to change the way start-ups are seeded. For every start-up, equity crowdfunding platforms offer new potentials to appeal to a different audience of investors than ever previously possible. Larry Downs on his Harvard Business Review blog calls this *Big Bang Disruption* (Downs, 2013).

While the potential is there for all start-ups, equity crowdfunding may be especially helpful if you are in a region where there is little qualified angel investment. The additional opportunity exists for you to advance your start-up by attracting qualified and now nonqualified investors under the equity crowdfunding platform. Political campaigns in recent presidential elections have capitalized on the small donor to accumulate significant financial resources. Can crowdfunding work for you?

Academic Crowdfunding

Are there any precedents for crowdfunding start-ups from academia? One success story comes from University College London in 2015. A spinout from the university called Chirp, which developed sonic data transfer, was supported through the university incubator. Chirp used the British investment crowdfunding platform, Crowdcube, the world's leading investment crowdfunding platform having both equity and debt investment options. Crowdcube itself has successfully funded 184 619 905 pounds to 435 successful raises through about 300 000 investors as of 2016.

Chirp raised 750 000 pounds on Crowdcube, well exceeding their target of 400 000 pounds. In just 7 weeks, Chirp had 365 investors. Most investments were less than $5000 pounds, so a large community of investors was necessary to achieve their goals.

What was Chirp's strategy? They laid out a comprehensive marketing strategy to build the buzz about their company. Chirp used branding, web presence, a well-polished video pitch, and a social media company to position themselves for the crowdfunding raise. They had the campaign already running before launching the crowdfunding request. In addition, they used anchor angels and friends and family who were lined up and ready to be the first investors for the campaign. The campaign was aided in a matching fund pledge from an early investor. In addition, Chirp developed new product features during the campaign and also announced new partnerships during the campaign. All of this progress, in the short time that Chirp was crowdfunding, drew in more and more investors until their target was met and then exceeded. Chirp accomplished the largest crowdfunding raise in 2015 for UK spinouts from universities.

In addition to university start-ups harnessing the power of crowdsourcing independently, like Chirp, some universities have partnered with crowdfunding platforms. The University of Utah was a pioneer in this area. Utah partnered with RocketHub for a Utah-specific crowdsourcing vehicle called University Tech Vault, a rewards crowdfunding platform, in 2012. The TTO in Utah established the partnership to help initiate funding for spinouts from the University of Utah. In their first offering, Utah raised $32 000 from 210 donors for their projects.

University of California Berkeley's Hass School of Business partnered with Indiegogo to help develop innovative leaders in their school in 2013. Like Utah, the Berkeley/Indiegogo partnership is a rewards-based crowdfunding platform. Projects have been funded with targets ranging from $2 000 to $25 000.

Over 20 universities in 2016 have their own crowdfunding platforms for fundraising for institutional advancement (strictly donor, not rewards or equity at this time). They pool alumni, including young alumni to support student, staff, and faculty projects as well as specific fundraising objectives, like research projects or lab renovations. As of 2016, there were no equity crowdsourcing sites for university start-ups. However, with 2016 changes in Title III, this may be an attractive option for universities going forward. Institutional advancement offices of universities are finding innovative ways to use crowdsourcing to target all alumni, but especially young alums, building university loyalty as receiving resources targeted for special projects associated with the institution.

It will be interesting to see how US university spinouts harness the power of crowdfunding. While reward crowdfunding is well established, in 2016, equity or investment crowdsourcing is still in its infancy. Is one preferable to the other for you? If your start-up is a consumer product, app, or service and you can deliver the product to your supporters, rewards crowdfunding may work well for you, especially initially where funding targets can be modest. For a business-to-business product or service or one with a 10–20 year presales cycle like a drug or energy solution, the equity crowdfunding model may be better. Some companies are using a combination of crowdfunding genres for different points along their development. For example, you could start with a Kickstarter campaign (rewards) and then go to MicroVentures (equity). Predictions are that equity crowdfunding will skyrocket in the coming years. How will universities take advantage of this opportunity? There may be conflicts of interest to consider if universities are equity holders in the start-up. The universities may be proactive in trying to partner with equity crowdfunding platforms to promote their start-ups, or they may develop their own platforms, like some are doing for donor crowdfunding. Regardless of the approach of universities, equity or debt crowdfunding may be a significant consideration for your start-up.

Venture Capital

Venture capital funds typically fund big on disruptive technologies. They are not interested in singles or doubles, only in grand slams. Grand slam innovative disruptors could be in any sector. The venture fund works by investors putting dollars into the fund, and the fund managers or venture capitalists, selecting, advising, and growing value in the start-up. The successful outcome from a venture-backed start-up could be IPO or sale of the company at which time the VC will reap the profits from their investment. They will distribute the profit back to the fund investors and keep a portion for the fund managers themselves.

A few university start-ups will attract venture capital funding right from the concept generation. These are rare and mostly limited to the best entrepreneurial scientists/engineers in the country (maybe 5–10 faculty at any given time). Others will build up to venture funding through other types of investment mentioned earlier, such as angel or crowdfunding initiatives or after graduation from an accelerator. Like all investors, venture capitalists want to maximize potential benefit and minimize risk. Many VCs will say that the technology is important, but they will bet on the team.

The deal with venture capitalists differs from the deals with economic development, angels, and crowdfunding in that there is always an equity deal with VCs. The company must have a valuation and equity will be taken according to the investment and the valuation. Because VCs are typically investing money to last you 2–5 years or until a predetermined major milestone (e.g., FDA approval), the amount invested will be large. While the VC investment will increase the post-money valuation of the company, it will also greatly reduce the founder's equity position (see example in the following). In addition, the VC will take a seat on your board of directors. This will give the VC influence over major decision-making for the company. Hopefully, you as the founder can select a VC with a shared vision to your own.

Most VCs review hundreds of deals each year. The best way to get in front of a VC is through an introduction. Here is where your network and that of your university, CEO, incubator, accelerator, and every other part of your innovation ecosystem come into play. Once invited for a presentation, there are many strategies to secure funding. There must be an alliance with your vision (think big, like bigger than $1 billion market), technology (IP, proof of concept, sales, or followers), finances, competition, and all other elements of your business plan. The most important, if not then second most important depending on the individual investor, is the team. You must be convincing, passionate, and engaging and have good comradery among the management team and a strong board and advisors. You will be the people who will make the technology work. Seasoned entrepreneurs can sometimes be given preference over novices. There are different preferences from different VCs. Most start-ups will target VCs that are in their domain, market size, and perhaps region. Every VC pitch yields feedback that you may choose to incorporate into your next VC pitch. The process can take 6 months to 1 year or more.

Venture capital is typically categorized by the level of investment and progress of the start-up. After the seed round (typically angels or crowdfunding) comes the Series A funding, typically enough venture funding to get to a targeted milestone over a few years. If that milestone is reached, the market still looks good, and continued investment is interesting to investors, then a series B and later a series C round can be considered. Any of these rounds can consist of more than one VC group, but one group will typically serve as lead investor, and this group will set the terms with the start-up. With each investment, hopefully, valuation will grow while unfortunately, your equity position will decrease. Companies that need the investment because they are still not profitable have few other options, such as a small business loan, usually because the business is still risky. With any investment, you would like to take as little as possible, but to be able to reach your targets to work your way to the exit as guided by your board. Often, university start-ups are measured by the amount of follow-up funding they receive, but in actuality, some companies need more (drugs), while others may be highly successful companies with less. This depends on your business model (bricks and mortar versus virtual) and sector.

Robert Adelson
Managing Partner
Osage Partners

Robert "Bob" Adelson built a highly successful venture business based on an observation from a little exploited academic policy and had found a way to leverage returns on academic spin-outs across a portfolio of universities.

This novel investment model has enabled Bob to raise the first ($100 M) and now second funds. Osage's model is clearly unique. Bob, through discussions with Lou Berneman, former head of the TTO at Penn, learned of a little-used clause in the contract of universities that licenses their technology to start-ups. The clause allows for the university to invest the same percentage of equity that they were allotted in the license agreement in all subsequent rounds of the start-up's financing (Series A, B, etc.). Most, if not all, universities were not taking advantage of this opportunity. Bob saw an opening.

If he could license the rights to invest in subsequent rounds of interesting start-ups, then he may be able to capitalize on the successful start-ups coming out of a university with a guaranteed equity position, but would not have to lead the round of investment or set the terms of the investment. In an additional twist, Osage decided to leverage its investment risk by licensing the ability to invest in subsequent rounds not from one start-up at a time and not one university at a time, but from selecting from the most interesting companies from 5 (later expanded to 8) different universities. If the university gives complete and exclusive rights to Osage to invest in future rounds, the university will share in Osage's profits. This allows Osage to leverage risk in that the fund does not pay out until the fund is profitable and does not rely on one company hitting a home run. The university gets additional capital from spin-outs without additional investment, even if their own spin-outs do not succeed, but the fund overall succeeds, leveraging the risk of the universities through diversification.

The 8 full original partners of Osage are Berkeley, Cal Tech, Columbia, Duke, Florida, Michigan, Penn, and Yale. There are also 60 affiliate partners. For the second funding round, Osage has increased the partner universities to 25, including some international universities. Osage has invested in 350 out of the 2700 university spin-outs/year.

Because of their vast amount of investment in university start-ups, Osage has collected what is likely the most comprehensive and powerful database on university start-ups including their management, investors, successes, and failures. This helps them to research new start-ups in which they invest and would be like gold to an entrepreneurship student (or TTO director) for analysis. Most TTOs are not generally privy to this information and don't really know how their spin-outs are doing.

One interesting observation that Osage made after analysis of spin-outs from their original 5 university partners for over 15 years was that university spin-outs don't usually have "break-out winners." The companies generally have a higher success rate than nonacademic start-ups; however, these are successful in the midranges. Osage uses a goal for company sale of $250 M or $5X investment. They also have seen that companies that use postdocs or professors as the management team typically fail. Osage believes that the faculty member should continue to innovate by remaining in the lab, fueling the next start-up with new discoveries. Another source of failure has been in start-ups that need $90 M, initially raise $2 M, and can't make the financing of subsequent rounds, being chronically underfunded.

Osage has a clear view of the role of the professor in the start-up based on his/her technology. First, the professor should be on the scientific advisory board. He/she should be sensitive to commercialization requirements and be market-oriented early in the process. Roles for professors can also be specific to sectors, where a life science sector might need the professor to help build network of sites for a clinical trial; engineering technologies might need the professor to have relationships with companies and in other sectors (IT) the professor can achieve a minimum viable strategy for a fast/cheap approach working along with management team. How about keeping some equity for that innovative faculty member? Bob suggests getting the university more equity so that the faculty member can increase his/her share. Bob also thinks that in the professor's first company he/she is in learning mode, but by the third company, VCs are willing to give them a much more involved role.

Bob Adelman has de-risked venture capital investment in university start-ups by partnering with the universities themselves and allowing them to partner with each other, providing an example of investment as a sharing economy.

University Venture Capital

Some universities have their own venture funds that exclusively fund faculty, students, and/or alumni from their university. While these funds may not be as large as Kleiner, Perkins, Caufield and Byers (KPCB) (Menlo Park, CA), there will be a much small field of competition. The first university venture fund sprung out of MIT and Harvard School of Business in 1973. From 1973 to 2010, there were 11 university venture funds launched in the United States (Croce *et al.*, 2014). From 1973 to 2010, these university venture funds invested collectively in 258 companies at $347 million. Information and computer technologies led the investments with 47.7% of deals and 44.7% of funding. Medical and health, biotech, and semiconductors/electronics were the next highest. Also included in investment were industry/energy, manufacturing, and non-high tech. Since 2010, more universities have announced venture funds, seeming to increase growth in this investment tool (Figure 9.3).

While there is debate over universities investing in risky start-ups, the fact is that many universities invest in venture funds (other than their own) already as

Percentage of the number of companies from
university fund investments 1973–2010

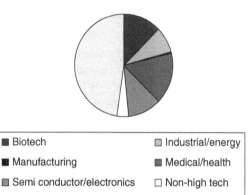

■ Biotech	□ Industrial/energy
■ Manufacturing	■ Medical/health
▨ Semi conductor/electronics	□ Non-high tech
□ ICT	

Figure 9.3 University venture fund investments from 1973 to 2010. *Source*: Croce *et al.*
(2014). Reproduced with permission of Springer.

part of their balanced portfolios. University pension funds and endowments from the State of California system currently invests $1 billion in external ventures and in 2015 started a $250 million venture fund of their own to invest in companies in the UC system. This offers a unique opportunity to university-originated start-ups.

When you have strong convictions about the opportunity for the investors, you can be confident in accepting money and performing to meet the milestones and timelines that you have put forth in your plan. The seed round is intended to de-risk the technology and build value in the start-up. It's difficult to put a dollar amount on the seed round because it's highly dependent on your sector. An IT business may need $300K to get to a product launch, or a biotech company may take $1–5 million before the technology is de-risked enough to bring in a venture capitalist in a series A round and $35–50+ million before it will be through clinical trials. Either way, the seed round financing should be sufficient enough to allow you to build targeted value and operate for a given period of time (6–12 months, typically). Setting milestones (and later achieving them) will be critical for the success of your company and for the integrity of your team in building a reputation that you are performers and can deliver on promises made. The seed round, financed by angels and others, is your first step toward realizing your goals.

How you structure your seed round is also highly flexible. You can take different approaches in setting up your seed round offering. One option is debt financing, which is essentially a loan to the company at a certain percentage interest to be payable upon a company financing round or sale and/or converted to stock at a discounted rate.

For example, you could raise a $1.5 million seed round from friends/family as convertible debt at 8% interest and a discount rate of 20%. This means at the sale of the company or the next round of financing (series A), the investors can take 1.08X their investment and receive stock at a 20% discounted rate. The discount is based on the valuation of the company at series A financing and the numbers of pre-money shares. The reason for doing this method of financing in the seed round is that it allows you to postpone setting a valuation of the company at the very beginning. Many start-ups believe this to be the most desirable offering for a seed round, and seasoned angles understand the methodology and are generally in agreement with this approach. However, some angels would prefer an equity position in the company for their investment.

When you give equity (stock) for investment in the seed round, you will first need to agree on a valuation for the company. At a very early stage, valuation can be difficult. There are typically no sales from an academic start-up on which to base a valuation, so then the company is valued purely on potential. The team, market opportunity, IP, potential product, and competitive landscape are all included in the valuation; however, there are no set rules on how this is accomplished. A negotiation will proceed until the investors and the management team has come to agreement. One way to bracket this problem is to search on pre-money valuations of comparable companies. Valuations of recent competitive or at least similar companies in your sector can help inform your negotiations with the investors and help you to land in a reasonable space. While these valuations are not always easy to come by, your TTO may have a good idea about typical valuations for the companies of your academic colleagues over the past few years. Your colleagues at incubators and accelerators who are supporting start-ups through the transition to funding are another resource for comparables. While it's important focus on the technology and potential of the product, the team of individuals who will be making the business materialize is a significant factor in valuation of the early start-up. Entrepreneurs and academic entrepreneurs who have had prior start-ups, even if the start-ups were unsuccessful, result in a bump in valuation over first-time entrepreneurs.

A high valuation is beneficial to the founders initially; however, if the company does not develop expected value through the seed round according to expectations, there could be a difficult series A round to follow with a devaluation, which is not positive. Undervaluing the company at the start is at the expense of the founders, and also not ideal. The challenge is hitting the sweet spot with very few guiding principles. The "cost" of the investment to the company should always be considered.

In any type of offering, in exchange for the investment, each of the founders will give up a portion of their equity. How much equity you exchange for investment will depend on the amount of investment you take in and the agreed valuation. These calculations are adapted from Bradley Feld's analysis (antiventurecapital.com).

Sample Problem

Let's say that for RegenLiv (from Chapter 6), 1 000 000 shares of common stock were issued initially with an initial valuation (also called "pre-money valuation" or "pre") of $2 000 000 ($2/share). The academic founder, Emma, had 40% equity position or 400 000 shares.

Pre-money valuation = $2 000 000
Pre-money shares = 1 000 000
Pre-money share price = $2/share
Emma's shares = 400 000

For the seed round, RegenLiv gets $1 000 000 in investment on the $2 000 000 pre-money valuation for a post-money valuation ("Post") of $3 000 000.

Post valuation = pre valuation + investment
= $2 000 000 + $1 000 000 = $3 000 000

RegenLiv now has to give $1 000 000 in stock to compensate the investors. This is not taken from the original pre-money shares. Instead, shares are added to the pool at the pre-money share price.

At $2/share (pre-money stock price), the investor pool will need 500 000 shares to pay for the $1 000 000 investment. This results in a total of 1 500 000 post-money shares in RegenLiv. The investor equity for 500 000 shares out of a total of 1 500 000 total post-money shares is 33.3%. Meanwhile, Emma has been diluted from 40 to 26.6%.

Investor shares = investment/pre-money share price
= $1 000 000/$2/share
= 500 000 additional shares to be issued
Post-money total shares in RegenLiv
= 1 000 000 pre + 500 000 new = 1 500 000
Investor equity = investor shares/total post-money shares
= 500 000/1 500 000 = 33.3%
Emma's equity = Emma's shares/total post-money
= 400 000/1 500 000 = 26.6%

At this point, the company uses the seed round investment and works to build additional value in the company. After 1 year, they have used just about all of the investment, have hit major milestones, and are ready to build more value in the company. They are ready for a series A round of financing. To keep the share price flat, the seed round post-money valuation now becomes the series A pre-money valuation. This is actually a new negotiation, and based on the milestone accomplishments of the seed round, series A pre-money valuation may be different, hopefully, higher. RegenLiv is asking for a series A investment of $10 million. We go through the calculations again.

Assume: seed round post-money valuation = series A pre-money valuation = $3 million
Series A investment: $10 million
Series A post-money valuation = seed post-money valuation
     + series A investment
     = $3 million + $10 million = $13 million
Series A share price = series A pre-money valuation/series A pre-money shares = $3 million/1 500 000 = $2/share
Investor shares = series A investment/share price
     = $10 million/$2/share = 5 000 000 shares
Series A investor equity = series A investor shares/total shares
     = 5 000 000/6 500 000 = 76.9%
Seed investors equity = seed investor shares/total shares
     = 500 000/6 500 000 = 7.7%
Emma's equity = Emma's shares/total shares = 400 000/6 500 000 = 6.1%

This example is only one way to look at financing a company. Your story may be quite different depending on your valuation and capital requirements. But the story is generally the same for most academics in that in the very beginning, you are central to the story of the new company. Without you, there would not even be a company. You are responsible for the innovation, targeting the market, developing a commercially viable product from the laboratory finding, bringing the CEO on board, helping to secure financing, staffing the company, and providing technical direction, just like Emma.

In actuality, the further the company progresses and in general, the more money that takes, the origin of the business may be less important to the company that it becomes. After the start, the value added comes from investment. We saw that Emma's equity position went from 40% at the founding of the company on the $1 million valuation (40 000 shares valued at $400 000) to $26.6% after the seed round (still 400 000 shares now valued at $451 127) to 6.1% after series A (still 400 000 shares now valued at $793 000). While Emma's equity position decreased dramatically as the company took in investment, the value of her shares did grow because the value of the company grew. Of course, with no real revenues at this time, the value of her equity is only realized if there is a buyer for the company at those valuations.

Bruce Robertson, Ph.D., MBA
Managing Director
H.I.G. BioVentures

Bruce Robertson finished his Ph.D. in Chemical Engineering at the University of Delaware and then started work in corporate R&D. After 8 years on the job, Bruce now reflects that he felt stifled by the confined thinking of the corporation at that time. He wanted to be innovative and use entrepreneurial thinking. This drive led him away from corporate R&D and into venture investment. Since that time, Bruce has been an active venture capitalist.

Through Bruce's impressive venture capitalist career, he has focused primarily on biotech. With this focus, he has invested in numerous companies that have their roots in university technology. As an advisor to Johns Hopkins University for translating discoveries toward commercialization, he has had additional experience interacting with and advising university start-ups.

Bruce has made some observations about technologies coming out of universities and how faculty members interact with the larger innovation ecosystem. He sees a pattern in venture deals with university technologies:

1) *Rock star start-up*: Where a VC group will invest in the people involved. Here the investment is in the professor and team around a game-changing idea around which a company will be built. This approach is most commonly found in the Boston area and VCs are betting on the person even more than the technology. And they bet big with $30–50 million investment on a technology just spinning out of a university.

2) *Discovery start-up*: Here a tech transfer deal could be made around a discovery, like a new molecule, and IP will be licensed from the university. In this approach, the faculty member is not central to the start-up and may not be asked to play a major role at the VC investment stage. The value is in the IP itself and what the start-up wants to do to exploit that IP with other scientists and engineers within the company structure.

Bruce sees the best way for a professor to successfully start a company is to build a network in the entrepreneurial community before you need it. To meet VCs, go to the venture capital conferences. With an introduction, the VCs will take a friendly meeting. Bruce thinks doing this early in your academic career, building the foundation for when you need it, will prepare you when the first time comes for you to spin out a company or license a technology. Most venture investments are made with people that the VCs know beforehand. If not known in person, that person should be at least known by a trusted colleague. Bruce emphasizes the importance of knowledge of the entrepreneurship ecosystem for faculty members who are interested in starting companies or spinning out their technology.

From Bruce's perspective, one of the biggest disconnects between venture capitalists and academia revolves around the valuation of the university technology. The discovery may represent years or a career's worth of research by the faculty member, who is obviously tied to the discovery and values the technology highly. The VC, however, will value the technology as a component of the business proposition in which the technology is only one of many important components. This sets two different perspectives of technology value between the VC and faculty. In another case, the VC may value the technology and IP, but may not need the faculty member to join the start-up. This is difficult, but happens more often than not.

How does the faculty member make financial gains through their start-ups? Bruce points out that if the technology has a long path to commercialization, like biotech or energy technologies, there will be serious dilution. Over time, the faculty member equity level could be less than 1%. For a faculty member to more likely make a profit from commercialization, Bruce thinks it's better to have "a portfolio of start-ups with a fraction of each." This strategy, Bruce points out, will mitigate the potential non-winners from the successful companies and the same strategies that VCs use in investing.

Bruce, like other VCs see value in academic based start-ups. This world is exciting with potential big impact, and that works for Bruce.

Building and Expanding Value for the Academic Founder

Is there a way for founders to maintain more of an equity position as the company progresses through the development and sales stages? One way is for you to maintain relevance to the company (Figure 9.4). Your start-up legacy should be a source of pride for you. However, compensation from the company will be based on your current contribution to the corporate mission at the time. In the beginning, you are critical to the mission of translating the technology, but how relevant will you be to the day-to-day operations of the company when production is going and the company has just hired 30 sales reps?

There have been numerous academic founders that have started successful companies that have gone to consumers or patients where the founder received very little compensation in the end. How does this happen? The nature of many businesses is that as the value increases, the closer the business is to the actual sales. Also, after the product is developed and is ready for launch, there can be much less need for the original faculty member who discovered the idea behind what has now turned into a real business with product engineers, sales and marketing teams, management layers, manufacturers or developers, human resources, and accounting (Figure 9.5).

Figure 9.4 Research and development is heaviest at the beginning of the start-up, while sales and marketing increase as the start-up progresses. To have a smooth transition between the two, communication and collaboration are needed between them in the company.

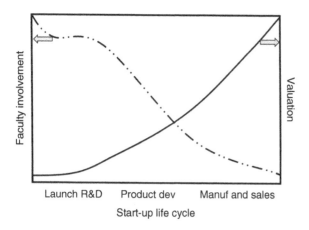

Figure 9.5 Faculty involvement in the start-up is high early in the start-up life cycle when the technology needs to be transferred to the employees of the company and valuation is modest. This can reverse through the life cycle of the company and is a risk for the academic founder monetarily.

How can you keep active in the company and show your value to the investors? In an interview for this book, one venture capitalist was asked about the extreme dilution of academic founders and the reply was "Hmmm, I never thought about that." The investors will not be looking out for you, only their investment, or they may be looking out for you in so far as it affects their investment. If you are useful to the company and the board is well aware of your contributions, then de-motivating you or getting rid of you entirely will not serve to the benefit of the company. One way to keep relevant is to show technical expertise on the board. Some ways that you may be able to provide key contribution to the start-up to keep your day job include learning about regulatory pathways and strategies and how the product can be fine-tuned to minimize this risk; keeping a pipeline of new innovations coming from your lab that will help the company to improve the product or expand in new ways; helping with scale up issues; and/or helping to recruit top talents to the company. While you may not be rewarded in additional shares, you may receive options, research grants to your lab from the start-up, and/or a consulting agreement with the start-up. Or, you may not be diluted quite as much as you would if you were a silent founder. Again, there is no set formula for your level of participation in the company and corresponding compensation from the company. You should be aware that this progression may occur and keep an open dialog with your CEO and investors about your desired level of participation and value add from your involvement to the start-up at every point along its trajectory (Figure 9.6).

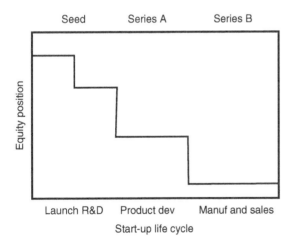

Figure 9.6 Faculty member equity stake in a start-up can decrease dramatically with increased capitalization of the company over the company's life cycle.

For some companies, academic and others, there is a phase called "founders fatigue." This is a syndrome where the initial vision of the company, enabled by the founders, has evolved into something beyond that initial vision or beyond the viable skill set of the founders. The founders, naturally and emotionally tied to the company, cannot separate their vision and contribution from the present-day state of the company, which might be quite different. At this point, the company management and investors may find that the founders are more disruptive than constructive to the current mission. They may dilute you even further to remove your control or buy you out. You need to be acutely aware of this possibility and try to continually sense from the management and investors how they are valuing your contributions through the process.

Is it worth it? That really depends. Every business in every sector is so different. The pace of development in mobile or health IT can be fast compared with medical devices, drugs, or energy solutions. For longer-term propositions, the founders need to do periodic assessments of personal benefit at different points during the life cycle of the company. Should you sell the company after a series A is complete because the dilution from series B would essentially wipe out significant personal financial benefit? Or, would the company value grow so much that even a tiny percentage would still be financially rewarding to you? Is the market rapidly changing so that your amazing technology is now looking like a "nice to have" rather than a "need to have"? Or is there a feeding frenzy among companies to buy technologies like yours? It may be time to sell.

Business decisions can become complicated based on the interests of the founders, management, and directors. Ultimately, the board will vote on the decisions to target more investments and prepare for a sale or an IPO, among other financial decisions. They will hopefully have the best interest of the company in mind with their decision-making and hopefully that is in your best interest as founder. Again, keeping a voting seat in the room where this is occurring will allow your voice to be heard and your vote to count.

Summary

Investors in start-ups are risk takers, as you are in bringing your discovery to commercialization. To recruit investors to finance your vision, a bulletproof business plan can help. Details of the business plan allow both the start-up management and investors to think through each step and strategy in launching the company. Investment can come in many forms, depending on your point in the development of the company. From angels in person or in the crowd to venture capitalists and corporate partnerships, you will need to present your business opportunity and deliver on promised milestones to continue to provide resources to get your start-up into a phase where you and the investors can realize gains.

References

Barnett, C. (2015), "Trends Show Crowdfunding to Surpass VC in 2016," *Forbes*, June 9, 2015.

Croce, A., Grilli, L., and Murtinu, S. (2014), "Venture capital enters academia: An analysis of university-managed funds." *Journal of Technology Transfer* **39**(5): 688–715.

Downs, L. D. (2013), "Crowdfunding's big-bang moment." *Harvard Business Review*, October 28, 2013. https://hbr.org/2013/10/crowdfundings-big-bang-moment (accessed May 31, 2017).

Freedman, D. M. and Nutting, M. R. (2014–2015), A Brief History of Crowdfunding, Including Rewards, Donation, Debt, and Equity Platforms in the USA.

Weisul, K. (2014), In Crowdfunding, All-or-Nothing Campaigns Are More Successful, Inc.com. Monsueto Ventures, June 14, 2014.

10

Your Roadmap: Avoid the Potholes

The best time to plant a tree was 20 years ago. The second best time is now.
—Chinese proverb

This guide has served not only to show you the general path toward spinning out a company from your lab but also to explore some considerations for the numerous decision points that you will be faced with as you progress through this process. The idea is that after you make the considerations at each decision point, you will choose wisely and continue your path forward. For all academics who want to translate their discoveries to start-up companies, there are numerous challenges along the way. Decisions in business need thoughtful exploration, just as those do in research, but the pacing of the decision-making is quite a bit faster in your start-up than in the lab. When faced with major decision points, delaying the choice can be as devastating to a business as making the "wrong" decision. It's all about continuing to move forward to your targeted objectives or milestones, whether that is accepting venture capital (VC) funding, launching an MVP, obtaining regulatory approval, or making your first $10 million in revenue. There may be decisions you make that you may later regret. For the most part, one poor decision may hurt, but not kill the company, and there is often a way to undo it if you can recognize the problem—the earlier the better. If you make a poor hire, you can fire the person. If you choose a poor CEO, you can work yourself out of the partnership (make sure you start with a good contract that allows for this). If you drive toward a product that ends up having little traction in the market, you can redesign and pivot in a new direction. The challenge comes in balancing when to keep with the plan and when to change course. The use of trusted advisors, board members, and partners can help you face these situations and offer perspective on the situation.

Academic Entrepreneurship: How to Bring Your Scientific Discovery to a Successful Commercial Product, First Edition. Michele Marcolongo.
© 2017 John Wiley & Sons, Inc. Published 2017 by John Wiley & Sons, Inc.

There have been several studies that examine the main causes for start-up failure. CB Insights surveyed 101 failed start-ups and found that there was rarely a single cause of a start-up's failure and that across the failures, the reasons for failing were quite varied (CBInsights, 2014). They listed and quantified the reasons that the start-up management gave for their failed businesses and allowed them to report multiple reasons. Their data analysis reports the reason and percentage that the start-ups cited that reason so the percentages don't add up to 100%, but they do provide a relative ranking of the major challenges to start-ups in their cohort. An analysis of these reasons is worth a look. Over 55% of the reasons cited were in the top seven causes.

1) *Building a solution looking for a problem, that is, not targeting a "market need" (42%)*
The main challenge to start-ups was choosing the wrong problem to solve because the solution did not satisfy a market need, which was reported as a main reason for failure by 42% of the start-ups. One company described their challenge:

> Start-ups fail when they are not solving a market problem. We were not solving a large enough problem that we could universally serve with a scalable solution. We had great technology, great data on shopping behavior, great reputation as a thought leader, great expertise, great advisors, etc., but what we didn't have was a technology or business model that solved a pain point in a scalable way.

This concept goes back to Chapter 3, and the critical idea of primary market research to help refine the product or service offering and to target if the product or service is a "nice to have" or "need to have." Even if you've done this analysis thoroughly at the start of the business planning cycle, things change as time progresses, and 5 years later, when you are ready to start selling, you need to be abreast of market conditions and need. For academics, this can be a particularly pertinent point because often the discoveries in the lab are serendipitous or they are examining a pathway or mechanism or working out a new theory and are not driven by market need from the get-go. In addition, some academics have historically discounted the role of marketing and marketing research in the advancement of the product, working toward an end goal that just wasn't there.

To avoid this pitfall, a continuous assessment of the market can help. Repeatedly probing pain points for your potential customers and trying out your solution with demos and review of data for the potential product with them can help to keep you on target so that all of the hard work has a payoff in the end with customers that are ready to jump on your product.

In the top 20 reasons for start-ups failing in this analysis, four of them were based on marketing. In addition to "no market need" (42%), also cited were poor marketing (14%), ignore customers (14%), and product mistimed (13%). Marketing matters.

2) *Ran out of cash (29%)*

After forming a company and getting initial funding, the decisions on how to wisely spend their resources and enable follow-up funding to continue progress derailed almost 30% of companies. The initial investment should be used to meet milestones that will help to build value in the start-up, driving the product or service toward launch and sales. Rounds of funding are typically necessary before a technology is ready for commercialization. To secure investors for subsequent rounds, start-ups need to build value and show progress on an upward slope. One start-up summarized their experiences in running out of cash.

> In fact what eventually killed (us) was that the company wasn't able to raise this additional funding. Despite multiple approaches and incarnations in pursuit of the ever elusive product-market fit (and monetization), (we) eventually ran out of money-and a runway.

It often takes quite a bit of knocking on doors to find an investor who is interested in your sector and solution and who is ready to invest in a company such as yours in the stage such as yours. The process can take months to a year. Almost as soon as you receive your seed funding, you will be strategizing and laying the groundwork for your next round. The challenge is to keep the pace of process (which requires spending money) so that you can build value quickly and to secure your next round of money. Management of cash flow is an essential skill that will make this possible along with assessments on hiring decisions, consultant time, marketing costs, equipment needs, legal fees, and all of the other costs that an early stage start-up will need to pay. Discipline and good planning can be a strategy to managing your burn rate. Things happen that are out of your control, and while you don't want to take too much more investment than is warranted for the stage of your company, very few start-ups complain that they have too much money. Additional financial-related causes for failed start-ups on the list were pricing/cost issues (18%) and no financing/investor interest (8%).

3) *Not the right team (23%)*

Companies that cited team problems generally reflected that they needed more diversity of their leadership in terms of expertise. Some companies regretted not having a chief technology officer from the beginning or thought things would have been better if the founder was really interested in business aspects. Sometimes the founders thought that they should have had more balance in their partners.

This brings me back to the underlying problem, I didn't have a partner to balance me out and provide sanity checks for business and technology decisions made.

When considering the founding team, a discussion of the merits of bringing in a partner with business expertise as a cofounder or CEO from the start was considered in Chapter 6. Especially starting a company from academia, where the training of scientific academics does not often include business teachings, the role of a trusted CEO-type for your company can provide the marketing, finance, cash flow, pricing, business planning, hiring, networking, pitching (to investors) that will balance your expertise, and interest in the technical aspects of developing the product or service. That being said, you as a founder still need to get up to speed on the business components of the start-up so that you can actively and knowledgeably participate in the decision-making. Investors usually bet on two things: the market potential and the team (and not necessarily in that order). To avoid common pitfalls in management, assembling the right team (or readjusting if you've assembled the wrong team) is one of the key aspects of placing your start-up on the path to success. Failure causes associated with the team make a few more appearances on the top 20 list as disharmony on team/investors (13%), nonuse of network/advisors (8%), and burn out (8%).

4) *Get outcompeted (19%)*
Competition is a reality of the playing field for any emerging start-up. Whether you're gunning to be first to market or to outperform the status quo, you will certainly have competition. Nothing brings on competition like a little success. In some cases, speed to market will help beat competition. Knowing who the market is and just what the market wants will give you an edge. Other times, the technology that you have protected with your IP will put you out front. Knowing who your competition is and analyzing their product offering as best you can help you to focus your own business, develop a niche, or take over the market.

5) *Pricing/cost issues*
Pricing may be one of the most difficult challenges for a start-up company. Even with primary marketing research, setting the pricing model and price points is difficult in light of actual scale-up costs including overhead and operations as well as the value proposition to the customer and their view of need of the product. Products priced too high or too low to make money were not viable.

Our most expensive monthly plan was $300. Customers who churned never complained about the price. We just didn't deliver up to their expectation.

Whether you are disrupting a technology or providing a value added to an existing technology, setting a successful pricing strategy is an experiment unto itself. If your CEO is not expert in pricing, then a consultant who is may be worth her weight in gold. Pharmaceutical companies have entire departments related to pricing because US pricing and reimbursement differ greatly from those in other countries, which have to be negotiated independently. For any business, along with pricing is understanding who exactly will be buying your product. In a hospital setting, is the doctor actually buying it or does an administrator who runs the unit? How many people in a business-to-business sale do you need for approval? The price and actual customer as well as sales cycle will be key to the uptake of your product or service.

6) *A "user-unfriendly" product*
Many companies have been derailed by the great concept, poor execution problem. For any product, the user must be able to easily engage with the product. Everyone has tried software that was clumsy or had too many options and steps needed to make it useful. The interface is wildly important to customer engagement. Some companies also design a product for an expert user when their customer base is more on the average level, overdesigning features and layers instead of making it easy for customers to navigate the product.

Ultimately I believe (we) lacked too much core game compulsion to drive enthusiastic mass adoption … Looking back, I believe we needed to clear the decks, swallow our pride, and make something that was easier to have fun with, within the first few moments of interaction.

Less than optimal product design can occur with more than software. Features of devices, processes, robustness of synthesis strategies, and packaging are critical in the usability of a product.

7) *I got this product. Now I just need a business model*
Numerous founders of failed businesses agreed that the business model was important. In particular taking a product and scaling it derailed many companies. The idea that there is a product that works on a local level, but cannot be distributed, or a material that can be made in a lab, but can't be scaled with reasonable costs, can be the challenge. Finding the business model that will enable that scaling to succeed or figuring a way around it is critical.

Although we achieve a lot…, we failed to create a scalable business. (We) didn't scale because we were single channel dependent and that channel shifted on us radically and suddenly.

Trying to imagine every next step as you are developing your product as far as sourcing, quality, validating, packaging, software licenses, alternative suppliers, and any other scaling challenges will let you get ahead of potential roadblocks.

Another survey of failed start-ups looked only at failed academic start-ups. In a survey of 36 TTO professionals who were part of AUTM, Terry Young, a former president of the organization, asked, "What are the top three reasons for failure of university start-up companies?" Here are the responses (Schwartz, 2010): Management Failure (22 mentions)

1) Failure to raise sufficient capital (15 mentions)
2) Innovation does not meet commercial need (12 mentions)
3) Geography (7 mentions)
4) Cultural factors (6 mentions)
5) Government laws, bureaucracy, and programs (6 mentions)
6) Infighting within start-up team (6 mentions)
7) Problems with IP (6 mentions)
8) Poor business plan (5 mentions)
9) Unrealistic expectations (4 mentions)

You can immediately see the overlap with the prior list of failures from nonacademic start-ups, especially with insufficient investment, market need, poor business plan, and management team. However, on the academic list, IP and government bureaucracy as well as cultural factors become dominant challenges. IP is significant in that valuation of most academic start-ups relies on IP initially and when there are problems with the IP by way of patent issuance or a tight patent space, leaving little room to operate, this can put an end to the start-up. Scott Shane in his research on 134 MIT spin-offs supported this observation with his finding that the number of patents held by a spin-off at the time of founding reduced the likelihood of the company failing (Shane, 2004). Shane also showed that a strong patent portfolio provided sustainable competition for the MIT spin-offs, allowing them to more often partner with established companies and allowing sufficient room to develop a broad technology within the range of the market. In particular, platform technologies with broad coverage allowed start-ups to pivot when necessary. Government laws and bureaucracy stunted start-up growth through protection of computer software and biotechnology in Europe. In the United States, SBIR programs were considered to stifle growth because they don't encourage "market-pulled technology needs." Cultural factors cited stagnation when the culture of the country stifled entrepreneurial spirit. Comments from the survey participants said that in some countries a failed start-up can damage an academic's reputation as a researcher, although in the United States, even a failed start-up is generally seen as a "badge of honor" and has little impact on the academics.

While some features of business development challenges are unique to academic start-ups, the major reasons for failure are common to all start-ups examined in these reports.

While it's important to consider potential pitfalls for start-ups, so that you can hopefully navigate around them, it's also interesting to look at some success stories. Arguably a wildly successful start-up (nonacademic, but still technology based) in the last decade is Uber. A brief look at the short but sweet story of Uber can offer additional lessons in component of a successful start-up.

How to Create a Successful Company

Example 1: Uber

While not an academic start-up, many lessons can be learned about what to do right by looking at the phenomenon of Uber, which was founded in 2009 by Garrett Camp and Travis Kalanick with $200K in self-funded seed investment. The value generation of this company in a relatively short period of time ($3.5 billion after 4 years, $40 billion 1 year later, and more than $65 billion in 2016) is staggering. Uber started as UberCab with the idea that you could request a black car limo service from an app on your smartphone, eventually disrupting most of the world's taxi service as it then existed. While comprehensive business analyses of Uber will continue to be performed by business scholars, here it is possible to analyze a few twists and turns in the successful launch of Uber that relates to the roadmap and decision points discussed in this book.

The Concept

The founders came up with the concept during a conversation about how hard it is to get a cab when it's raining and you have luggage. The idea to have an app on your smartphone that will allow you to request a driver was conceived in 2008, and by 2009 they had a working prototype and self-funded the seed of $200K, setting up in San Francisco in the offices of another start-up (keeping costs low).

Market Research

A year later, in 2010, UberCab (as they were then called) had demonstrated the service in New York (in three cars) and San Francisco, learning by doing. By the fall of 2010, they used this proof of concept as well as the uptake in customers who used the service to build value in the company and to secure $1.25 million from First Round Capital.

Intellectual Property

Uber had an early strategy using utility patents to cover their business methods and then protected logos and icons with trademarks. In addition, they used design patents to protect their app's user interfaces (screens). Methods patents were added to protect algorithms to impose surge pricing (IP Watchdog, 2016).

Proof of Concept

To see if the feasibility shown in the prototype analysis held up, in 2011 Uber launched the car hailing service in New York City with 100 cars. Within 6 months, they had 6000 users and had given 20000 rides. In the same year, they opened service in Chicago, Washington, and Paris. Their model was validated.

The Team

Garrett Camp and Travis Kalanick were friends and founded the company together. Each had prior start-up experience and successful first exits that enable them to have some time and capital to invest in Uber. Early on, in 2010, they named Ryan Graves as CEO. Later that year, they reviewed their management strategy and replaced Ryan with Travis, and Ryan became COO, under friendly terms. As of 2016, Ryan was a board director and SVP of global operations of Uber Technologies. Garrett served as the chairman continuously from 2009.

Financing

Financing at Uber was swift, to say the least. Why was that? The taxi business is far from exciting to most people. However, the rise of the sharing economy put ride-sharing in an interesting place. It was definitely a hot market. However, a need was already established for a car-ride service. The innovation and business model made the start-up interesting to investors. In addition to the sharing economy, mobile was hot at the time. The founders both had prior start-up experience, lending credibility to their ability to execute. They had demonstrated the product in those first tries in New York and San Francisco; they were using IP to protect the product/service as they progressed. What started as a focused product (simply put an app that could allow you to grab a black car) was expanded to become a platform technology that now includes non-black car rides (UberX, 2012), a bike service in Manhattan (UberRush, 2014), a moving and delivery service in Hong Kong (UberCargo, 2015), a meal delivery service (UberEats, 2016), and a driverless car service launched in Pittsburgh in 2016.

An amazing confluence of events must converge for success like Uber has enjoyed. This would not have gotten very far without financing. Investment was built based on the initial investment of the two founders putting some "skin in the game." This was quickly followed by early investment by First

Round, who took an early risk. Subsequent demonstration of execution by Uber and market need, timing, scale-up, and expansion to other markets, built value, drawing investors every step of the way. Valuation has far exceeded the considerable investment in Uber. The 2016 investment in Uber was over $11.6 billion, and the corresponding valuation was over $65 billion.

Challenges for Uber

With such impressive success, what can be the worry for a company in such great shape as Uber? One challenge is their success, which has encouraged numerous similar companies to launch including Lyft, SafeHer, Didi, and others. Still, Uber dominates the way globally with services in 66 countries and 507 cities in 2016. Now the diversification of its services will require others to invest considerably to keep up. Another challenge is the regulatory hurdles that Uber faced through first vetting drivers and complying with transportation regulators in states and cities in the United States and globally. Several states have sued Uber for violating regulations. In addition, Uber was challenged with their business model of utilizing drivers as consultants, rather than employees, which will need to be addressed and also poses a risk to the company.

In this brief overview of Uber, there are lessons to be learned. The management team needed to adapt and reposition itself over the course of development of the enterprise. This can be difficult, but for Uber, it worked out with wild success and business relationships were maintained. The culture that was established early by the management team was that everyday matters. The speed of development, financing, proof of concept, scale-up, and diversification around the platform is astonishing. That can't happen without a culture that encourages and rewards drive to target goals but also supports risk-taking and innovation. The biggest innovation has been that of the founders that recognized a market need when everyone was more or less getting by with traditional black car services and the process for requesting them. Mobile platforms made this possible; the widespread use of smartphones and infrastructure of connectivity in cities were recognized as a foundation to build the business model. Hard work and market feedback helped to take a good idea and make it into a viable (or way more than viable) business. Can you incorporate any of these principles into your start-up?

Example 2: Genentech

The phrase *Gen*etic *En*gineering *Tech*nology formed the basis for naming Genentech in 1976. The company was founded by Herbert Boyer, a then associate professor of biochemistry and biophysics, and Robert Swanson, a venture capitalist. Genentech was founded on a "simple" method for isolating and amplifying any gene or DNA fragment and moving it with controlled precision. This technology formed the basis for the founding of the biotech industry. Genentech synthesized insulin and human growth hormone in the early 1980s and was an established leader in biotech through its sale to Roche in 2009 for $46.8 billion. It was a long and interesting road over the 33 years between 1976 and 2009. One of the most significant stories is how Genentech was founded. In *Genentech: The Beginnings of Biotech* by Sally Smith Hughes (2011), the story of scientific discovery, patenting and founding are documented, along with proofs of concept, early products and sales agreements, scale-up, and IPO.

Discovery

In 1972, Herbert Boyer from UCSF and Stanley Cohen from Stanford met at a conference in a deli in Waikiki. They were working on DNA with Boyer focusing on the enzymes that he could utilize to clip DNA into fragments and map its structure to become restriction enzyme research and genetic manipulation. Cohen was a medical doctor with a focus on research and clinic and an interest in plasmids, using them to transport genes and DNA fragments into bacteria. With Boyer's method for clipping DNA and Cohen's plasmids, they together discussed the idea of a way to join and clone DNA molecules. The drive to explore this concept brought the two together, despite their very different personalities, although both were "workaholics and passionate about their science." The realization that the collaborative experiments were successful came shortly after the meeting in Hawaii, in early 1973 when their gel electrophoresis measurements proved that they had recombined and cloned DNA. The discovery of a straightforward method for cloning DNA was published within 1 year of their first meeting in Hawaii.

Intellectual Property

The story of the discovery seems much easier or at least shorter than the process of patenting the technology. The discovery became top news in the United States in 1974 with a front-page article in the *New York Times*. With all of the publicity, the director of Stanford's Office of Technology Licensing, Niels Reimers, learned of the discovery. He contacted Cohen to discuss patenting the invention. Remembering that this occurred before the Bayh–Dole Act (1980) and that few basic scientists considered patenting their basic research, Cohen was surprised. At the time there was a belief that discoveries related to health should be open access. Cohen finally agreed to allow a patent to be filed but decided to forego the one-third potential payout to him from any licensing agreements and instead donated that to Stanford, saying that he wanted to help the university. Boyer agreed to file the patent but did not forego his UCSF portion of potential payout. Stanford and UCSF petitioned the government for the ownership of the IP since it was NIH sponsored (the work was performed before Bayh–Dole) and permission for the universities to own the potential IP was granted.

The patent process turned into a 6-year battle with numerous political casualties. There were controversies about the technology being safe, which was taken up for discussion by the National Academy of Science and National Institute of Medicine who requested research guidelines for safety for the newly emerging field. In a letter by the committee and signed by 10 prominent scientists, including Boyer and Cohen, the community agreed to stop all work until a Recombinant DNA Advisory Committee could advise the NIH director on scientific matters about recombinant DNA research. At the conference discussions turned frantic and seemed like a "scientific witch hunt," which Boyer called "a nightmare."

At the same time, the patent effort was pulled into the political safety debate with critiques to Stanford and UCSF on their patenting to profit from basic scientific discovery. Cohen and Boyer suffered much criticism as the inventors of the controversial technology and that fact that they were pursuing a patent around the discovery, which could benefit human health.

Aside from the political challenges, the US Patent and Trademark office was unsure of how to decide on the patent of a biological process like DNA cloning. After much review, the government decided that biological patents could be granted. The patent finally issued in 1980.

The Team

In 1976, Boyer was having thoughts of the potential industrial uses for the DNA cloning technology but had not pursued how to proceed on this front. He was approached in his lab one day by Bob Swanson, who had recently been fired from Kleiner, Perkins, Caufield and Byers, the VC group, after one of his companies was failing. Swanson was interested in starting a company around the DNA cloning. Over a few beers, he and Boyer decided to launch a formal agreement. Boyer thought that since Swanson knew about how to get funding, he might get support for a few postdocs in his lab; it was a tough funding climate for research. He also knew that he needed someone with business savvy to move the discovery toward commercialization. Swanson had one of the best recombinant DNA experts in the country interested in participating as the company's research adviser, recruiting scientists and giving the start-up scientific legitimacy. They each put in $500 and entered into a contractual agreement.

Market Research

Where to start? Boyer gave Swanson a catalogue of protein structures to select small hormones for possible first targets. Swanson did his market research and decided on insulin, which was then derived from animals. A human insulin was of known amino acid sequence that would help in making the hormone. It was a potentially achievable target with clinical relevance and a (then) $100 million growing market worldwide.

Financing

Swanson put together a six-page business plan. After a failed try with a California banking family, he went back to Kleiner and Perkins, his former bosses at the VC firm. The VCs were used to investing in risky businesses but almost all of the early-stage companies that they had supported had at least some sales. This was new. There was not a product, just the idea, the patent application, and a storm of controversy over the safety of the approach. Knowing Swanson, they recognized this passion and determination to make the business a reality. However, it was Boyer's calm and comprehensive layout of the equipment, personnel, and space that needs to achieve his milestone goal that helped to convince Kleiner and Perkins to fund them with a $100 000 investment. Perkins took a seat on the board along with Swanson and Boyer, and Genentech was founded.

Perkins suggested that they contract early research and they did, guided by Boyer. While the team has shown that the DNA would function *in vivo*, no one had shown that you could make a protein in bacteria. Boyer pulled a few collaborators into the process. They were working on making a nonmarketable hormone peptides in bacteria, specifically somatostatin. Boyer thought this could be the proof of concept needed to prove out the technology and help to secure more funding. Swanson was not in support of this approach and wanted to continue to push for insulin, since that was the market target. Like in many businesses, there was push and pull between the two, but Swanson eventually agreed and Genentech supported the collaborators of Boyer. (Interestingly, at the same time of these discussions, the collaborators submitted a grant to NIH for the same experiment and were soundly turned down because NIH thought that it was an "academic exercise" with no practical merit.) The team worked out new methods while working through new safety rules from the biosafety offices and developing new analytical technique to see what they've made while trying to make it. During the experimental period for the proof of concept, Swanson was extremely anxious and pushing everyone to get things done. He had a lot riding on the experiments going well and his career and reputation at stake. After a total fail, they regrouped with a new approach and succeeded in bacterial synthesis of somatostatin. It took just 7 months of research and was then 1977. Amazingly, this was only 4 years after the discovery of recombinant DNA. To achieve this goal, the company had spent $515 000 (a "lean but effective manner"). This was accomplished by running research in contract and university labs, not leasing and equipping their own lab facility. They did not hire employees but used the staff and students in the research facilities before they knew the technology would work.

In 1978, Swanson completed a third round of private investment securing $950 000 at $8/share. Now it was time to get a facility, hire scientists, and drive toward insulin development. Boyer was key in recruiting young scientists, trained in latest techniques. Competition in the field of insulin cloning was rising, and very strategically Boyer was able to recruit both senior and junior scientists to consult with Genentech (for shares, fees, and research grants to their labs). This way, Genentech was able to tap into all of the leading minds of the time, securing a technological foundation for the company beyond that of the founder. Swanson at the same time was trying to partner with a major pharmaceutical firm for the deeper pockets that would be needed to take the molecules through marketing and sales. After trying a few companies, his vision aligned best with Lilly, the leader in animal derived insulin who was looking for a way to expand the amount of insulin to serve a growing market and took a chance on Genentech, supporting them with $50 000/month. In 1978, Genentech succeeded in developing human insulin from DNA cloning in bacteria. They secured an IPO in 1980 and raised $38.5 million, making the founders millionaires. Insulin was FDA approved in 1982. Lilly bought the rights to market the insulin. Next came the synthesis of human growth hormone in 1985 and another licensing partnership to Roche. After that, Genentech started on its own products, launching, and selling. Two decades later, Genentech was sold to Roche for $46.8 billion.

When considering an analysis of the story of Genentech, it is interesting to see so many reflections of the trials of start-ups:

- Getting the right team, which they seem to have in the business partner with prior experience (including failure) and an academic scientist
- A lean start-up model, using contract labs with expensive facilities and top scientists to do their research through proof of concept, keeping costs down
- Breaking barriers for funding and regulatory and patenting challenges (which actually set the tone for our current methods of doing business)
- The passion driving excellence in research with a focus on market and speed to get there
- Understanding the competition and trying to bring academic competitors and top scholars on board

For a start-up facing what seem like insurmountable obstacles, Genentech is inspiring in its ability to work through roadblocks and create value from academic discoveries.

Summary and Going Forward to Your Successful Venture

There are so many lessons to be learned in entrepreneurship. No two companies take the exact same path and use the exact same strategy. This book is meant to be an introduction to the considerations that you might make as you begin your path in entrepreneurship. It is a guide for the very specific subset of entrepreneurs who develop our businesses based on an innovation discovered in the academic research lab. There are unique challenges to starting a business from academia in that university relations must be managed along the way. Very few of us initially set out to study business and become entrepreneurs, so we are learning on demand by whatever means we can from local start-up boot camps to more formal NSF or NIH I-Corps programs to reading this book. What we are trying to learn is a systematic way to develop a company from a research finding in our particular academic setting, all while keeping our challenging day jobs.

My sincere hope is that by reading this, you have now learned steps to start your company in an efficient manner. While this process takes time, this book is intended to streamline your learning of the process and let you get down to filling in all of the pieces. From first protecting your IP to developing your management team, licensing your technology from the university, and financing your company, this book is intended to guide you through each step.

Although there is a considerable amount of strategy and hard work in getting to the point of having a financed start-up, it is really only the initiation of the path to building the company. There will be many more steps and decision points and lots more hard work going forward to make your company a viable entity to survive in the highly competitive marketplace outside the walls of academia. From this point forward, there will be additional resources to guide you along the journey. Please see a list of a few you may consider in the Suggested Reading section.

The rewards from starting a company, for me, happen when I see employees working in an office and lab on product that just was not there before and would not have been there unless I did the work to discover the technology and launch the company. Reward also comes from the stimulating interactions as the company moves forward, working with great people and developing strategies for success. The start-up community is a close knit and helpful one full of interesting people. The best reward is seeing a technology that I conceived become product and, for my discipline, that product is used for treating patients, enhancing their quality of life. Research is a powerful tool and innovations that come from research have the power to change our world for the better. A major way to effect that change is through commercialization of those innovations. I wish you the best of luck!

References

CBInsights (2014), The Top 20 Reasons Startups Fail, https://www.cbinsights.com/blog/startup-failure-reasons-top/ (accessed May 13, 2017).

Hughes, S. S. (2011), *Genentech: The Beginnings of Biotech*. Chicago and London, University of Chicago Press.

IP Watchdog (2016), http://www.ipwatchdog.com/2016/07/23/uber-ip-patents-trademarks-copyrights/id=71167/ (accessed May 13, 2017).

Schwartz, D. (2010), Tech Transfer eNews Blog. Survey suggests top 10 reasons university start-ups fail. http://techtransfercentral.com/2010/07/14/survey-suggests-top-10-reasons-university-start-ups-fail/ (accessed May 31, 2017).

Shane, S. (2004), *Academic, Entrepreneurship: University Spinoffs and Wealth Creation*, New Horizons in Entrepreneurship Series. Cheltenham, UK and Northampton, MA, Edward Elgar Publishing.

Suggested Reading

Allen, T. J. and R. P. O'Shea (2014), *Building Technology Transfer within Research Universities: An Entrepreneurial Approach*. Cambridge, Cambridge University Press.

Blank, S. and B. Dorf (2012), *The Startup Owner's Manual, The Step-by-Step Guide for Building a Great Company*. Pescadero, K&S Ranch Publishing.

Chesbrough, H. (2006), *Open Innovation: The New Imperative for Creating and Profiting from Technology*. Boston, Harvard Business School Publishing Corp.

Freedman, D. M. and M. R. Nutting (2015), *Equity Crowdfunding for Investors, A Guide to Risks, Returns, Regulations, Funding Portals, Due Diligence and Deal Terms*. Hoboken, John Wiley & Sons, Inc.

Horowitz, B. (2014), *The Hard Thing about Hard Things, Building a Business When There Are No Easy Answers*. New York, Harper Collins.

Hughes, S. S. (2011), *Genentech: The Beginnings of Biotech*. Chicago/London, University of Chicago Press.

Osterwalder, A. and Y. Pigneur (2010), *Business Model Generation: A Handbook for Visionaries, Game Changers, and Challengers*. Hoboken, John Wiley & Sons, Inc.

Outlaw, S. (2013), *Cash from the Crowd*. Irvine, Entrepreneur Press.

Ries, E. (2011), *The Lean Start Up, How Today's Entrepreneurs Use Continuous Innovation to Create Radically Successful Businesses*. New York, Crown Business.

Shane, S. (2004), *Academic Entrepreneurship, University Spinoffs and Wealth Creation*. Northampton, Edward Elgar Publishing.

Shimaski, C. (2014), *Biotechnology Entrepreneurship, Starting, Managing, and Leading Biotech Companies*. Amsterdam, Elsevier.

Spenser, P. L. (2006), *The Art & Science of Technology Transfer*. John Wiley & Sons, Inc., Hoboken.

Theil, P. with Blake Masters (2014), *Zero to One, Notes on Startups, or How to Build the Future*. New York, Crown Business.

Ury, W. L., R. Fischer, and B. Patton (1991), *Getting to Yes, Negotiating Agreement without Giving In* (2nd Edition). New York, Penguin Books.

Academic Entrepreneurship: How to Bring Your Scientific Discovery to a Successful Commercial Product, First Edition. Michele Marcolongo.
© 2017 John Wiley & Sons, Inc. Published 2017 by John Wiley & Sons, Inc.

Key Terms

Angel investor Investor who will fund the earliest, first stages of financing a company. Sometimes a group or fund, but most likely individuals such as friends, family, and independent certified investors.

Business plan A guiding document that may be in the form of a written document or slide presentation that outlines key features of your business offering and the detailed plan of execution for the start-up company.

C-Corporation (C-Corp) Legal entity of incorporation that separates entities from their owners where income is taxed at the corporate level and again when it is distributed to owners. This structure must be used if a company goes public.

Common stock A security that represents ownership in a corporation. Common stockholders are at the bottom of the priority ladder for ownership structure and in the event of a liquidation, after all other bondholders, debtholders, and preferred shareholders have been paid in full. Typical stock issued to founders.

Conflict of interest (COI) Conflict that arises when you have an interest in both sides of a negotiation.

Copyright Protection provided to the authors of "original works of authorship."

Crowdfunding Using a web-based platform to secure funding for a project, loan, or company with small contributions from numerous people (the crowd).

Design patent New, original, and ornamental design for an article of manufacture.

Exclusive license Licensing intellectual property wholly, with no other entity able to use the IP.

Freedom to operate (FTO) Determining whether testing or commercializing a product can be done without infringing on the intellectual property rights of others.

Academic Entrepreneurship: How to Bring Your Scientific Discovery to a Successful Commercial Product, First Edition. Michele Marcolongo.
© 2017 John Wiley & Sons, Inc. Published 2017 by John Wiley & Sons, Inc.

Incubator or accelerator Physical space where a start-up can launch the business. They have different resources and terms depending on the incubator. Most are temporary until financing allows the company to move out of the incubator.

Intellectual property (IP) Patent, trademark, or copyright that legally protects a discovery.

Limited liability corporation (LLC) Crossover between corporation and partnership where partners are taxed personally, but there is no corporate tax.

Nondisclosure agreement (NDA) or mutual nondisclosure agreement (MDA) Contractual agreement between parties that outlines the secrecy to be observed during confidential discussions. NDA is typically a one-way agreement with one party sharing and another just listening, while the MDA is typically used when both parties are disclosing confidential information. Either document must be signed by both parties to be valid.

Nonexclusive license When IP is jointly owned, all parties are able to use the IP but no one party is able to exclusively use the IP (generally considered weaker than exclusive).

Non-provisional patent application "Full" patent application can follow a provisional patent application within 1 year of the provisional application's filing or can be filed directly without a provisional application. This application will be fully prosecuted.

Option Financial derivative that offers the buyer the right, but not the obligation, to buy or sell a security or other financial asset at an agreed upon price during a certain period of time or a specific date.

Patent cooperation treaty (PCT) International filing for intellectual property that allows your patent to be considered for protection in 148 countries simultaneously.

Plant patent Invention or discovery of asexually reproduced, any distinct, and new variety of plant.

Preferred stock A class of ownership in a corporation that has a higher claim on the assets and earnings than common stock. Typical stock issued to investors.

Proof-of-concept center (POCC) Specific source of funds and services that help support a laboratory discovery or concept through the feasibility phase (prototype or critical experiment) that will better prepare the technology for commercialization by license to an established or start-up company.

Provisional patent application Patent application that holds the invention date for 1 year but will not be fully prosecuted. Some countries will publish provisional patent applications online.

S-Corporation (S-Corp) Legal entity of incorporation that protects shareholders, but profits are taxed at shareholder level, not at corporate level. For businesses less than 100 shareholders.

Small business innovation research (SBIR) Federally supported program that can be granted to a small business where 66% of the work must be done by the company and the remaining third can be subcontracted to an academic institution.

Small business technology transfer (STTR) Federally supported program that can be granted to a small business where 40% of the work must be done by the company (the remaining 60% can be done by an academic institution).

Technology transfer office (TTO) Many possible names, but the office at the university that provides support for protecting the intellectual property of members of the university; also may be involved in licensing technologies to companies and helping to start-up new ventures.

Trademark Word, name, symbol, or device that is used in trade with goods to indicate the source of the foods and to distinguish them from the goods of others.

Trade secret Any practice or process of a company that is generally not known outside of the company.

Utility patent Used for any new and useful process, machine, article of manufacture, or composition of matter, or any new and useful improvement thereof.

Value proposition Establishing the value (not price) of your product or service to the customer.

Venture capital Investment that comes from a fund dedicated toward start-up companies.

Index

a

academic crowdfunding   160–162
academic research
  partnership models   118
  social capital needed for   12
  toward commercialization   76
accelerators   129–140
  characteristics of   131
  success start-up   139
American Association of University
  Professors   31, 57
angel investor
  certified   150
  early-stage companies by   84
  groups/networks   17, 153–154
  individual   151
  qualified investment   160
angel-like investment   154
Association of University Technology
  Managers (AUTM)   5

b

Bayh–Dole Act 1980   5, 6, 186
board of advisors   105
board of directors   102–105
Boh's analysis   123
break-even analysis   147
bricks-and-mortar company   107
Bureau of Economic Analysis
  (BEA)   3

business consultants   105–106
business development
  component of   12
  consultant   106
  execution phases of   51
  strategy for   154
  from university/regional   78
business management   89
business model   181
business partnership   16
business plan   92
  break-even analysis   147
  competitions   125–126
  components   143–144
  cycle   178
  different stages of   144
  financing plan   147–148
  intellectual property   145
  market need   145
  market size   145
  milestones and projected
    budget   148
  pricing strategy   146–147
  product definition   144
  product solution and differentiation
    in marketplace   145
  value proposition   146
  written document   144
business success, creating
  framework   45

*Academic Entrepreneurship: How to Bring Your Scientific Discovery to a Successful Commercial
Product*, First Edition. Michele Marcolongo.
© 2017 John Wiley & Sons, Inc. Published 2017 by John Wiley & Sons, Inc.

business-to-business
  product/service   74, 162
  sale   181

c
C-Corps   93
CEO
  compensation   97
  decision-maker   93
  entrepreneurial skills   89
  equity   104
  personal characteristics   88
  strong business partner   89
  trust in leadership of company   88
cofounder   90
co-inventors   14, 31
  patent equally   32
commercialization
  academic research toward   76
  component of   15
  drive for   60–61
  FTO   33, 146
  initial stages for   117
  innovation toward   15
  and market potentials   51
  path toward   2
  plan with technical and
    business   81
  product/service   21, 31, 146
  research innovations   8, 82
  road to product   21
  start-up for   116, 149
  technology assist   16
  translation research   11, 113
  university flow   13
  university research, core principles
    of   81–82
common stock   97, 99
comprehensive marketing
    strategy   161
confidential information   26
conflict
  between student and faculty
    member   90

universities inherent between   60
  university inventor/founder   63
conflict of interest (COI)   70
consulting agreement   15, 97
  start-up   173
  TTO   59
consumer markets   46
convertible debt   167
Cooperative Patent Classification
    (CPC) system   39
Copyright Act   1976, 23
Copyright Office of the Library of
    Congress   23
corporate accelerators   138
corporate attorney   70
corporate investment   154
corporate investors   154–155
corporations
  C-level position   95, 104
  existing, license agreements with
    58–62
  license IP   5
crowdfunding
  academic   160–162
  debt-based   156
  equity   157
  intrastate   160
  investment   161
  platforms   152, 155–156
  power of   161
crowdsourcing
  in debt   156
  equity   157, 160, 161
  investment   161
  power of   161
  strategy   158

d
debt-based crowdfunding   156
debt financing   92, 137, 158, 160
decision-making
  board of directors   102
  CEO   93
  equity holders   103

founders and equity holders   105
  start-ups   95, 117
defensive publication   36
de-risk technology   15, 16, 146
design patents   22
direct university–corporate
    license   60
due diligence   33, 69

e
employee management   108–110
entrepreneurs
  business networks of   89
  characteristics of   7, 115
  market need   45
  relationships between faculty
    members and student   116
  social capital of   78
  success   45, 88, 152
  translates knowledge from
    universities   7
entrepreneurship
  business student in   122
  culture of   133
  review of   3–5
  students for education in   81
  study of   7–8
equity   68, 99
  CEO   104
  crowdfunding   157
  dilution of   100
  for future investors   110
  investment   136
  negotiation   100
exclusive license   15, 64, 67, 70
existing corporations
  license agreements   58–63
  market need by   60
experienced entrepreneur   117, 123

f
faculty inventor   15, 58
faculty member
  equity stake   173

not participating   122
  participation   119–122
fail-fast test   77
first-to-file patent system   27
formal education   123–124
for-profit accelerators   138
for-profit corporations   129
founders
  conflict   63
  fatigue   174
  shares   96, 97
  term sheet for RegenLive
    99–102
freedom of information laws   26
freedom to operate (FTO)   21, 33
  commercialization   146
  infringement   42
full-time management   95

g
GI Bill of Rights   4
graduate student
  education in entrepreneurship   81
  postdoc university spin-off   122
  university start-ups, early stages
    of   113

h
The Hard Thing About Hard Things
    (Horowitz)   110
Hayter's analysis   124
high-tech start-ups   8
hybrid company   107

i
I-Corps   145
incubators
  academic innovation
    ecosystem   133
  characteristics of   131
  competitive selection process   132
independent board members   103
innovation ecosystem   12
inside board members   102–103

intellectual property (IP)
  business plan   145
  exclusive license   67
  invention protecting   70
  law   1, 21
  management of
    university-generated   57
  patentability opinion   145
  patenting and public disclosure
    25–36
  for product development   60
  protection of   34
  TTO   62
  types of   22–25
International Patent Classification
  system   39
invention
  business development for   46
  contribution   32
  patentable   24–25
  with patent application   31
  patent law   24
  protection of   31, 70
  title of   40
  TTO   43
inventors
  document type   36
  patent law   31–32
  property rights   22
  TTO   58
investment infusions   18
investment risk   69
investment strategy   69
investors
  academic crowdfunding   160–162
  angel investor groups/networks
    153–154
  corporate investors   154–155
  crowdfunding platforms   152,
    155–156
  in debt crowdsourcing   156
  economic development
    organizations   151

equity crowdfunding   157
  friends and family   150
  FTO and rightfully   33
  future equity   110
  individual angels   151
  initiators, effect on   158–159
  invested in incubator's start-ups   133
  investors, effect on   159
  local incubators/accelerators   150
  management   124
  negotiations of license agreement   57
  patentability opinion   34
  platforms, effect on   159–160
  potential   55
  Rule 506(b)   157–158
  Rule 506(c)   158
  type communication   144
IPO   156

j
JOBS Act   157, 158

l
Leahy–Smith America Invents Act   27
The Lean Start-Up (Ries)   77
license agreements   15
  early-stage   60
  with existing corporations   58–62
  great deals for universities   60
  investment option in university to
    start-ups   69
  option agreement   69
  shared between university   63
limited liability corporations (LLCs)
  93, 94

m
management structure
  board of advisors   105
  board of directors   102–105
  consultants   105–106
  employee management   108–110
  independent board members   103

inside board members 102–103
outside board members 103
subcontractors 106–108
management team risk 74
marketing risk 56
market need
  business plan 145
  critical 47
  hypothesis 46
market-pulled technology needs 182
market research 45
  primary feedback 15
  search phase 52
market risk 74
market size 14, 51, 55
  business plan 145
  intellectual property 145
market value 54
minimum viable product (MVP)
  55, 177

n
NASDAQ Stock Market 6
National Science Foundation
  (NSF) 4
  Innovation Corps (I-Corps) program
  46, 52, 56
NIH 33
  I-Corps program 98
nondisclosure agreement (NDA) 14
  one-way 26
nonexclusive license 5
nonprofit organizations 129
nonprovisional patent application
  24, 30, 32, 145
nonuniversity incubators 132

o
Old-Corp 58–61
one-way non-disclosure agreement
  (NDA) 26
Open Innovation (Chesbrough) 3
operating agreement 110

option agreement 69
options 87
outside board members 103

p
patent
  anatomy of 34–41
  coding and structure 34
  design 22
  front page of 39
  public disclosure 25–27
  reading 42–43
  reissued 36
  risk of interfering 31
  selling invention 22
  standard field codes for 37–38
  types of 22
patentable information 26
patentable invention 24–25
patent application
  data collect 48
  process 25
  publication 36
patent attorney 26, 33, 34, 146
Patent Cooperation Treaty (PCT)
  14, 145
patent examiner 30
patent fees 15, 58, 68
patent law 21, 24, 33, 34, 43
patent strategy 34
plant patents 22
Porsche effect 8
postdoc entrepreneurs 124
postdoctoral students 16, 17, 113, 114
potential investors 55
preferred stock 97
pre-money valuation 168
primary marketing research
  definition 56
  feedback 15
  pricing model 180
  quantitative data 145
principal investigator (PI) 70

product commercialization   21
product development cycle   55
product-market fit   179
product/service
    of benefit   54
    business-to-business   162
    commercialization   1, 31
    international market potential for
        31, 125
    patent landscape   33
    primary market research   178
    technical aspects of   180
    technical risk of   13
    university innovation in   114
proof-of-concept (POC)   16, 70
    component to developing   86
    experiment, failure of   77
    killer experiment   98
    management team risk   74
    market risk   74
    regulatory/reimbursement risk
        73–74
    technological risk   73
proof-of-concept centers (POCCs)
    assist in technology
        commercialization   16
    economic development
        organizations   78
property rights
    FTO   33
    to inventors   22
provisional patent application   24, 30,
    31, 98, 145
public disclosure
    information   26
    patent   25–27
public offering   115

q
qualified angel investor   151, 160

r
regulatory/reimbursement risk   73–74
reissued patent   36

research agreement   15, 59
risk assessment   84
royalties   15, 64, 68
    license negotiation   69

s
S-corps   93
search phase   51
    value proposition   54–56
Securities Act of 1933   157, 158
serial entrepreneur   124
series A *see also* preferred stock
    financing   137
    investment   136
service rights   23
Small Business Administration   137
Small Business Innovation
    Development Act   1982, 83
Small Business Innovation Research
    (SBIR)/Small Business Technology
    Transfer (STTR)   16, 35, 70,
    82–84, 134
social capital
    for academic research   12
    networks of   11
start-ups   5–8
    academic preparation   16
    accelerators   130, 139
    business management   89
    business partnership   16
    CEOs   87
    decision-making   117
    early stage   8–13
    existing corporations license
        agreement to   63
    failure of university   182
    graduate and postdoctoral student
        perspective   17
    incubators   130, 133
    investment option in university
        license agreements   69
    investment strategy   92
    investment success   152
    leadership   108

license agreement   63
life cycle   172
management   63, 64, 68,
   87–110, 152
partnership with cofounder   92
predetermined deal structures
   for   64
pricing/cost issues   180
research and development   172
revenue over time for   55
securing investors   17
success accelerators   139
through commercialization   149
university IP licenses to   16, 62–70
statutory invention registration   36
students
   leadership ability of   114
   spinning out from university for
   116–119
subcontractors   106–108
successful company
   challenges for   185
   discovery   186
   financing   184–185, 188–189
   intellectual property   184, 186–187
   market research   183, 187–188
   proof of concept   184
   team   184, 187

t
technical markets   46
technical risk   84
technological risk   73
technology assessment   82
technology transfer   5–7
technology transfer office (TTO)   26,
   29, 30, 32
   independent of   59
   internal university relationships   64
   market analysis   51
trademark rights   23
trade secret   23–25, 34
two way/mutual non-disclosure
   agreement (MDA)   27

u
universities
   attorney   70
   COI   70
   commercialization, component
      of   68
   equity   68
   failure of start-ups   182
   graduate student/postdoc
      spinout   122
   incubators   132, 133
   inherent conflict between   60
   initial licensing fee   60
   inventor/founder conflict   63
   invest in venture funds   165
   investment option in license
      agreements   69
   IP licenses to start-ups   62–70
   legal fees   68
   license agreements   57, 63, 67
   net/gross profit   69
   patenting process   27–34
   pension funds and endowments   166
   preferred disclosure   25
   royalties   64
   spinout   115–119
   start-up   16
   TTO   57–70
   typical patent policy   32
   venture capital (VC)   165–168
   venture funding for   68, 166
university-based accelerators   138
up-front payment   15
US patent system   3
USPTO   22, 30
   database   41
   trademark/service mark   23
   trade secret   23
utility patents   22

v
value proposition
   business plan   146
   search phase   54–56

venture capital (VC)
  building and expanding value
    for academic founder
    171–174
  funds   81, 164, 177
  investment   100, 155
  MVP   177
  universities   165–168
venture capitalists   11, 69, 84

venture funding   68
virtual company   106–107, 148

w
World Intellectual Property
  Organization (WIPO)   31

y
Y Combinator   136–138